ACTIVISTS IN THE DATA STREAM

The Practices of Daily Grassroots
Politics in Southern Europe

Alice Mattoni and Diego Ceccobelli

First published in Great Britain in 2024 by

Bristol University Press
University of Bristol
1–9 Old Park Hill
Bristol
BS2 8BB
UK
t: +44 (0)117 374 6645
e: bup-info@bristol.ac.uk

Details of international sales and distribution partners are available at bristoluniversitypress.co.uk

© Bristol University Press 2024

The digital PDF and EPUB versions of this title are available open access and distributed under the terms of the Creative Commons Attribution-NonCommercial-NoDerivatives 4.0 International licence (https://creativecommons.org/licenses/by-nc-nd/4.0/) which permits reproduction and distribution for non-commercial use without further permission provided the original work is attributed.

British Library Cataloguing in Publication Data
A catalogue record for this book is available from the British Library

ISBN 978-1-5292-3963-8 paperback
ISBN 978-1-5292-3952-2 ePub
ISBN 978-1-5292-3953-9 ePdf

The rights of Alice Mattoni and Diego Ceccobelli to be identified as authors of this work have been asserted by them in accordance with the Copyright, Designs and Patents Act 1988.

All rights reserved: no part of this publication may be reproduced, stored in a retrieval system, or transmitted in any form or by any means, electronic, mechanical, photocopying, recording, or otherwise without the prior permission of Bristol University Press.

Every reasonable effort has been made to obtain permission to reproduce copyrighted material. If, however, anyone knows of an oversight, please contact the publisher.

The statements and opinions contained within this publication are solely those of the authors and not of the University of Bristol or Bristol University Press. The University of Bristol and Bristol University Press disclaim responsibility for any injury to persons or property resulting from any material published in this publication.

Bristol University Press works to counter discrimination on grounds of gender, race, disability, age and sexuality.

Cover design: Andy Ward
Front cover image: Stocksy/Catherine MacBride
Bristol University Press uses environmentally responsible print partners.
Printed and bound in Great Britain by CPI Group (UK) Ltd, Croydon, CR0 4YY

To Domenico, Agata, and Martino.
Alice

To Simona, Emilia, and Gaia.
Diego

Contents

List of Figures and Tables		vi
About the Authors		vii
Acknowledgements		viii
1	Everyday Grassroots Politics in the Data Stream	1
2	Activists' Quest for Information Amid Data Abundance	29
3	The Multiple Patterns Towards Visibility During Latency Stages	55
4	Algorithmic Visibility and Activists' Management of Reputation	78
5	The Accelerated Times of Activists' Organizational Work	100
6	The Creation of Connections Between Activists and Their Audiences	123
7	The Fragile Interactions Between Activists and Journalists	145
8	Activists' Practices and Agency in the Data Stream	167
Methodological Appendix		182
Notes		202
References		203
Index		221

List of Figures and Tables

Figures

1.1	Socio-material practices as constitutive entanglements of the material, the symbolic, and the social	20
A.1	An example of a media in practices map	186
A.2	The interview guidelines	188

Tables

1.1	The four practices that emerged from the analysis	21
A.1	The 20 most common configurations of actions–services–devices in each country (practice of political organizing)	193
A.2	The 20 most common configurations of actions–services–devices in each country (practice of sustaining connection)	194
A.3	The 20 most common configurations of actions–services–devices in each country (practice of information gathering)	195
A.4	The 20 most common configurations of actions–services–devices in each country (practice of gaining visibility)	196
A.5	List of research participants interviews (names are fictional)	197

About the Authors

Alice Mattoni is Associate Professor in the Department of Political and Social Sciences at the University of Bologna (Italy). She conducts research and has published extensively on the dynamic interplay between media – digital and otherwise – and grassroots politics in international journals, including *Big Data & Society*, *European Journal of Communication*, *Communication Theory*, *Information, Communication and Society*, *International Journal of Communication*, *Journal of Information Technology & Politics*, *Social Movement Studies*, and *Visual Studies*. She is the author of *Media Practices and Protest Politics: How Precarious Workers Mobilise* (Routledge, 2016) and editor of *Mediation and Protest Movements* (Intellect, 2013), with Bart Cammaerts and Patrick McCurdy, and of *Spreading Protest: Social Movements in Times of Crisis* (ECPR Press, 2014), with Donatella della Porta.

Diego Ceccobelli is Senior Assistant Professor in the Department of Social and Political Sciences at the University of Milan (Italy). He has published extensively in the fields of political communication, comparative politics, social movements, media, journalism, and leadership studies in international journals, including *International Journal of Press/Politics*, *Journal of Political Marketing*, *European Journal of Communication*, *Journal of Information Technology & Politics*, and *Journalism Practice*.

Acknowledgements

This book is the result of a long journey of research. We have received many forms of support along the way, all of which have been essential to the production of this work.

First of all, we would like to acknowledge the funds provided by the Italian Ministry of Universities and Research, which supported the PiCME – Political participation in Complex Media Environments (Grant Agreement Number RBSI14GUJE) – research project, on which this book is entirely based. We would also like to thank the Scuola Normale Superiore, the University of Bologna and the University of Milan: the first hosted the PiCME research project for its entire duration, while the other two are the universities where we both ended up after our experience as researchers at the Scuola Normale Superiore. Both constitute the vibrant academic communities in which the book was written.

Also, we would like to warmly thank all the research participants in Greece, Italy, and Spain who decided to contribute to our empirical research by sharing their expertise on digital media and grassroots political participation, in the case of experts, and their daily experiences with the use of different forms of media and technologies, in the case of activists, politicians, and journalists. Without their willingness to share their stories, this book would not exist.

Some colleagues supported us in various ways during the empirical data collection phase. We would like to thank them: Emiliano Trerè, who participated in the initial phase of the PiCME research project as a postdoctoral fellow, contributing to the initial development of the empirical research and collecting some empirical data in Spain; Angelos Evangelidis, who acted as a country expert for the case of Greece; Aloia Alvarez and Xavier Alcalde, who helped us with the transcriptions of the interviews we collected in Spain.

As we moved into the analysis of the empirical material, we discussed our initial findings with many colleagues who were generous enough to comment on our work, provide feedback, and suggest further lines of interpretation, either in formal settings or in informal conversations. We would like to thank them for this: Marco Deseriis, Anastasia Kavada, Elena Pavan, Christoph Raetzsch, Dieter Rucht, and Lorenzo Zamponi.

We would also like to thank all the colleagues who discussed first drafts of this paper in the various conferences where we presented our first empirical results: the European Communication Research and Education Association (ECREA) conferences in 2016, 2017, and 2018, the International Communication Association (ICA) conference in 2017, the European Consortium for Political Research (ECPR) conferences in 2017 and 2018, the Italian Association of Political Communication (AssoComPol) conferences in 2016, 2018, and 2019, and the Italian Political Science Association (SISP) conference in 2019.

We are also grateful to the colleagues who provided useful feedback on some of the book chapters: Ester Sigillò, Alice Fubini, Anwesha Chakraborty, Michele Grigolo, and Andrew Chadwick. Andrea Hajek proofread the entire manuscript and Valentina Tomadin helped us with the production of the book: they were indispensable in the final stages of writing the book and we express our appreciation to them. We would like to thank Paul Stevens, editor at Bristol University Press, for his enthusiasm for our book and his continued support throughout its production. The two anonymous reviewers also helped to strengthen our work and we thank them for this.

Although this is something uncommon to read in the acknowledgement section of a co-authored book, we also would like to thank each other, since this book would have never seen the light without our mutual support. Alice would like to thank Diego for all his hard work in collecting the data, for sticking with her in a rather demanding data analysis effort, and for his unwavering optimism about this whole editorial project, even in the most difficult moments of writing the book. Diego would like to thank Alice: she has been much more than a co-author of this book, but undoubtedly a fundamental mentor in his professional growth and in his life. Without her, who knows where he would be professionally today. To her, the greatest gratitude.

As a final round of appreciation in these acknowledgements, we would like to thank our families and friends for their support throughout the research and writing of this book.

Alice thanks the extended family of Cynar, whose friendship once again proved invaluable during the COVID-19 pandemic, when the series of *spontan* online meetings and long WhatsApp chats, both collective and individual, were essential to finding some relief during the most stressful moments of the lockdown in Italy. She is deeply grateful to Carla, a sister of choice, who has always supported this book project from afar in many ways. And to Ale, another sister of choice, who has been an invaluable witness and companion in many adventures and misadventures. Then, Alice would also like to express her immense gratitude to her mother, Verena, for indispensable support throughout the research project and the writing of the book, to her brother Andrea, her sister-in-law Rebecca, and her nephew Vittorio for all the joyful moments she spent with them in the past years. Finally, Alice would like to thank her husband, Domenico, and their two children, Martino and Agata, being aware that these two lines of thanks are little compared to the million reasons, moments, and feelings she would have to list to explain how immensely grateful she is to them for being a constant source of strength in her life.

Diego thanks his wonderful family. Writing a book is an adventure that you know begins when it starts, not when it ends. In the journey that led to the publication of this book, there have been many encounters, life changes, moments to persevere and move forward. Being able to do so while enjoying the unwavering support of my entire family, none of them excluded – my wife Simona, little Emilia, my mother Franca, my father Mauro, a brother and sister as splendid as Valentino and Simona, and a precious grandmother like Lucia – is a privilege that fate has chosen to grant me, and without which I would never have had that essential tranquillity, enthusiasm, and joy of living to manage the ups and downs that come with writing a book or simply being a young scholar today. To fate and pure luck, which have bestowed this fortune and privilege upon me, something beyond my control and personal choices, a final sincere thank you.

1

Everyday Grassroots Politics in the Data Stream

This book is about the subtle, daily interactions that activists have with digital media and digital data during their ordinary political activities, that is, when they are not involved in massive demonstrations in the streets. Once mobilizations have reached their peaks, activists continue to work – day after day – to achieve their long-term objectives. Beyond the short-lived moments in which they manage to involve hundreds of thousands of people in protests, they are constantly immersed in the daily activities that sustain the engagement of their organizations in the political realm. In order to do so, they speak with other activists, write reports, engage with journalists, and talk with their supporters. These and the other countless actions that activists perform on a daily basis are undoubtedly made possible through face-to-face interactions. Even more frequently, though, these actions take place thanks to digital media: activists meet other activists via Zoom, write their reports collaboratively in Google Docs, engage with journalists through their Twitter[1] accounts, and talk with supporters on their movement organization's Facebook page. Consequently, activists – some of whom are the subject of this book – spend a considerable amount of time engaging in a wide array of media. While some of these media are analogue, most of them are digital: together they immerse activists in what we conceptualize as a heterogeneous, ubiquitous, and perpetual data stream with which activists have to come to terms.

In the following chapters, we will examine how activists deal with this data stream, in which digital and non-digital media intersect. We will draw on fieldwork we conducted between 2016 and 2019 and which we will discuss at length in the Appendix at the end of this volume. The empirical research was based on expert interviews, in-depth interviews with activists, maps of the activists' use of digital media, and a careful reading of their documents and statistical data on digital media usage. We collected these data in three Southern European countries: Greece, Italy, and Spain. Although there are many similarities between the activists in the three countries, we will demonstrate that they all engage in digital media and make sense of the data stream in different ways during the quiet moments of grassroots politics. Depending on the country under examination, the activists we interviewed employ different types of digital media to perform the same kind of action. For instance, while Twitter is deeply intertwined with the practice of gaining visibility in Spain, this is not the case in Greece and Italy; at the same time, Italian activists mainly depend on Facebook to get the information they need, but in the other two countries it is of little value in this regard. Additionally, the activists in Italy, Greece, and Spain interpret the same type of digital media – and the challenges that come with it – in different ways. For example, the Greek and Spanish activists see social media platforms like Facebook as a risk to their privacy, while in Italy they seem to be less concerned with this issue.

Hence, beyond offering an overview of how Southern European activists employ digital media when they are not protesting in the streets, this book also casts light on the extent to which global social media platforms, such as Facebook and Twitter, and instant messaging services, like WhatsApp and Telegram, change their role and meaning depending on where the activists use them. We will demonstrate that, even in countries that are very similar to one another because they belong to the same geopolitical area, the activists' use of the same digital media for daily grassroots political activities may be different. We will pay full attention to these differences to reveal how activists encounter the data stream in the place where they are located and, in this way, experience the processes of digitalization and datafication in various and sometimes unexpected ways.

At the same time, we also highlight some features that make instead the relationship between activism and digital media in the three countries similar. The most prominent similarity is related to the practices that activists in the three countries engage in when they are not involved in street mobilizations. In the course of this book, we show, in fact, that two practices that are usually little studied by those researching these topics, seem instead to be very relevant for activists, in moments of latency. These are the practice of building connections and maintaining them, and the practice of information gathering. The latter, in particular, seems to be so important as to be able to anchor the other practices to it. We also show how a fairly well-known practice, that of seeking visibility for one's political exploits during moments of mobilization, nowadays overflows without delay even in moments of latency. We bring to light the importance of building and maintaining a good reputation to cope with the constant care that an always-on visibility requires of activists. Also, we illustrate how traditional media are far from being forgotten: they remain an important reference point for activists. And this in spite of the fact that, as we show in the book, the relationship between activists and journalists working in these media has become complicated over the years, also due to the increasingly precarious working conditions of information professionals. Overall, then, we discuss how, in a highly digitalized and data-driven world, face-to-face interactions acquire an important significance for maintaining activists' agency in relation to digital media and the data derived from them.

Before getting into the heart of this book and unpacking the findings discussed in the previous paragraph, we will first explain what we have done in the past few years and how we will present what we have learned during this research journey. To begin with, in what follows, we will unveil the theoretical and analytical architecture that lies behind this book. We will start from what we already know about the relationship between digital media and activism in times of protest. Drawing on research that has been conducted on this subject matter in recent years, we will summarize the most relevant changes that digital media have introduced in social movements during mobilizations. After that, we will turn our attention to those moments in which activists are not out in the streets voicing their demands. We will do this by explaining why it is important to focus our attention on these moments of latency and on the ordinary routines of grassroots political engagement. Next, we will describe some of the theoretical tools that we employed to carry out our research, which served as a compass when investigating the activists' political engagement and their use of digital media in the three Southern European countries. In a nutshell, we will first present the overall media-related processes in which we situated the activists and their daily political work at the grassroots level in the present day: digitalization and datafication. Then, we propose to use the concept of data stream as an interpretative key to understanding how digitalization and datafication occur in the concrete daily experience of activists. Subsequently, we go a step further and focus on the analytical architecture that sustained our research, namely practice theories. We will explain why we decided to rely on practice theories, discuss some of its main developments in the study of media and social movements, and describe the specific media-in-practice approach on which our investigation is based. The next section, instead, unpacks the first relevant finding of our research, presenting and comparing the four main practices that the activists in Greece, Italy, and Spain engage in through digital media: the practice of getting information; the practice of political organizing; the practice of gaining visibility; and the practice of sustaining connections. In the very last section of the chapter, we will present the book's overall structure.

Activism, digital media, and big data in times of protest

Activists have been using digital media to organize protests ever since the dawn of the Internet, well before the creation of social media platforms like Facebook, Twitter, Instagram, or TikTok. Already in the early 1990s, activists began using emails, Bulletin Board Systems, and dedicated computer networks – such as Peacenet and Econet – to exchange information and support their struggles (Myers, 1994). Since then, the history of activism has always been closely intertwined with technological developments. Digital media have taken on an increasingly important role in enabling activists to support their mobilizations, both nationally and transnationally. It is no secret that the grassroots movement for globalization, which developed in the late 1990s, was supported by the use of mailing lists and the creation of the independent information site Indymedia (Häyhtiö and Rinne, 2008); more recently, the mobilizations of the Arab Springs, the Occupy Wall Street movement, and other coeval protests also leveraged social media platforms and the widespread use of smartphones (Gerbaudo, 2012; Mattoni and della Porta, 2014; Tufekci, 2017; Fominaya, 2020).

This increasingly strong connection between social movements and digital media in various parts of the world has stimulated the publication of a wide range of studies on the matter. Scholars have wondered how and with what consequences digital media support protests, transform social movements and, ultimately, promote political change from unconventional places of politics. As a result, today we know a lot about how activists use digital media to sustain their campaigns and their protests. More specifically, we could say that digital media can be held responsible for four main transformations in the realm of social movements and activism.

First, digital media contributed to the hybridization of their repertoire of communication. Indeed, contemporary politics revolve around media hybridity and activists have to navigate the media logic that characterizes both older media (for example, the mainstream press) and newer media (for example, social media) (Chadwick, 2013). Along the same line, it is possible to argue that digital media sustain different forms of hybridity in contemporary activism, spanning from the more traditional online/offline combination to those forms of hybridity that will become even more important in the near future, such as human/non-human arrangements (Treré, 2018). In this regard, when activists started to actively employ digital media in the late 1990s, most of the time they used these in combination with older media technologies, like the print press, and media outlets with a longer history, like television broadcasts. It is hence basically impossible to consider digital media without inserting these into the broader repertoire of communication (Mattoni, 2012) that activists employ and which have become, year after year, increasingly hybrid.

Second, digital media and the Internet have changed the way in which activists protest in the public space, hence bringing about a deep change in the repertoires of protest of social movements. Not only have these repertoires broadened to include forms of protest that can occur only online, hence creating an additional repertoire of electronic contention (Costanza-Chock, 2003), but they also allow activists to depend less on the sharing of the same space and time of protest (Earl and Kimport, 2011). Additionally, and probably even more importantly, more traditional collective actors – like social movement organizations – become less central in the repertoire of protest that today revolves instead around the political engagement of individuals, often in an aggregated form, far more so than in the past (Earl and Kimport, 2011).

Third, digital media contributed to the modification of some of the social movements' organizational forms, also changing the way activists coordinate their mobilizations. In this regard, the use of social media platforms such as Twitter and Facebook have considerably changed the organizational structures of contemporary protest. While older forms of collective action persist in the present day, newer forms of connective action where individuals engage online without any collective organization are becoming more and more important (Bennett and Segerberg, 2013). In other words, digital media, and social media platforms more specifically, contributed to reverse the relationship between organization and communication, the latter having the power of shaping the former in contemporary grassroots politics (Gerbaudo, 2012). The constant flow of mediated interactions between activists, their allies, supporters, and bystander publics that occur through Facebook and Twitter generates a form of liquid organization of protest that assigns the most important roles to the communicators within the movements (Gerbaudo, 2012).

Finally, the very existence of digital media and their appropriation by activists have set in motion a brand-new imaginary of what activists can do and how they do it in the framework of their mobilizations. In the anti-corporate globalization movement that emerged at the end of the 1990s, with anti-summit demonstrations taking place in Seattle, a culture of networking arose that characterizes this movement and is deeply tied to the emerging internet technologies of the time and their potentials (Juris 2008). Far from being a mere tool in the hands of activists, then, the emerging Internet infrastructure of the late 1990s already proved to have a strong impact on what activists thought of their grassroots political engagement and its potential. The imaginary that activists construct around the technologies that they employ can be seen at work in other mobilizations as well, as in the case of anti-austerity movements (Treré et al, 2017; Treré, 2018) – which make use of social media – or in that of the so-called movement parties (Mercea and Mosca, 2021).

Beyond these four aspects, scholars interested in social movements and digital media have recently had to confront themselves with yet another relevant technological transformation: the spread of algorithms and big data. In this regard, scholars speak about the emergence of data activism: a form of activism that frames the data and their use as contentious issues, hence focusing on 'data-as-stakes' or considering the data as a central element in repertoires of protest, thus defining them as 'data-as-repertoires' or 'proactive data activism' (Milan, 2017), meaning that activists collaborate, organize themselves, and engage in collective actions through data (Gutierrez, 2019). Existing literature has cast light on how activists integrate data into various types of mobilizations: for example, the use of data to support initiatives against corruption (Mattoni, 2017b; Odilla and Mattoni, 2023); the autonomous creation of a National Index of Male Violence in Argentina, in the framework of the feminist movement #NiUnaMenos (Chenou and Cepeda-Másmela, 2019); and the InfoAmazonia project's use of data crowdsourcing and satellite images, including data sources, to provide information about environmental threats and related issues in the Amazonian region (Gutierrez, 2019).

Another relevant feature is the activists' engagement not in big data itself, but in the algorithms that regulate the production and circulation of information on social media platforms. For instance, the Spanish activists who participated in the 15-M mobilizations in 2011 consistently appropriated the Twitter algorithm to create trending topics about their protests to raise the interest of the general public and, even more importantly, of journalists working in legacy media (Treré, 2018). However, algorithms may also alter some of the dynamics that characterize social movements, and the algorithms that support the functioning of social media platforms create a different politics of visibility that put individual activists, rather than their movement organizations, at centre stage (Milan, 2015). Social media platforms can also enhance forms of content production that are individualized and, therefore, contrast with the otherwise collective efforts to craft messages which are the expression of movement organizations (Barassi and Fenton, 2011). Furthermore, algorithms that sustain social media platforms can even create technological barriers to grassroots activism: including the development of filter bubbles for activists and their audiences; and an excessive emphasis on social media metrics in order to gain popularity (Dumitrica and Felt, 2020). At the same time, algorithms might also facilitate collective action, for instance through the creation of links among distant activists; the assemblage of otherwise scattered information; and the augmentation of the reach of activist mobilizations (Etter and Albu, 2021).

In this section, we have given a concise overview of the relationship between social movements and digital media, algorithms, and big data during moments of mobilization. However, some questions remain to be answered as to the quiet moments of grassroots politics in between protests. What happens when the streets are empty, activists go back to the ordinary routines of their organizations, and demonstrations stop being trending topics on Twitter? What is the role of digital media and digital data in the practices of social movement and civil society actors when the spotlights are turned off, and nobody is watching them? In the following section, we will explain why these two questions, which this book seeks to answer, are so relevant.

Digital media and big data during the quiet moments of grassroots politics

Activists do not disappear the moment a public protest ends, and there is a good wealth of literature that teaches us how important stages of latency are for social movements. Indeed, contentious collective action rests on social 'movement areas' where we find 'a multiplicity of groups that are dispersed, fragmented and submerged in everyday life, and which act as cultural laboratories' (Melucci, 1989: 60). It is exactly during these moments of invisibility that activists engage in the creation of 'new cultural codes [that] enable individuals to put them into practice' (Melucci, 1989: 60). Stages of latency, though, are not just moments in which activists take part in the production of meanings. For instance, the impact of small incidents happening in the daily life of an activist group may outline new directions for this group, changing its capabilities to engage in future collective actions (Blee, 2012). There are, also, 'social movement scenes' that exist before and beyond the peak of protest; these are networks of different yet interconnected, countercultural spaces, which have the function of promoting an 'active engagement in the movement as a low-pressure context in which people are exposed to movement norms' (Leach and Haunss, 2009: 270). In short, those moments in which protesters are in the streets or engaged in some form of visible collective action to make their demands heard are sustained through 'the crucial, undramatic day-to-day activities necessary to consolidate the work of a movement's "ritual public displays" into significant impact' (Reed, 2019: xxi). Similarly, social movement organizations might carefully craft their communication strategies long before the protests took place, as happened in the Spanish 15-M mobilizations that erupted in 2011 (Fominaya, 2020). It is clear, then, that these moments of latency are relevant to social movements since they allow activists to build their political commitment and sustain their future protest activities. Furthermore, these are moments in which potential protest participants may develop an interest in the contentious matters that social movement actors care about and struggle for.

Stages of latency are becoming ever more important because the repertoire of contention of grassroots activists is broadening, increasingly embracing forms of collective action that do not require people to go down to the streets to obtain their scopes. Especially in countries that have been struck by the 2008 economic crisis, such as Greece, Italy, and Spain, scholars have observed an increase in what they call direct social actions: collective actions that aim at transforming certain aspects of society by means of the very action itself (Bosi and Zamponi, 2015). Although they might be confrontational, these types of actions do not put the expression of dissent in the streets and squares of contemporary urban spaces at the centre of the debate, in part because they do not address governmental actors in order to change society. Direct social actions became even more relevant, and evident, during the COVID-19 pandemic, when activists across the world could not hit the streets to demonstrate as a result of social distancing measures. Nevertheless, activism did not disappear: on several occasions, it took the form of direct social actions, with people engaging in solidarity actions to sustain the most vulnerable individuals in societies (Pleyers, 2020).

More generally speaking, even those grassroots activists that privilege public forms of protests – including demonstrations, occupations, and strikes – live these stages of intense protesting as punctuated moments in between longer periods of time, during which they remain politically engaged, though not necessarily and continuously in public. It is in these periods that grassroots activists define and redefine themselves, their unwritten norms, and their shared routines. In these moments of latency, digital media and digital data remain in the hands of activists who are engaged in the routine activities of grassroots politics. As we will make clear in the following chapters, it is exactly during these periods of grassroots political engagement – far removed from massive mobilizations – that we may better appreciate how grassroots activists employ digital media at the peak of mobilization, when the streets are full of protesters and Facebook's pages are packed with posts about demonstrations. This is because it is in these moments that activists also experiment with and reflect on how to use digital media to sustain their activities. In other words, we see the moments in between protest peaks as periods in which activists' interactions with digital media tend to sediment and stabilize. Hence, it is by looking at what happens during these ordinary moments of grassroots politics that we can truly understand the peculiarities of an activist's reliance on digital media and the digital data related to them, among which big data, also during protest peaks. In other words, the challenges posed by digital media are always relevant for activists, both when they mobilize and when they decide not to engage in public protest and related activities. In the next section, we will reflect more in depth on this issue by unpacking two relevant transformations in current societies: digitalization and datafication.

Mediatization, digitalization, and datafication

When activists who are involved in movement organizations work toward the achievement of their political projects, they face societies in which the presence of media – and not just the digital ones – is deeply ingrained in all human activities. This phenomenon has been called mediatization and refers to a meta-process according to which the main social processes in our societies are mediated through media of all kinds, ranging from radio and television to the most recent, innovative Internet applications (Hepp, 2013). Obviously, mediatization is not a novel meta-process. Well before the emergence of digital media, for instance, scholars interested in political communication have observed that politics – more precisely, institutional politics – were increasingly mediatized. Already in the 1960s and 1970s, activists had to come to terms with the logic of mainstream media, as in the case of the movement organizations belonging to the civil rights movement in the United States, which had to deal with the need and ability of the press and television to turn the movement's leaders into political celebrities, with serious consequences for the movement itself (Gitlin, 1980). Similarly, in the 1990s, leaders and members of political parties adapted to the logic of the mainstream press and broadcast television, changing the way in which they interacted with their supporters, colleagues, and opponents (Mazzoleni and Schulz, 1999; Kepplinger, 2002; Strömbäck, 2008).

In the present day, mediatization touches the very fabric of our societies, much more so than in the past decades, because all social processes rely on a wide array of infrastructures of communication not only at the global level but also on a far more limited scale, like the micro experiences of people in their daily lives (Couldry and Hepp, 2016). Mediatization also changes over time, and it does so in waves according to the specific configuration of media technologies that is dominant in a specific epoch. Current societies are characterized by two interlaced waves of mediatization: digitalization and datafication (Couldry and Hepp, 2016).

Digitalization is related to the invention of personal computers, computer networks, the Internet, and mobile phones (Couldry and Hepp, 2016). The rapid diffusion of all three technological innovations brought along several deep transformations, including the convergence of older and newer media in the daily experience of people (Jenkins, 2006), but also the overall increased relevance of the digital in all spheres of individuals' daily and social lives (Lupton, 2015). Datafication is strictly linked to the proliferation of big data and data analytics, which led to an unprecedented, automated quantification of many aspects of social lives that were not so heavily quantified before (Kennedy, 2018; Couldry and Mejias, 2019). Referring to this process, scholars have spoken about datafication to signal the transformation of information about human beings and their activities into data that can be easily measured, aggregated, and profiled, often for the purpose of producing economic value (Kennedy, 2018; Couldry and Mejias, 2019).

Through this book, we aim to enrich the literature on mediatization – and on the mediatization of grassroots politics more specifically – by looking at this meta-process from the perspective of the activists themselves. This is something scholars have seldom done, although there are of course valuable exceptions. Concerning digitalization, research on 'subactivism' puts the ordinary unfolding of grassroots politics at centre stage, capturing 'a kind of politics that unfolds at the level of subjective experience and is submerged in the flow of everyday life' (Bakardjieva, 2009: 9). In this case, the attention is directed toward individuals who have no kind of political affiliation, neither formally nor informally. Yet, the author argues, they contribute to the making of politics from the margins of their everyday experiences, with the Internet sustaining their actions. But there is also research that focuses on activists involved in progressive movement organizations to explore what impact their daily use of digital media in Italy, Spain, and the UK had on their self-perception as activists as well as the tensions that arose from the encounter between the activists' political cultures and the culture of digital capitalism (Barassi, 2015a).

As for datafication, the continuous interaction that people have with data throughout their daily lives has also been a quite marginal line of investigation; scholars have mostly focused either on the power actors who produce and employ big data or on the less powerful, but still technologically skilful, actors who work on the accountability of big data usage (Kennedy, 2018). A promising line of research in this direction lies in the exploration of data activism, which 'consists in ways of collaborating, organizing and taking action via software and data seeking to create unconventional narratives and solutions to social problems' (Gutierrez, 2018: 2). Data activists engage in the datafication of our societies, either resisting or exploiting it in the framework of their mobilizations; they do this quite straightforwardly by organizing their collective actions around the negative consequences of datafication, or seeking to employ various types of data – not necessarily big data – to support their struggles (Milan and Van der Velten, 2016).

However, in societies that are highly digitalized and increasingly datafied, all kinds of activists – not necessarily only data activists – stumble upon various types of data in which they are immersed owing to the use of various types of digital and non-digital media. And they also deal with a wide range of digital media, while at the same time still engaging with other types of media, including the mainstream press. Hence, in this book we take a step further and consider all those everyday moments in which activists engage in various forms of data while not necessarily and not always thinking about themselves as data activists in the first place. On the contrary, they frequently consider themselves as promoters of civic actions, political organizers, or activists who simply fight for the causes they care about and, in doing this, attempt to raise awareness and influence policy makers. Yet, while doing this, they cannot avoid engaging in many types of data that are deeply ingrained in their daily routines as activist and go well beyond big data. To capture such a multifaceted engagement with digital media and digital data, we look at activists' interactions with digitalization and datafication through the analytical lenses of the data stream. The next section introduces this concept and discusses its main features.

Activism, data, and the data stream

In order to fully understand what the concept of the data stream refers to, we propose adopting a broad perspective on data, namely one that rejects the idea that the concept of data is synonymous with big data and also as a shorthand for digital data. The notion of data was not born with the advent of electronic computing devices; over the centuries, it has taken a semantic trip, frequently changing its central meaning in scientific communities. The term 'data' was originally considered as the plural of 'datum', from its Latin origin, which is a given that refers to a simple and incontrovertible fact (Poovey, 1998). Next, the notion changed its meaning and became almost synonymous with empirical evidence resulting from an experimental scientific process. In the present day, instead, data are mainly defined as pieces of information (Rosenberg, 2013). As is clear from this brief and not exhaustive excursus, regardless of their primary sense, data have never been associated with any specific format or support: we may well have digital data, but data also come in analogue forms, taking many shapes. While this viewpoint on data is nowadays probably not conventional in media studies, it is certainly not uncommon in other fields of research. For instance, Sabina Leonelli (2016) proposes considering data as 'any product of research activities, ranging from artifacts such as photographs to symbols such as letters or numbers, that is collected, stored, and disseminated in order to be used as evidence for knowledge claims' (77). While the author focuses on the production of knowledge in the field of biology, her observations resonate with what we understand as data in the framework of grassroots political engagement. Scholars focusing on data activism have already widened their perspective on data suggesting that this type of activism involves not only activists' interactions with big data but also with various forms of digital data used to create knowledge and increase public awareness about contentious issues as well as to sustain protest campaigns and mobilizations (Milan and Van der Velten, 2016). Broadening our view on data even further, we propose to think of data as a series of any unit of information (Gitelman and Jackson, 2013), coming in a variety of formats – including written texts, quick chats, long conversations, numerical strings, and different types of visuals, to name a few – that activists engage with in their daily political work.

Another relevant aspect of data is that, although activists engage in them in their many forms, not all data may be meaningful to them. This is because an inherent feature of data is their relational nature (Manovich, 2011), which renders them intrinsically tied to the situation in which they are constructed, gathered, and employed, as well as to the interpretation being assigned to them (Borgman, 2016; Leonelli, 2016). Indeed, while some data may mean nothing to one activist, the same data may produce information that is relevant to another activist. This happens because it is not the data that carry information, but the encounter between the data and other actors – not necessarily human – who select, store, process, and combine various types of data to obtain relevant information. Hence, the notion of data is not synonymous with information, in that activists must engage in data and act on them to obtain the information that they need. This can happen through algorithms or manually, that is, through spreadsheets and software or reading and underlining written documents, respectively. Even more importantly, activists seldom engage in just one type of data at the same time. Indeed, activists frequently create data that are not necessarily produced through high-tech tools, but which could be vital for the goals of their movement organizations and their constituencies (Gabrys et al, 2016). Furthermore, these data may at times be scattered, difficult to gather, or not yet gathered; they may be small in comparison to the magnitude of big data, but they require an extended activist effort to be integrated consistently into the activists' broader repertoire of protest (Mattoni, 2017a).

To take the manifold interactions that activists have with various digital and non-digital data (and media) into serious consideration, we propose employing the concept of the data stream, which is the core element of our analytical framework. Before considering its main qualities, it is worth spending a few words to clarify what we mean by data stream in the context of this book. The data stream is a popular concept in computer sciences, where it is used in connection with real-time analytics and defined as a 'sequence of items, possibly infinite, each item having a timestamp, and so a temporal order' (Bifet et al, 2018: 8). Data streams, then, refer to concrete data instances that various types of devices continuously produce, including sensor data produced through devices ingrained in the urban setting, phone call metadata produced by telecommunication companies, and social media data produced by the interactions of their users (Bifet et al, 2018).

In this book, the data stream is a heuristic that we employ to acknowledge and, at the same time, emphasize the interactions that activists have with a broad range of data when they engage in grassroots politics. In short, we consider the data stream as a heterogeneous, ubiquitous, and perpetual sequence of data that are generated through various technological devices – from the most high-tech ones to those closer to the low-tech side of technology – that activists interact with when they engage in grassroots politics, both during the peak of mobilizations and when protests are absent. The data stream therefore not only includes big data: it goes beyond it, in that it also encompasses data that may be simultaneously smaller and thicker, like the information that activists collect about their opponents and the political context in which they are embedded. For this reason, we argue that the data stream – as we understand it – is heterogeneous in terms of both the logic according to which the data are produced and circulated and, of course, the type of data that activists interact with. Indeed, data come in the form of concise and precise numbers about the social world and the social interactions that constitute them, but also in the shape of lengthier descriptions of the same social world that are generated through words and visuals. Such heterogeneity requires activists to deal with pressing challenges, which often leads them to make difficult choices, compromises, and trade-offs that enable them to extract meaningful information and then use these to perform various activities. In this regard, it is important to note that – as we have already stressed when we discussed the notion of data – the data stream, in itself, also does not equate with information: activists have to interact with the data stream to select, aggregate, and transform relevant data so that these can become crucial information. At the same time, the data stream is also ubiquitous, since activists can never position themselves outside it. They may decide to slow down its rhythm, but they are never able to disconnect from it completely. Finally, the data stream is perpetual, because it is constantly unfolding: it rarely stops, and although activists can decide not to engage in it in a certain moment, they also know that, in doing this, they are missing something because the data stream does not cease to exist when they refrain from interacting with it.

These qualities of the data stream are deeply connected to what activists do in their daily engagement with grassroots politics. In the case of activists who belong to movement organizations, as is always the case with the activists discussed in this book, this makes the activists' experience of the data stream both individual and collective. It is individual because each activist is dealing with data from their unique position in the world, including their demographic characteristics. But it is also a collective experience because what activists do and say about data is always linked to their participation in a collectivity, namely the movement organizations to which they belong, where activists learn from each other, make collective decisions, and orient their actions thinking as a whole and not just as fragmented individuals.

Moreover, the data stream and its qualities place activists in a direct, if somewhat unsettling, relationship with two aspects of social movements: the temporal and spatial dimensions of movement organization, which are relevant even when mobilizations are not taking place and activists are engaged in other, more everyday projects and tasks. While we will discuss the issue of temporality in more detail later in this book, it is worth noting that the flow of data is not necessarily tied to a specific location, as the data involved can be generated at the international, national, or local level. For example, some activists and social movement organizations may well engage with data developed by supranational organizations, such as anti-corruption data curated by the World Bank or labour data curated by the International Labour Organization. But even in these cases, these data are embedded in the efforts of specific movement organizations, which are always located somewhere and therefore have a local dimension. While acknowledging that the data stream undoubtedly has a national and international dimension, in this book we focus on how activists experience it in the local situations from which they engage in grassroots politics.

Finally, the data stream is produced partly inside and partly outside movement organizations. Activists are not the only ones producing data that converge in the data stream. Many of the political actors with whom they interact also participate in the construction of data: a politician's speech broadcast on television, a journalist's article in a national newspaper, the images posted on Instagram by activists' supporters. These are all examples of data that activists do not directly produce, but that nevertheless converge in the stream of data they encounter in the course of their daily grassroots political engagement. From this perspective, activists are simultaneously in the position of producers and consumers of the data stream: they contribute to it when they create and share social media content, but they also consume it when they read newspaper reports or receive instant messages, among other possible data. It is therefore worth noting that the data stream is not something that only activists experience and contribute to: other actors also come into play and engage with the data stream, from their specific perspectives and not always necessarily in the context of political participation. However, in this book we focus specifically on how the data stream is a relevant analytical lens for understanding many types of activities that shape activists' political engagement, including activists' use of data to organise their next political campaign; activists' production of data when participating in public debates; activists' collection of data on potential allies to facilitate gaining their trust; or activists' search for data to understand the current political situation.

While being a relevant heuristic for our research, the data stream is not the book's direct object of study. Indeed, we do not seek to measure the data stream, for example through its magnitude and velocity. Rather, we aim to understand how activists deal with the data stream as a whole and in its components, the challenges that it poses to them, and the agency that they exercise in its regard. In other words, we look at the extent to which the activists' interactions with digital media during their daily political engagement allow them to interact with the data stream or, to be more precise, with the various sequences of data that constitute it – ranging from social media data to legacy media data, from website generated data to data coming from face-to-face interactions. The presence of different sequences of data within the data stream is a direct consequence of the coexistence of various forms of mediatization in our societies. As Couldry and Hepp (2016) point out, mediatization developed in waves throughout history: mechanization put printing technologies at its core; electrification revolved around broadcast media; digitalization was strictly linked to the development of the Internet and the Web; and datafication is, instead, centred on all those applications and platforms – including social media – that produce, aggregate, and profile user data with the help of algorithms. Despite having developed in different historical moments, these four waves of mediatization do not exclude each other. Rather, they tend to live side by side and, in some instances, even overlap. This is also what happens to the data stream: sequences of data created through social media platforms and, more generally, various types of digital media develop in parallel – sometimes also overlapping – with less high-tech and non-digital sequences of data in various activist practices. Before briefly outlining the types of practice that emerged as relevant in our research, the next section explains in more detail the theoretical approach that underpins this book and the research on which it is based.

A practice approach for the investigation of activism in the data stream

So far, we have discussed the main conceptual tools that we will employ in this book. In this section, we will illustrate the analytical architecture that sustained our research. Again, our objective was to understand how the activists in Greece, Italy, and Spain embed digital media and other types of media in their daily political work: which digital media they use, to perform which actions, and for what reasons. To reach this goal, we decided to start not so much from the digital media in themselves, but from the actions that the activists perform; this will allow us to see what the role of digital media – and other types of media – in these actions was. Hence, we put the activists' practices at the centre of our investigation and mainly relied on practice theories to sustain it.

Practice theories first emerged about five decades ago. The work of prominent sociologists like Pierre Bourdieu (1977) and Anthony Giddens (1979) set the basis for a so-called first wave of practice theorists; these attempted to resolve certain prevailing dichotomies in the social sciences, including those opposing agency and structure, individuals and societies, subjects and objects. A second wave built on the previous one, while also expanding both the conceptual vocabulary and the fields of application of practice theories (see Postill, 2009). In what follows, we will draw on this second wave of practice theories, with the purpose not of providing an exhaustive presentation of its qualities and features but, rather, of leading the discussion toward the main topic of this section: the application of practice theories in studies that deal with media, at large, and with grassroots politics in particular, including social movements and civil society actors.

Although practice theories display a diverse collection of assumptions about the place and role of practices in societies, they certainly share some relevant characteristics. To begin with, they all consider practices as the most significant locus of the social; in so doing, they promote an understanding of societies that focuses on the analysis of how social actions are enacted, performed, and produced, rather than on the actors' intentions (Cohen, 1996). Practice theories therefore partially shift the attention from the actors to the things that the actors do. Although they do not deny the existence of social actors, social processes, and social institutions, practice theories indeed consider practices as the constitutive elements of societies or, to use Kevin McMillan's words, 'as one of the main building blocks of social reality: they are the basis upon which institutions persist, social structures depend and historical processes unfold' (McMillan, 2017: 21). From this viewpoint, practices – while they are, of course, inherently social – do not wither away in the social realm, other levels of existence being equally important in practices, as we will discuss in more detail later.

Several fields in social and political sciences have begun to explore the potential of practice theories. Scholars in international relations (Bueger and Gadinger, 2018), the sociology of consumption (Warde, 2005; Halkier et al, 2011), ecological economics (Røpke, 2009), science and technology studies (Gad and Jensen 2014), and organizational studies (Orlikowski, 2007; Nicolini, 2010) have developed their own perspectives on how a practice approach may foster a more grounded understanding of the topics that pertain to each of their fields of reference. A similar direction has been taken in the sociology of media (Bräuchler and Postill, 2010), in which several scholars have started to investigate media through a practice theory lens, focusing on diverse media-related phenomena such as journalism (Ahva, 2017), videogames (Roig et al, 2009), and political communication (Driessens et al, 2010).

A terrain that has proved fertile for the development of a practice approach is that located at the crossroads of the sociology of media, political sociology, and political sciences: this book is situated at the same interdisciplinary intersection. In the past decades, studies on media practices in grassroots politics and social movements have flourished. Taking on Nick Couldry's suggestion to look at media as neither texts nor institutions, but rather as a nexus of doings and sayings that goes beyond the usual distinction between media producers and media consumers (Couldry, 2004, 2012), scholars with different disciplinary backgrounds have employed a media practice perspective in order to investigate the multifaceted relationship between media and social movements. This literature has three clear merits: it has contributed to rendering studies on social movements less centred on one specific type of media device or platform at a time, less inclined toward a generalist understanding of the relationship between media and movements, and less prone to a deterministic, structural reading of the role of media in social movements (see Mattoni, 2017b). As a result, studies on the subject matter that have developed in recent years acknowledge the interconnected use of different types of media within social movements, take into account the contexts in which activists use media, and highlight the agency that social movement actors exercise over media, including mainstream media.

By analysing the media practices of social movements, scholars have certainly moved away from a media-centric perspective that puts media – and digital media – at the forefront of theoretical explanations of how social movements develop in societies, hence avoiding deterministic conceptions of media technologies. This shift from a media-centric to a media-centred approach to the study of grassroots politics has had its positive sides: scholars not only stopped – to a great extent – treating digital media as a force capable of determining the shape of a social movement, but they also constructed rich narratives of the many types of interactions between grassroots activists and digital media. However, when looking at this body of knowledge, it is clear that those studies that embrace a practice approach do so in different ways.

In the first instance, certain scholars study *media as practices* in the framework of social movements and grassroots politics, thus focusing on certain types of media that are different from mainstream media, like alternative media (Atton, 2002) or citizen media (Stephansen, 2016). By looking at these media from a practice approach, scholars pay attention to how, among other things, citizen media come into being through practices, how citizen media practitioners interpret these practices, and how citizen media as practices may orient other practices that are not directly linked to citizen media (Stephansen, 2016). A similar approach can be detected in some studies of hacktivism, which is not only considered in terms of its direct intervention in the so-called cyberspace, but rather as a radical media practice based on certain types of technological objects and entrenched with specific meanings related to what technologies are and should be (Milan, 2015).

A second way of looking at media and social movements from the perspective of practice theories is by focusing on practices that are related to the media, that is to say, *media-related practices*. Scholars seem to have privileged this viewpoint when analysing the activists' engagement with media, hence examining the extent to which activists simultaneously do things with and say things about a broad range of media: from mainstream to alternative, from digital to non-digital media. Scholars have focused on the way activists reacted to the presence of mainstream media during their protest actions (Couldry, 2000; McCurdy, 2011), explored 'activist media practices' and the implied interactions with media professionals and media objects (Mattoni, 2012), investigated the multiple tactics that activists scout when creating alternative media and interacting with mainstream media (Jeppesen et al, 2014: 24), and considered how activists appropriate and develop media technologies (Kubitschko, 2018).

Finally, it is possible to approach media and social movements by considering *media in practice*. To study media in practice means both to consider how different types of technological devices and services that sustain media intermingle with a given practice and, at the same time, to examine how such devices and services are actually used in the practices as they happen. Despite this stream of research being the least explored in the extant literature, there are some valuable exceptions. In this regard, scholars have focused on the role different types of media have in the practices of information production, distribution, and consumption that social movement organizations engage in (Kaun, 2016) and looked at how various types of media, mostly digital, are included in activists' practices during mass protests (Dumitrica and Felt, 2020).

In a similar way, in this book we investigate how the media interact with and affect different types of practices that are performed in the daily life of grassroots activists. However, we expand the media in practice approach to capture, at the empirical level, the data stream that simultaneously constitutes and is constitutive of the activists' practices. This decision is linked to what has emerged from the analysis of our data: while we started from the activists' practices and the role that digital media played in them, we soon realized that other relevant aspects emerged from these materials, namely the activists' daily interactions with many types of data through their use of digital media, social media platforms, and algorithms. For this reason, we decided to broaden our perspective to include not just media, but also data in practice.

In order to do this, we will draw on the work of practice theories scholars who consider practices as a dynamic heuristic device that is made up of several elements. Despite the existence of many types of practice theories, there seems to be a certain agreement among scholars, who tend to consider practices as heterogeneous bundles of multiple elements within which the activities that individuals perform in their daily lives are just one of many features. For instance, Andrea Reckwitz (2002) suggests that a practice is 'a routinized type of behaviour which consists of several elements, interconnected with one other: forms of bodily activities, forms of mental activities, "things" and their use, a background knowledge in the form of understanding, know how, states of emotion and motivational knowledge' (250). Similarly, Reijo Savolainen (2008) argues that practices are 'embodied, materially mediated arrays of human action (or activities), centrally organized around shared understanding' (24). Finally, Elisabeth Shove and her collaborators also outline three main elements that characterize practices: material features through which individuals perform practices, including their bodies; knowledge and skills related to how a practice could, and sometimes should, be performed; and the meanings that individuals assign to what they do and the contexts in which they do this (Shove et al, 2012). Finally, Theodore Schatzki (2002) also stresses that practices are an 'organized nexus of actions' (77) that are linked through a practical understanding of how to perform those actions, explicit rules on how those actions should be performed, a teleoaffective structure that presupposes the ends of the practice, and general understandings about specific aspects related to the practice. According to these authors, the various elements that constitute a practice are interconnected up to the point that it cannot be reduced to any one element; in other words, it is not possible to understand a practice simply by focusing on the mental activities that it entails, or on the background knowledge that is mobilized to sustain it. It is only by considering a practice as a whole, composed of all its elements, that we can access, analyse, and understand it.

With this aim in mind, in this book we will employ a definition of practice according to which practices are a nexus of actions. Actions and practices are linked because the former are the 'concrete, particular, datable events' of which 'practices are simply their generalized form – a class of such events whose various members share certain attributes' (McMillan, 2017: 21). However, limiting practices to the actions that belong to them would be reductive, for when we look at practices we also see the bodies of those who perform the actions, the objects they use, the other people they relate to, the motivations behind the action and, additionally, the perceptions that guide them (Reckwitz, 2002; Schatzki, 2002). Furthermore, as Reckwitz (2002) argues, practices are never simply focused on the individual who performs them: not only the individual who acts knows how to implement and understand practices, but also those who observe the individual. Drawing on Schatzki's understanding of practice (2002), we argue that activists who perform a certain practice seem to know how to engage in specific actions (for example, producing a post for Facebook), follow rules that are related to that practice (for example, choosing the right moment to post content on Facebook), draw on a teleoaffective structure that somehow defines their end goals (for example, becoming visible beyond the social movement milieu), and start from a general understanding of certain key dimensions that characterize the social world in which they act (a general understanding of politics, journalism, and their mutual relationship).

At the more operational level, we need to make an additional move. Drawing on Susan Scott and Wanda Orlikowski's reading (2014) of Kate Barad (2007), we too will consider practices as 'constitutive entanglements' of different dimensions that present themselves as deeply interlaced, with each of them being constitutive of the other and of practices as well. However, while the two authors focus on the connection between the social and

Figure 1.1: Socio-material practices as constitutive entanglements of the material, the symbolic, and the social

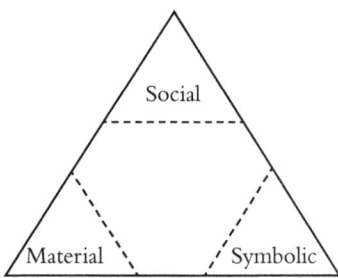

the material, we look at practices as constitutive entanglements of three aspects: the social, the symbolic, and the material (Figure 1.1).

In our operational definition of practices, then, we consider practices as social because they imply a series of actions that are performed through interactions between social actors, but also because they are foundational elements of the social world as we know it. Furthermore, they need social recognition to be performed (see Gherardi, 2009). At the same time, we consider practices as material because they also include non-human actors, such as technologies and protocols. Indeed, when individuals perform practices, they always use various types of objects that become an integral part of the practice (Haddon, 2011). Finally, we consider practices as symbolic because they are imbued not only with meanings that individuals assign to social actions and to the technological objects that they employ to perform these actions, but also with a broader knowledge – either implicit or explicit – of the way practices themselves should be performed (Siles and Boczkowski, 2012). The social, material, and symbolic traits of practices are therefore all entangled in the more concrete and tangible bundles of actions that activists perform on a daily basis; we can also see such entanglements at work in the practical understandings, rules, teleoaffective structures, and general understandings that organize the practices. In the next section, we will briefly introduce the first pivotal finding of our investigation, that is, the four practices that appear to be most central in the daily political engagement of the activists in Greece, Italy, and Spain.

Four practices of grassroots politics in the data stream

Our investigation and the related data analysis have revealed that activists employ digital media and other types of media to perform four main practices throughout their daily grassroots political activities. Overall, activists pay a lot of attention to the coordination of such activities in the first place, although they also want their movement organizations to be visible beyond the inner circles of fellow activists; and they want to stay updated on what other political actors are doing and, at the same time, create and nurture a wide set of relationships. Starting from the activists' purposes, then, we have named the four practices as follows: the practice of political organizing; the practice of gaining visibility; the practice of information gathering; and the practice of sustaining connection.

While in the following chapters we will describe more in depth what role the data stream and different sequences of data play in each of these four practices, this section provides a bird's eye view of the four practices as well as their general differences and similarities. On the whole, each of the four practices entails both activities that are specifically tied to that practice and others that encompass different practices. Indeed, while boundaries between different practices may exist – as Schatzki also observes when discussing practices – they are often tied to one another in complex configurations; the reason for this is that they could share the same activities. However, practices are ultimately distinct from one another, because in each of them the nexus of doings and sayings that belong to them is kept together by specific combinations of practical and general understandings, rules, and teleoaffectivities (Schatzki, 2002). Furthermore, what stands out as a particularly relevant finding of our empirical investigation, is that the practice of information gathering plays an anchoring role towards the other three practices. It is hence quite surprising, as we will stress more later in the book, that there is scarce literature on activism and such practice. Going back to the four practices, we consider two main dimensions according to which we can differentiate between them and, in so doing, put an emphasis on what renders them similar (and dissimilar) to one another (Table 1.1).

Table 1.1: The four practices that emerged from the analysis

	Mundane practices	**Political practices**
Backstage practices	Information gathering	Political organizing
Front-stage practices	Sustaining connection	Gaining visibility

Backstage and front-stage practices

While all practices are performed in public through bodies and with the involvement of various objects, some of them are specifically oriented toward people who are outside the inner circles of the movement organizations that activists belong to. Others, instead, are oriented toward people that are part of the movement organization of which activists are part of, like other fellow activists and the movement organization's members. In this regard, we differentiate between front-stage practices, which aim at reaching a broad range of distant actors, and backstage practices, which mostly involve actors who are already tied to activists and their movement organizations. Indeed, although the boundaries of an activist's organization may be blurred, and even more so when we are dealing with grassroots and informal types of civil society actors, it is always possible to identify certain activities that remain mostly in the backstage, as opposed to others that are performed front-stage. Activities that are part of the practice of political organizing are oriented toward the coordination of the activists' daily work; planning a meeting or setting up an assembly are activities that allow movement organizations and activist groups to continue to exist day after day. These activities, often happening backstage, are hidden from the public eye and even taken for granted by those who perform them. As such, they go unnoticed and remain invisible. Activities related to the practice of finding relevant information also mostly occur in the background, and they imply activists' search for pieces of news that could be useful to them; reading the news and watching television could be included in such activities as well as browsing the web and looking for specific types of data related to the activists' interests.

Directly oriented toward the establishment or maintenance of the activists' relationships with journalists, supporters, and potential allies are, instead, what we have called the practice of sustaining connections that are meaningful for activists and their political work. This practice includes activities of the following kind: replying to comments on the Facebook pages of activists' organizations, taking a weekly informal beer with a policy maker so as to maintain a potentially useful relationship, but also keeping the conversation going in WhatsApp group chats or meeting with members of the activists' organizations in order to learn more about their needs and hopes. Finally, the practice of gaining visibility is oriented toward the development and preservation of a public presence through which activists and their organizations can be followed by other actors, including their (protest) targets, the bystander public, potential supporters, and fellow activists. Almost by definition, then, this type of practice focuses on the front stage of activists' organizations. More related to the use of media technologies and interactions with journalists than to the other three types of practices, the practice of gaining visibility include activities such as producing videos about the activists' initiatives, holding press conferences, and publishing content on Twitter.

Political and mundane practices

When discussing practices, Schatzki makes a difference between dispersed and integrative practices (2002: 88). The former are somewhat simple and can be found in different domains of social life: describing and questioning, for instance, are two practices that can be related to several realms, some of which are also very different from one another. The latter are complex practices that are usually performed in specific domains of social life, such as voting and cooking (Schatzki, 1996). When analysing our data, we found a similar difference. While none of the four core practices that turned out to be relevant can be considered as dispersed in the strictest sense, it is true that two of them are core practices of activists' movement organizations, whereas the other two – although relevant for activism – can also be linked to non-political, mundane realms. From this point of view, the nature of these practices is, so to speak, generic and not strictly related to the field of political participation. In fact, activists perform these practices even outside their movement organizations, when they are not directly engaged in their daily political activities.

The practices of political organizing and the practices of gaining visibility are strictly tied to the domain of grassroots political participation. The organizational patterns that civil society actors may follow are many, diverse, and changing over time, but the presence of some kind of coordination plays a pivotal role for activists. The same can be said for visibility; whether obtained through the coverage of the mainstream print press or thanks to trending hashtags on social media platforms, popularity beyond the circles of fellow activists and their movement organizations is a precious resource. Both organizational patterns and visibility are intimately tied to the political work that activists and their movement organizations perform on a daily basis. Thus, the quest for visibility puts the activists' grassroots political engagement at the centre, and not their private lives or other activities that they may carry out independently from politics. Similarly, the organizational work that activists do is inherently political, linked to the reach of specific – albeit sometimes shifting – political objectives. This is what renders the two practices strongly related to the realm of politics, and not to the other sphere of social lives in which activists are also situated.

The practice of sustaining connections and the practice of information gathering, instead, can also be performed in other, more mundane domains of the social lives of activists that are not necessarily tied to the realm of grassroots politics. Hence, although being relevant for grassroots politics, both these practices are performed well before and beyond the political commitment of activists. In other words, when activists perform activities such as reading website content or listening to radio programmes in search of information that could be useful to them, they also do so for reasons other than that of supporting their daily political work: they may want to know how to cook something properly, what the latest weather forecast is, or how to fix a broken window. Obviously, each of these types of information can also be linked to the activists' political engagement: knowing how to prepare a social dinner to raise money for their organizations; checking the weather to estimate how many people will join a sit-in they have organized; fixing a broken window in the organization's headquarters without paying money for it. Nonetheless, it is undoubtedly true that activists knew how to find information even before becoming activists, and they will continue to do so independently of their activist commitment. At the same time, activists do not reply to text or email messages that they receive on their phones and laptops only to maintain relationships that are useful to reach their political goals. Rather, their practice of sustaining connections may support their affective networks of kin, friends, and acquaintances; engaging in a continuous exchange of messages can help to continue family conversations when living far away from one another, or strengthen a relationship that will become central to providing care for activists beyond their political engagement. Again, we are dealing with something that does not necessarily pertain to the realm of grassroots politics, and that activists knew how to deal with even before they started their political engagement.

Organization of the book

So far, we have sketched the overall theoretical and analytical framework that guided the empirical investigation on activists' daily engagement with digital media and digital data in Greece, Italy, and Spain. We have also presented one preliminary finding of our fieldwork: the fact that four practices are particularly relevant during latency periods for activists in the three countries, as outlined in the previous section. The rest of the chapters in this book present in more detail how activists deal with the data stream in the context of each of these four practices.

Chapter 2 focuses on the practice of information gathering. Throughout the chapter, we argue that a relevant part of the daily political work of activists entails the constant collecting, assembling, and storing of various types of data that activists try to transform into relevant information. We will illustrate how activists seek to retrieve data from a multiplicity of media devices and services, spanning from newspaper articles published in printed media and radio programmes that they listen to when driving to social media platforms accessed through smartphones and tablets. We will also show that the type of data they seek to retrieve is related to different political actors. For instance, legacy media may provide information about the ongoing political debates within the ruling political parties and other institutional political actors; and social media are useful to check how the public debate is developing within activist circles. Finally, we will describe two challenges that affect the practice of information gathering: the multiple temporalities that characterize the data stream, and the data overload that activists experience in the practice of information gathering. Activists are constantly immersed in data sequences of mediated information, which they complement with face-to-face interactions either to verify what they have learned through media or to access information that would otherwise remain hidden from the public space. Activists use the presence of multiple temporalities to their advantage; the slowness with which they manage to collect data through their face-to-face relationships is crucial in giving activists those interpretive tools that enable them to derive information even from data arriving at a higher speed. At the same time, in this chapter we demonstrate that the practice of information gathering cannot be accomplished without all the filtering activities through which activists bring order to the abundant (and fast) set of data that they interact with on a daily basis.

Seeking information is certainly relevant for activists in times of quiet politics, and this is often the first step before engaging in other practices. These include the practice of gaining visibility, which is important for activists also when they do not need to make their public protests visible beyond the streets and squares where they physically happen. Chapter 3 explains how activists and their movement organizations follow different patterns to make themselves visible beyond the inner circles of their supporters. We argue that legacy media like television, radio, and newspapers, far from being neglected media of the past, remain a crucial venue for activists to gain visibility. In this regard, we will discuss the trade-offs that activists have to face if they want to become data sources for legacy media. Next, we will consider the important role of social media platforms for activists and their movement organizations. Finally, we will discuss alternative media that often take the shape of a non-digital soapbox for their political views. In this case, too, we argue that alternative media still play a role for activists and their movement organizations also when it comes to granting them visibility among specific types of audiences.

Chapter 4 focuses on another crucial aspect for activists and their movement organizations: algorithmic visibility. Using commercial social media platforms on a regular basis, activists have daily experiences with the algorithms that govern their operations, also in terms of gaining visibility for their published content. However, activists do not control these algorithms and, more importantly, rarely understand how they work. As we will explain in the chapter, activists implement three different strategies in order to manage algorithmic visibility: first, they aim at acquiring and maintaining a good reputation for their movement organization; second, they constantly and carefully manage the individual dimension of their movement organizations, which embodies a meticulous and strategic curation of the activists' social media accounts; third, activists may prefer the quality of the content they produce and pour into the data stream to its immediacy. They therefore choose to use stationary digital devices – such as computers and laptops – to process the data related to their activities, producing high-quality content. In short, caring for the reputation of their movement organization, paying attention to the online behaviours of the individual activists who are part of it, and producing high-quality content are three strategies that the activists in the three countries under examination implement to increase the possibility of being visible on social media platforms and, more generally, online, thus exceeding and countering the logic of algorithmic visibility as much as possible.

Chapter 5 shifts the attention to a practice that, unlike the practice of gaining visibility, takes place primarily in the backstage of movement organizations: the organization of one's own political work, which is vital for maintaining a movement organization and preparing it for those times when it is necessary to take to the streets. In this chapter, we will show that it is primarily digital media that lead the way in this practice. The widespread use of digital media, in particular smartphones and certain services such as instant messaging, is not without problems, though. The chapter focuses on three challenges that activists face in their daily political actions: the acceleration of the time of politics; the dissolution of the boundaries between the sphere of political engagement and other spheres of activists' lives; and the risk of privacy breach through surveillance activities. These three challenges have an important impact on the daily organization of political activities, even at the collective level. Nevertheless, we will demonstrate that activists manage to exercise a certain level of agency by developing strategies that allow them to cope with these challenges. A particularly relevant strategy is the ability of activists to reduce the pace of the data stream in order to rediscover a slower tempo of politics. Moreover, activists make a differentiated use of various digital services to restore those boundaries that otherwise disappear, namely between public and private life, between political activities and activities not primarily dedicated to politics. Finally, activists resort to face-to-face, unmediated interactions to secure a higher level of privacy and to escape surveillance. However, these types of interactions are a luxury that few movement organizations can afford on a stable basis, especially when it comes to movement organizations acting on a national scale. Paradoxically, in a world where digital media are pervasive and facilitate many organizational tasks, sharing the same physical space for an organizational meeting becomes a valued activity, even if it is not widely practiced in the absence of resources that can move activists across the country, from one city to another.

Chapter 6 considers another very important practice for movement organizations during latency stages: the ability of activists to establish relationships with other social actors, both inside and outside the environment of their movement organizations. In other words, this chapter focuses on the practice of sustaining connections. We will again show that, although several activities may help to generate trust through the use of various media technologies, including instant messaging applications, the activists in the three countries put face-to-face interactions at the centre stage. More specifically, we will focus on the actions that are directed at three types of audiences, at the same time discussing – for each of them – the various ways in which activists embed digital and non-digital media in the practice of sustaining connections. First, we will examine how they keep alive their connections with other movement organizations and potential allies, like political parties and policy makers. In this case, the activists in the three countries assign a primary role to face-to-face interactions. Second, we will consider the relationship between activists and those who are already supporters of their movement organizations. In this case, the activists' choices vary: while some movement organizations privilege face-to-face interactions, others prefer digital media, in particular social media platforms, and still others consider various types of digital media as complementary to each other. We end the chapter with a discussion of one relevant finding of our research, namely the strong emphasis that activists put on writing as a means of sustaining their connections, also because of their widespread use of instant messaging platforms and emails, and the consequence that this has for their grassroots political engagement.

The three publics that we have previously outlined are not the only ones with whom activists connect. There is at least one more actor that is extremely relevant for movement organizations, given its central role in the practice of sustaining connections: journalists and their media organizations. In Chapter 7, we will describe how activists first perceive the broad, multifaceted, and changing field of contemporary journalism, and then engage in activities to handle and nurture at best their daily connections with journalists, especially when they are free from the pressure of participating in street protests. More specifically, we seek to understand how activists deal with three specific challenges that they have to face when seeking to establish long-lasting connections with journalists in Greece, Italy, and Spain. First, we will consider the strong political parallelism between legacy media and institutional politics. Activists are aware of the fact that it may not be enough to nurture a relationship of trust with journalists who work in highly politicized news outlets, since the news-making process also involves news values that are imbued with political considerations. Things become even more complicated when we consider the employment conditions of the journalistic workforce in the three countries: journalists are increasingly precarious and mostly work freelance outside the newsrooms. This means that activists also need to adjust to news-making routines that are dramatically different from those of journalists in permanent employment. Both these aspects have an indirect relationship with the data stream; in this case, activists seek to become relevant data sources for journalists, feeding them the data that their movement organization elaborates on the contentious issues that they care about. Doing this amid the political parallelism of news organizations and the labor precarity of the journalistic workforce is particularly challenging for activists. Finally, the chapter deepens one aspect that has already surfaced, when we spoke about the practice of political organizing: the relevance of privacy and the protection of personal communications. We will discuss this topic from the perspective of the relationship between activists as data sources for journalists.

Chapter 8 works as a conclusion and summarizes the main findings of our research from a theoretical perspective. First, we will separately discuss the four practices concerning both digitalization and datafication, considering them not as separate from one another, as we have done in the previous chapters (for analytical reasons), but as practices with many points of contact that in fact frequently intersect with each other. In this regard, we also argue that the practice of information gathering anchors the other three practices, as it has both theoretical and empirical consequences for the study of daily grassroots politics in stages of latency and, also, of social movements in times of mobilization. We will subsequently shift our focus to the issue of the activists' agency in the data stream, recalling its three features, namely the fact that it is heterogeneous, ubiquitous, and perpetual. In light of these three characteristics, we will discuss an aspect of the activists' agency by considering the role of hybridity for the activists in the three Southern European countries, their skilful recourse to face-to-face interactions, and their ability to slow down the fast pace of the data stream when necessary. Finally, starting from our research, we will formulate a number of hypotheses about grassroots politics, social movements, and the data stream, suggesting further lines of research on this subject matter.

2

Activists' Quest for Information Amid Data Abundance

Kosmas works as a press agent within a Greek union. He agreed to do an interview with us and decided to meet us at his office. When we arrived in front of his desk, there was something that immediately attracted our attention: several piles of newspapers and weeklies were occupying a significant portion of his working space right next to his desktop computer. Without moving the newspapers and weeklies from his desk, Kosmas told us to sit in front of another little table next to his. The presence of the print press was so noticeable in his office that it was one of the first things we ended up covering in the interview. Kosmas explained this presence as follows: "Of course I am reading newspapers as well. If you work for a press office, it is an imperative to read newspapers … If you want to have a wider view of what is happening, you have to read some leading papers in Greece as well."

As a press agent, Kosmas always needs to remain up-to-date on the main issues at stake within Greek political agendas, including the reactions to relevant political events of the key political actors, be they political leaders, single parliamentarians, or unionists. However, Kosmas was extremely clear to us concerning the role of legacy media such as newspapers in fulfilling this task: he cannot rely simply on Greek newspapers: "I most prefer to have a look on TV and social media as well, because social media transfer the first views of key opinion leaders about what has been said. You have a very early image of how some players absorb the key messages coming from the political arena."

What is problematic, for Kosmas, is the timing of the print press; since newspapers are published the day after something happens, they may provide good commentaries while being unable to follow the political debate as it develops live. For Kosmas, to know what to say and when on the day of the event, but also to be able to steer the discussion within his own movement organization, means searching for information on what other political actors say as they say it. In this regard, social media are the best option; according to Kosmas, they are able to convey the very first viewpoints of key opinion leaders in Greece about political events and, additionally, about what other relevant political actors have said. Through social media, it is possible to understand – almost live – how political actors interpret what other political actors have just said. This is vital for Kosmas: when something big is at stake, like a massive demonstration, he privileges social media over more traditional news sources. However, as he reminded us several times during his interview, "the newspapers are still setting the ordinary media agenda in Greece".

After having commented on both legacy media and social media, Kosmas showed us the private monitoring news platform through which he keeps a regular eye on the media coverage across a wide spectrum of media outlets, which are not necessarily specialized in the production of news. He commented on the platform while showing us how it works on his computer:

> 'I have a privilege [in] using this platform because sometimes I am over-informed. I have a broad view of what is happening [when] using this media platform. This is a private monitoring news platform but they are not producing news, they are reproducing printed media. I'll show you on the screen: this is the news, all the sections – industry, energy, environment, corporate governance and labor issues, finances, and so on. I click on that and this is all the previous information regarding labor issues today. This is media coverage. You also have TV, radio, and social media. And if you learn how to use this platform, you can dive deep [into] the news very quickly.'

Kosmas's words effectively convey one of the challenges he faces on a daily basis, as do many of the other activists we interviewed in the three countries. Searching for information does not only mean knowing where to find it and having the right tools – even in the form of a digital platform – to spell it out. For research to be fruitful, one must also know how to put together not only the most relevant but also the most solid information. To do so, activists must orient themselves in a data stream in which data are abundant but scattered, hence demanding to be recombined; only thus can they constitute key information for activists, allowing them to carry out their daily grassroots political engagement at their best.

As we will see later in this chapter, both legacy and social media produce important data sequences for activists, albeit with differences. More specifically, when considering the material side of such practice, we will show that activists rely on three main configurations of data sequences. First, activists may read printed newspapers, watch television, and listen to the radio, either online or offline. When they do so, they collate a series of news sources that are relevant to them, or they employ the press review put together by someone else in their organization. Second, activists may use social media platforms to understand what people are saying and therefore gather information not on specific topics, but rather on a more general climate of opinion that is useful to fine-tune the medium-term goals of their activists' organizations. Finally, activists may rely on automated services that combine their chosen settings and expressed preferences on what they want to be informed about with a selection of news that the service's built-in algorithm considers relevant for that activist.

In so doing, activists alternate and combine data coming in at different paces and in different formats on a daily basis. They do not prefer one over another; they need all of them, but as we will show in this chapter, sometimes it is difficult for activists to combine them to shape meaningful information. On the one hand, activists have to take into account the existence of different data temporalities: although the data stream is generally continuous and always available to activists, not all the data sequences that activists engage in come at the same rhythm – some are extremely fast, others just fast, and still others are slow. On the other hand, activists have to deal with the fact that they enter into contact with data in a seamless way, hence dealing with data overload that makes it difficult, sometimes even impossible, to transform data into information that is meaningful to them. To cope with these two challenges, activists need to exercise agency over the data stream, and they do this in two different yet interlinked ways. First, we will show that they employ multiple temporalities to their advantage: the slowness of some data sequences, like those derived from face-to-face interactions, serves to better interpret faster data sequences, like those coming from social media, framing them in ways that resonate with the activists and their needs. Second, we will discuss the different methods through which activists engage in data filtering and data ordering activities: from the rare employment of algorithmic support via the much more common recourse to personal knowledge of different types of media to a reliance on the support of reference people, including other activists. Before proceeding with this discussion, however, we will briefly define the practice of information gathering in order to explain why it is important to activists in their day-to-day actions.

Defining the practice of information gathering

Regardless of its format and pace, information is always extremely relevant for activists who need to know what is going on, how they can make their decisions, and thanks to whom; this depends on how they can coordinate the workflow within their activists' organizations and strategize collective actions and mobilizations. Activists need information to understand what opportunities they have to act successfully so as to obtain political change or, on the contrary, when it is better to step back and wait for the right moment to mobilize. In this regard, social movement literature stresses that activists need to perceive, and gain knowledge of, the opportunities that a political system or a political conjuncture offers them in terms of mobilization (Goodwin and Jasper, 2004). Along the same lines, activists also need to understand what the best message would be to connect with the general public, and who their potential supporters and likely allies would be when they mobilize. Again, social movement scholars have pointed out the relevance of framing for activists (Cress and Snow, 2000; Ryan and Jeffreys, 2019): constructing the right message and producing a compelling worldview is not just a matter of luck. When activists engage in grassroots politics, they must know what to say and to whom, and while this may sometimes be a simple matter of intuition, most of the time they know how to reach the public because they have gathered relevant information before going public with their mobilizations. Even the specific moment in which a message should be released – for example when to launch a press release and through which channels – requires activists to gather information on how media professionals work (Ryan, 1991).

Activists find information through interactions with other people who are able to provide already filtered information and, at the same time, they also conceived the Internet, broadly speaking, as an accessible and always updated source of information (Savolainen, 2008). Additionally, the aggregation of information coming from older and newer media is one of the main praxes through which activists might 'obtain up-to-date and accurate information from various media platforms so that they can make correct judgments about their subsequent actions' (Lee and Chan, 2018: 5). In short, activists perform the practice of information gathering through different types of actions, in which older and newer media play opposite roles but sometimes blend, and the many services that activists employ are combined – from social media to instant messaging platforms, from institutional websites to radio programmes.

As such, there certainly are many similarities between the way in which activists handle information in the realm of grassroots politics and more common practices of information gathering that people generally perform in contemporary societies when they navigate the political realm. In this regard, people find information through different activities, ranging from active information gathering, when people consciously look for information that is relevant to them and their lives, to non-direct monitoring, when people find information in a somewhat serendipitous manner, namely in moments and situations in which they are not actively searching for information (McKenzie, 2003). In most cases, information practices are needed to manage the large amounts of data that people are confronted with. As we live in a media environment with many choices, where people have a wide range of information sources at their disposal (Prior, 2007), the ability to find better ways to manage a considerable amount of information without the need for in-depth exploration, interaction or understanding of this information (Andrejevic, 2013: 4) is what matters most to people, and certainly to political actors such as activists. In the framework of this book, we define the practice of information gathering as a practice including all those activities that activists perform in the deliberate and concrete attempt to produce information that is relevant for the aims and functioning of the grassroots political work of their movement organizations. Viewed from this perspective, the practice of information gathering can be considered to include both activities through which activists select, order, and access different types of data sources, and those through which activists collect, store, and assemble data into meaningful information for other activists.

Generally speaking, the practice of information gathering is certainly relevant for activists in times of mobilization, but for several reasons it is also crucial during times of latency, when activists routinely engage in such practice. In the remainder of this chapter we dig deeper on this topic, starting in the next section from legacy media, which are still carrying precious and unique values for activists, even in the mature stage of the digital era and at the dawn of datafication – the last wave of mediatization they have to cope with.

The centrality of legacy media for accessing the public discourse of political elites

Domenico holds an important position in an Italian national association that has anti-corruption as one of its core contentious issues. During the day, he is generally very busy, constantly immersed in the coordination of his association's activities. Apart from a glance at the main headlines of the websites of legacy media, he does not have time to indulge in a careful reading of the daily news and related commentaries, not even online. He is even less interested in looking for more in-depth coverage of the contentious issues that interest him and his fellow activists, and he does not watch television during the day, also for lack of time. Although he typically dedicates moments to his family during dinner, it is during the night that Domenico carves out some time to go beyond the hectic daily routine that defines his political involvement. It is in those moments of tranquility that he can focus on receiving news on what is happening in the world, and he does this mostly through television programmes, which Domenico views mostly via YouTube or the online platform of the Italian national broadcaster, RaiPlay. He finds it particularly useful to watch the same programme more than once, for example when something is not clear and he wants to be sure that he has grasped what has been said, that he understands the core message conveyed by the people speaking on the TV show. Finally, on some days of the week, Domenico also buys a selection of national newspapers in their print edition, because they are accompanied by magazines that he reads to find inspiration for his activist work; after reading them, he selects the articles he finds most interesting, he cuts them out of the magazine, or the newspaper, and includes them in a paper archive that he keeps at home.

Despite the presence of both older and newer technological devices and services in Domenico's and other activists' activities of information gathering, legacy media are still central to retrieving relevant knowledge on what happens in the world. The sources of information that activists employ most frequently in Greece, Italy and Spain are media outlets that produce news and that are accessed either in their traditional format – like newscasts aired live on television – or in their digital counterparts, namely websites that publish news online. Overall, the Greek activists we interviewed seem to be a bit more skeptical about legacy media and more prone to search for information primarily through the Internet; more specifically, they tend to consult news websites that only exist online. The Italian and Spanish activists we interviewed, instead, seem to share a very similar way of searching for information, with television newscasts being the most relevant source, followed by national newspapers, news websites, and radio programmes on current affairs. National newspapers in their printed form, the oldest type of media device, are still considered relevant outlets where activists may find useful news for their daily political work as well as for their movement organization as a whole.

Beyond news websites that only exist online, hence without a printed counterpart, activists consult newspapers and television programmes in their digital format as well, accessing printed newspapers and their online websites through their smartphones and computers. They do this by employing a wide array of devices and a combination of services so that each activist develops a preferred way to access media content. There is, then, a strong fragmentation when it comes to how activists read newspapers and watch television to search for information, although they frequently access these media online, in their digital formats.

For instance, going back to Domenico's statement about watching television mostly on YouTube, we need to underline that his way of accessing information is common also among the other Greek, Italian, and Spanish activists we interviewed. Television programmes do not disappear, in that activists still access their contents and use them to make sense of the contentious issues that they care about. However, they seldom access television content through the material objects that were once the only way to access these contents, like the television set located in the headquarters of a movement organization. In sum, television is still relevant, but mostly in its digital form online, as David from Spain also explains:

> 'So, what do I watch on television? Normally debates, programmes where you will develop an opinion. I watch very little television and I just try to get an idea of what they think in the political debates that

are usually aired. If I want to watch the news shown on television I watch it on the web page of the television channels, that is, I am already watching what TVE has, what its news is.'

In a similar way, many of the activists we spoke to told us that they constantly read newspapers during the day, but not their printed versions: they prefer the newspapers' websites. This is the case of Riccardo, who told us that "I always have the newspapers open, I leaf through them several times a day." Another frequent way of accessing the content of the print press is, once again, through online press reviews that are compiled and published online, as Emilia explains when speaking about her daily habits related to her work as an anti-corruption activist in Italy:

> 'I buy the newspapers before coming here, to my office. ... and I immediately look for the issues that concern us. At the newsstand I essentially buy La Repubblica, Il Corriere and Il Fatto Quotidiano. But then we have access to a press review where I look for news on crime, mafia, and corruption.'

In this example, the press review includes the same articles that have been published in the newspaper's print edition albeit in a digital format, which recalls the private monitoring news platform we referred to when we summarized our interview with Kosmas at the beginning of this chapter.

In other cases, although this rarely emerged in the interviews, activists gathered legacy media contents through social media platforms because they followed the profiles of specific outlets, as Gianluca told us:

> 'I [get information] through the social pages of the newspapers as well. From the Huffington Post I always get the sponsored thing: for example, if the latest news about a politician appears in the Huffington Post, I take a look at it. I follow *The Guardian* on Facebook and then its articles appear. And the same for many newspapers: I follow them on Facebook and when an article comes out I take a look at it, through the social media pages of the various media.'

Interestingly, in this case, the dividing line between information gathering in an active as opposed to a more passive manner (through Facebook advertising) is rather thin. Gianluca gets information via a social media platform through both sponsored and unsponsored posts. When it comes to the former, activists passively receive information from news media outlets. In the case of the latter, instead, activists actively decided to follow certain media outlets so as to receive their posts. As we will see later in this chapter and also in Chapter 4 devoted to algorithmic visibility, managing contacts is an action that is strictly linked to the practice of information gathering: having a solidly trusted pool of contacts enables activists to receive the information that is most interesting for them 'by proxy' (McKenzie, 2003), without having to search for it each time from scratch.

Contrary to what happens in the case of newspapers and television, radio is more linked to specific locations and less accessed in its digitalized forms (for example podcasts). Those interviewees who mentioned radio as a means of searching for information listen to radio programmes early in the morning, while having breakfast at home. For some of them, this is a very strong habit that allows them to obtain an encompassing view of the main news of the day, especially when they listen to press review programmes, as Diego points out when speaking about his and his activist organization's needs in Catalonia:

> 'Since we are multimedia [actors], the radio is the essential instrument early in the morning, in my case. Some people also watch television. But in my case, radio is fundamental, because it allows me to do other activities … In my case, early in the morning, I listen to the radio, and to more than one station to contrast [different news] … So the radio is essential to know the top news stories. And it coexists with the rest, with Internet, with the mobile phone, with newspapers.'

While newspapers, television, and radio seem to be equally important for the practice of information gathering, the main difference between the former two and the latter is their relationship with the physical space in which activists are situated. This holds particularly true for Italy, where newspapers and televisions are ubiquitous since activists access their digital versions virtually anywhere, while the radio is accessed more in specific locations (for example at home, in the car) and not much listened to in its digital format or through mobile devices.

Despite such differences, interviewees from all three countries under examination declared experiencing legacy media in a similar way when it comes to their reliability. On the one side, activists acknowledged that these media have an authoritative role: the news that they publish really matters to the ruling political elites as opposed to the noise that can be found on social media platforms (Langer and Gruber, 2021). On the other side, activists were also aware of the intrinsic bias that characterizes political reporting in television newscasts, radio programmes, and newspaper articles. In countries where the political parallelism of the press is still strong, for example in Southern European countries (Mattoni and Ceccobelli, 2018), activists are well aware of the political interests that guide mainstream media, which are therefore almost considered as political actors. The perception of news media as biased among activists is certainly not a novelty (Gitlin, 1980;

Couldry, 2000; McCurdy, 2011; Mattoni, 2012). Our empirical investigation conducted in Greece, Italy, and Spain shows that this is still the case.

In Greece, especially after the economic crisis and the related protests of 2011 (Sotirakopoulos and Sotiropoulos, 2013), activists became even more skeptical about the ability of mainstream media to provide valuable information, as Kosta suggests:

> 'The field of newspapers has changed very very much. I used to check the newspapers very often, but nowadays there is no newspaper that I really trust. I only buy [a] newspaper [that is close to] the government or … the party that is going to govern next if I want to see [what] their political views [are] directly.'

Activists consider newspapers in Southern Europe are (still) as biased when providing information, and they may read them just to learn the viewpoint of their political counterparts. In other words, according to activists, newspapers are the de facto voice of an institutional political actor, whether it is the ruling party coalition or the opposition. The mainstream press is therefore also the means through which the ruling elites speak to each other, as Mauro points out when speaking about Italy: "I don't underestimate television stations or printed newspapers, because they are full of coded messages to the members of the ruling class; they are almost always a mouthpiece for the capitalists."

By describing Italian printed newspapers and television newscasts in this way, Mauro highlights their opacity: because the messages are encrypted, they are not immediately clear, neither to the broader public nor to the activists themselves.

Conversely, activists consider social media platforms like Facebook and Twitter as somehow transparent platforms through which messages are exchanged in a fairly transparent way not just among those who count most in the political realm, but also among their challengers at the grassroots level. Furthermore, they have the potential to convey not just national voices, but also international ones. Regardless of the fact that these platforms are apparently regulated through proprietary algorithms and hence not transparent at all (Sloan and Warner, 2018; Shin, 2019), when activists compare them with older media (that is those deeply linked to institutional political actors), Facebook and Twitter seem more straightforward in giving activists the information they are trying to obtain. Indeed, while the mainstream press includes a few voices and selects only a limited amount of topics to be covered daily, social media give back a huge amount of information on any possible issue. In this regard, then, activists consider mainstream media as actors that give prominence to certain issues and put many others in the background. A platform like Twitter, instead, is not able to do so. What we are dealing with here is one of the tensions that we will discuss in relation to different practices presented in this volume: that between the immediacy and the quality of the data that activists encounter through the data stream. In this specific case, it is the tension between the activists' need to have immediate access to information, on the one hand, and the equally important need to have access to quality information, on the other. In short, news on television may be partial, but at least it is salient. What social media platforms circulate is a richness of content that comes from a variety of actors; yet, it would be difficult for activists to give prominence to the information that they obtain through Facebook and Twitter. This aspect of social media is extremely relevant for activists, as we will see in the next section.

The reconstruction of grassroots political debates via social media and algorithms

While legacy media gives activists important data to reconstruct the debate developed by institutional political actors, social media allows them to understand what opinions are circulating most within the movement networks that they belong or relate to. Our interviews show that activists also want to understand what other people think about current political events that are related to their daily political work. It is important for them to know how other people interpret the world in which they also act, mainly concerning the facts that are more directly linked to the specific contentious issue that they are working on. Activists want to know what other activists – among others – think about current affairs, how they comment on the latest events, and what their viewpoint on them is.

In order to do so, they read posts on social media platforms, in particular Facebook. While activists employ Facebook in all three countries that we investigated, Italian activists spoke about this social media platform most frequently, with regard to the practice of gathering information about what other people say on current affairs. Gianluca and Domenico, for instance, mainly employ Facebook for this reason:

> 'Facebook is more to understand what is going on, what issues are being discussed, and even among people who are not part of my affinity group in the strict sense, but I follow [them] and I look at what they have written.'

> 'I also use social networks to observe what happens in the world and in the world of anti-Mafia, so I see the anti-Mafia that takes decisions with its gut, I see the anti-Mafia of the fans, I see the more meditative anti-Mafia.'

It is through Facebook, then, that the activists try to reconstruct the grassroots political debates about the contentious issues that they focus on during their daily political engagement. Moreover, some of them may use this social media platform to reconstruct how the different souls of the social movements that they belong to differ, interact, and dispute. Other activists, instead, highlight that Facebook is useful to know what people think about certain contentious issues. In this regard, Domenico explains that "Facebook is useful to understand the way the wind is blowing", while Federico says the following: "I frankly believe that around twenty per cent of the total public opinion is here on Facebook, which is composed of the angriest people. I need to look at Facebook to understand this minority part of public opinion."

While the activists consider a social media platform like Facebook as the place to understand people's attitudes and opinions on current affairs, there are also other digital media that the Southern European activists mentioned during our interviews. Together with Facebook, Twitter is the other social media platform that they referred to most, while others – such as Instagram, YouTube, Reddit, or even TikTok – were at the very margin of their practice of information gathering, at least in the specific moment of the interview. Regarding Facebook and Twitter, the activists regularly assigned very different tasks and symbolic meanings to them. If the former makes them feel that they can enter more into contact with strong-tie networks, such as their peers and the very personal circle of friends and acquaintances, it is mainly the latter that helps them to extend their views to the broad array of media, political and social actors involved in the contentious issue that they care about, as studies on this subject matter have observed (Valenzuela et al, 2018).

Gathering information on activists' audiences is just as relevant as looking for the latest opinion leaders' viewpoints on the facts of the day. As we will see in Chapter 3 related to the practice of visibility, the online presence of activists and their movement organizations is relevant to ensure a constant visibility in the public space even in moments of latency, when they are not engaged in collective actions that are meant to get the media attention. Such online presence is obtained mostly through the use of websites and social media platforms, like Twitter and Facebook, which constantly produce information about the audiences that interact with the activists' organizations online. It is not just a matter of understanding when people are accessing these online contents, but also from which devices they do so, and with what reactions. David, for instance, explains that his organization knows from which devices its audiences look at the content that it publishes on its website:

> 'The first thing we did is an analysis of when people watch us, the devices in which they watch us. So, we discovered that in our federation people very much like to see us on the computer: most of them have [saved] us [among their] favourites and we have already discovered at what times

and from where they watch us. We have fewer people who watch us from Android devices, for example from mobile phones, than from computers. That is one thing that we have to keep changing because for a long time our page had some problems and it was not on the Web, that is, it did not load well on the Android system. So what happened? That it looked the same as on the web page. Now it looks different, because we have had to evolve, obviously, and change. ... That's why people watch us less on mobile devices than on computers. What is our audience, then? There is one part of our audience that watches us on the computer, and that watches the web page. Then we have another [part of our audience] that begins to be increasingly important, which is when you send news and see how that news suddenly goes like wildfire on WhatsApp [and] you start to see that this news has many more visits. Then, we began to realize that we must put some news on WhatsApp and Facebook and Twitter to fly more.'

Having this information is vital for David's organization, which adjusts its online communication strategy to be more effective. Additionally, observing an increase in the website traffic related to certain news items once they had been circulated on WhatsApp, David's organization decided to invest more in social media, using it as a vehicle to increase the number of readers on its website. In this case, the practice of information gathering passes through the use of data analytics related to the website, to discover when and from which device people access the organizations' online content, but also through careful observation of the more multifaceted data stream that involves not just one but several online services and platforms.

While data analytics represents a relevant source of information, our interviewees did not use it systematically. Those who mostly used it either had the skills to understand data analytics or were able to do so because their organizations had invested resources toward this activity. For instance, Carlos – who works for a trade union organization in Spain – tells us the following:

'Every week we prepare a report on social networks, [and] once a month we prepare a report on our reach, both in traditional media and social networks, [with] a more in-depth analysis. But every week we analyze not only how we are doing but also how concrete actions that we have developed have worked. ... We do this through analytics ... we have also hired the services of specialized agencies and one of them is specialized in media analysis, impacts, and social networks.'

Carlos's organization believes in the power of data analytics, which is systematically embedded in the practice of information gathering when it comes to knowing more about the organization's audiences and how they interact with its various online services. It does not do this by itself, though: rather, it outsources this service to an external agency that is specialized in data analytics. However, only a few interviewees have their organizations invest money in this type of service. While in many cases we are dealing with resource-constrained organizations, others that may have had a budget to invest in data analytics decided to do otherwise. This means that having the material resources to pay for these services is not a sufficient condition: the organization first needs to recognize the relevance of professionals in data analytics as well as the importance of data analytics for their organization.

When this does not happen, as was usually the case with the movement organizations that we considered for this study, the practice of information gathering in relation to one's audience is developed starting from activists' observations of what occurs in their information channels. We found examples of this in all three countries, as the following extracts from our interviews with Enrique, Fabio, and Delphina demonstrate:

'We have a platform on which we can check the activities of our Facebook and Twitter profiles. And we watch them, but we do not do it on a daily basis. [We notice that] "we have gained followers", or that "there are more people", or that "this article has had more follow-ups in recent months". Things like that, but not obsessively, not on a daily basis … no.'

'I'm gonna go on Twitter and see what kind of reply we got. There you can see … When we published our book on [basic] income, we published it for free and had an infinite number of downloads. Every night I went to see the Tweets with this news. Late in the evening, I check what has happened on Twitter. If there are 40 retweets, I try to figure out which of our Tweets people have retweeted.'

'As for Facebook, I'm also interested in the number of likes. If there is a positive or negative interest. I'm also interested in comments. I did some research and saw that more engagement is triggered when there is an image. When there is an image, there are more likes. When there is a video, it depends on the content.'

In other cases, activists engaged in an even more in-depth analysis of their audiences' reactions when they publish something online. It is not a matter of data analytics and the big numbers that come with it, but rather of a fine-grained analysis of the comments that people leave on posts and tweets on Facebook and Twitter, respectively. In the following extract, for instance, Daniela explains that two people in her organization systematically read all the comments that they received on Facebook to moderate them, and also to check for interesting and useful reactions:

> 'Obviously, we have two people who moderate the comments, so if something is interesting they will report it to us. This activity of responding to comments is essential because it is part of establishing boundaries. One thing is what we communicate, then it is essential to know how we are perceived, of course, from the outside. So the comments make us do a reality check in relation to the proposition, the idea that we have of ourselves. So they are very important, we take them into account for this [reason], to adjust our approach. For example, a video is not very clear and the comments show that our argument is not so clear, and then we react, we respond, we have reactive lines in the most critical situations; we have recorded a series of recurring comments, so we are putting together a FAQ section and every time we receive a comment that might be replied through them, we reply to the comment by sending the link to our FAQ section.'

So far, we have seen how activists employ a combination of basic amateur data analytics and fine-grained reading of comments in their social media profiles to understand what their audiences think about their organizations. In this case, algorithms remain in the background of the practice of information gathering, but there are other cases in which they have a more prominent role. This happens with pervasive services like Google News and similar platforms, and also with Google, which is often the first point of access to the vast world of online information. Activists are aware of this and they may try to act upon the algorithm, as Eustratios explains: "You can personalize Google news. For example, I have interests in tourists, hotels, restaurants and that sort of thing, so I get, every day, at least 10 emails from Google news. This is my primary information source."

In other cases, activists acknowledge the impact of algorithms and their opacity on the process of selecting information, as Mauro from Italy and Julia from Spain observe, speaking about Google:

> 'My first act to find information is in the Google search engine ... it is clear that by using Google I have a greater "efficiency". Given that I am a user, I do not know the algorithms put in place by Google. Maybe it makes me find links that are only a tenth of what I was looking for.'

> 'Nowadays, whoever does not want to be informed does so out of choice, because with Google and the Internet you have access to web pages of labor organizations, you have access to laws, press articles,

you have access to a lot of things, so we can consult all that and we can discuss it among ourselves.'

While Mauro told us that Google is the very first service that he employs to find information, the role of algorithms in the practice of information gathering can be even more multifaceted when activists combine a number of web services to look for whatever interests them online. A telling example of this is the following observation by Ruben, a Spanish activist: "In the morning I wake up ... and open Reddit, I open Menéame, I open the RSS and look at the interesting contents of the last 24 hours. And I open like about 200 tabs, 200 links that I review."

The combined use of Reddit, Menéame, and RSS to find "interesting contents" reveals a combination of ranking algorithms – as in the case of the social news aggregators Reddit and Menéame – with RSS feeds, which do not rely on ranking algorithms.

Algorithms, then, are not alone in determining the kind of information that activists can find about the facts of the day; in most cases, they are embedded in the practice of information gathering, together with other media services that could counterbalance them. This is because activists think that being able to obtain the right information at the right time is also a matter of navigating a multifaceted ensemble of media devices and services, in which they can contrast news and pick up the facts that seem more accurate. The Greek labor rights activist Kosmas, for instance, says that "of course, if you want to have a broad [base of] information it's imperative to use different devices, different resources"; Agata, an Italian activist who works on anti-corruption issues, explains that her organization engages in "an overall mapping of media, not only of social media; and it is from such general mapping that all starts, knowing that each media [outlet] has its own function". Algorithms are therefore not to be seen as working in isolation when it comes to the practice of information gathering because activists select and combine a variety of tools to learn what they need to know about the world around them. This seems to mitigate their weight in determining, in a linear way, what activists decide is worth noticing – and trusting – when it comes to information related to their daily political engagement.

The multiple temporalities of data for activists

So far we have seen how activists include various types of media and devices in their practice of information gathering to obtain data about various types of actors, be they political or not. In this and the next section, we will instead explore how the practice of information gathering necessarily comes into contact with three key qualities of the data stream as a whole: its heterogeneity, its ubiquity, and its perpetuity. In particular, the interviews conducted in the three countries clearly demonstrate that the heterogeneity of the data stream leads them to experience the presence of multiple temporalities. In fact, activists strongly link their perception of fast or slow media to the ability of the media themselves to publish and disseminate news in a given time, which can be instantaneous, as in the case of social media platforms, or deferred, as in the case of the print press. It is precisely the switching between instantaneous and deferred time within the practice of information gathering that shapes the activists' formulation of a general understanding of digital media as information media. What is also interesting to note is that activists also identify differences within the simultaneous timeframe that normally characterizes social media platforms. There are, in fact, social media platforms that are able to produce data more simultaneously than others, as recounted by Vicente, the co-founder – together with other media practitioners – of a small grassroots collective of video makers in Spain.

For him and the other members of the collective, it is highly relevant to be constantly up to date on what is going on in their city, but also at the national level. One thing he spoke of at length during our interview was the huge difference between Facebook and Twitter. He is rather annoyed by the former, which he only accesses through the group profile of his collective; he seldom uses his private one, having even uninstalled the platform's app from his smartphone. He thinks that Facebook is not very fast in providing the required information, especially when he needs to track the most recent posts of his collective. Moreover, Facebook is full of older people, and there are so many of them that Vicente can no longer find any interesting posts. This is why he infinitely prefers Twitter: with its 140-character posts, the micro-blogging platform is quick and light. Also, its population is vibrant and able to point out the most stimulating contents. Twitter, he says, is "there, right what you need".

When contrasting Facebook with Twitter, Vicente makes a difference between those social media platforms that are slow in giving the information he needs and others, which are instead very fast. While many scholars have pointed to digital media – and social media platforms more specifically – as being able to support an almost live exchange of information among its users (Van Dijck and Poell, 2013), Vicente's short account suggests that, for activists, the wide array of media devices and services, and their combinations, is much more nuanced. Moreover, when looking at our data as a whole, it is clear that such nuances actually depend on the context in which the practice of information gathering takes place. On the one hand, what counts considerably is the whole ensemble of media devices and services that activists employ to look for the required information and that contribute to shaping the meanings assigned to each of them. On the other hand, and related to this, it also depends on the country in which activists engage in grassroots politics, which to some extent renders certain media devices and services more popular and others less central in the daily lives of activists.

Being slow or fast is a contextual quality, which is always relevant because it points to the preferred media devices and services that activists employ when looking for content that matters to them in the framework of their daily political work. For instance, Facebook could be considered slow, but there are other means of receiving information whose slowness in providing data necessarily couples with information that is already old. This is the case with television newscasts and printed newspapers. Related to this, David says that he knows that people usually watch newscasts on television to get information about what is going on. However, he explains that he and his fellow activists consider television news too slow for them:

> 'The newscast at 8 in the morning already comes with news that happened the night before. If you want to know what is currently happening, web pages are the ones covering live what is going on. And Twitter is always much faster than television … Therefore, television is useful to get opinions on facts, but informatively it does not have the level of update that we constantly need, because the newscast is at 8 am, then at 3 pm, and then at 9 pm. The web pages and Twitter are running all day. I know that a lot of people stand in front of the television, but we actually do not need to know what information the television is covering and talking about.'

Twitter is always operative and therefore accessible whenever someone wants to access it; television news comes at fixed times of the day. The former is fluid and provides a stream of live information that never stops; the latter is more like a provider of information that is regulated top-down, following a rhythm of political communication that is not in tune with the activists' needs when it comes to obtaining relevant information there and then, as it is often the case with those who engage in politics from a grassroots position and with limited material resources. In this regard, Agata suggests that Twitter resembles a "news press agency" that points to the relevant contents, which can subsequently be explored independently from the platform, by looking for information on the Internet more broadly.

At the same time, Twitter can also be perceived as slow in comparison to yet other platforms, as we will also see in the following chapter. In Ruben's words, Reddit is – together with 4Chan – the place where viral content first spreads, at an extremely fast pace, before reaching Twitter. Of course, it is a matter of some hours, and the delay may not be very significant for many of the interviewees who do not use 4Chan or Reddit to obtain information. What is interesting, though, is that for some activists it may be determining if they receive information even only a few hours after it has been circulated for the first time, hence demonstrating the incredible acceleration of the time of politics even in periods of latency when people are not engaged in any relevant form of collective action.

Activists amid data abundance

Many of the activists we interviewed told us that they access information about what is going on in the world first thing in the morning. Emilia, for instance, says that she takes her smartphone and searches for news when she is still in bed; later on, when she is having breakfast, she checks her emails as well. When they are working toward their political goals, then, activists constantly perform the practice of information gathering. Martino, from Italy, says that "every five to ten minutes I check the home page of Repubblica and Corriere della Sera. I refresh their homepages. I always have them on". Carlos, from Spain, goes along the same line when he explains that "during the whole day, we are doing an analysis and diagnostic work: for example, we are continuously testing what appears in the digital media, in the information agencies … This is constant." Moreover, activists search for information not only when they are devoting time to their grassroots political engagement, for example when they are in the headquarters of their civil society organizations; they also do this when they are somewhere else and doing something that is not related to their political engagement in the first place.

This continuous access to a wide variety of news sources allows activists to gather a large array of data about who is saying what about the issues that matter most to them. Indeed, the practice of information gathering implies a constant connection, through various types of media, with what is happening inside and outside the world of movement organizations and the networks in which they are engaged. This seamless connection is entirely in line with one of the qualities that characterize the data stream, namely its ubiquity: the data that activists need are always there, and all they have to do is reach for their smartphone to access them. The result is that activists have immense amounts of data at their disposal, and in the most varied formats: from the prime minister's statements on Twitter to the analysis of the political phase that fellow activists post on Facebook; from a politician's opinion piece on the leading national newspaper to the WhatsApp comments they received from their supporters. Nevertheless, while activists can access sequences of data that are continuous and heterogeneous, they risk not being truly informed, not understanding how the political debate of their interest is developing, and failing to be in tune with what the people who might support them are experiencing and saying. In short, activists risk dealing with cacophonous, ever-changing sequences of data that they cannot control and may potentially overwhelm them. The possibility of this risk emerged from many of the interviews we collected in the three countries, and is well summarized by Fabio:

> 'Speed sometimes also means superficiality, because you have a communication that in some cases dizzies you. At a certain point,

you can't do it anymore, because there is so much communication, as communication channels and communication actors have increased. If I had to think about all the networks on income that exist around the world, if each of them already sends ten Tweets a day ... except that you would not have time to read, but it becomes just a quantity of information that you no longer process.'

Fabio also mentions the speed with which he comes into contact with large amounts of information, an aspect he shares with many of our interviewees, like Kosmas:

'We are over-informed, and the information coming from [the] Internet sometimes is very stressful, the velocity of feeding news media demonstrates is stressing to everyone who wants to be part of this movement. Too much information: you have to react, you cannot absorb all the information, and many times you don't even understand what you are reading.'

The result is a general understanding of the information environment that presents too many stimuli happening all at once, which activists cannot process. As a further consequence, activists try to escape this continuous and incomprehensible cacophony of data. This is why the practice of information gathering also includes activities through which activists act more decisively on the data stream, by filtering and ordering data to make sense of them: in fact, to turn them into information. These activities are also a necessary consequence of the transformation of the journalistic profession and the newspapers' impact on people's ability to inform themselves, as Stefano argues:

'In the past we did not have direct access to the news; what we perceived were those [events] of which we were either direct witnesses or [indirect witnesses] because they were told to us by communication professionals who made a selection of the news. We were sufficiently guaranteed that those [events] were true, real, because there had been the mediation of a professional. They were listed to us according to priorities, defined by communication professionals, which we accepted. We had no access to other news, so that was our perception. Now we have indistinct access. Some news items are mediated by professionals, others are news items that ... we do not always have the ability or time to assess, [to] verify.'

Stefano refers to the process of disintermediation, according to which media professionals like journalists no longer have a monopoly on mediating between news sources and the broader public. Like politicians, news sources increasingly speak by themselves and let their voices be heard through their own communication channels, including social media platforms. At the same time, the broader public knows how to access relevant news sources, follow their communication activities online, and avoid altogether the mediating role of journalists in explaining what the situation is with a certain contentious issue. Disintermediation in the realm of political communication has been studied with regard to the general tendency of contemporary political actors to speak 'directly' to both their fellow citizens, in particular via social media (Engesser et al, 2017), and more specific sets of political actors, such as populist leaders (Bracciale and Martella, 2017).

In the framework of our study, it is clear that disintermediation may also have a disorienting effect on activists: when so many of their potential interlocutors produce news by themselves, constantly spreading their viewpoints on this and that matter, activists like Stefano face the problem of understanding where to find useful data on a subject matter.

Filtering activities

The previous section shows that searching for information is not enough. Better still, it reveals that the practice of information gathering is not as linear as it may initially seem. In a world in which everyone makes themselves heard through social media platforms, and professional journalism has lost its monopoly on providing news, activists need to filter the data they find in the course of their research. In this section, we will demonstrate that they do this in different ways.

In the rare cases of activists who belong to movement organizations that have a good deal of material resources at their disposal, they may relegate the activities of filtering and ordering information to ad hoc platforms, as we have seen in the opening section of this chapter, when Kosmas showed us the platform he uses to filter all the information related to a given topic. However, this does not seem to be a common activity among the activists we interviewed in the three countries: in fact, almost all of them exercise their agency in more direct ways, without resorting to specialized filtering platforms.

Some interviewees start from themselves and their knowledge of the subject matter to critically discern what information they can trust – and hence retain as relevant for their political work – and what information they should dismiss because part of the more general noise that characterizes the overload of information. Relying on one's own knowledge of the context in which the daily political work is performed is relevant both when applying these filtering activities to newer and older media. As for the latter, Delphina, an anti-corruption activist from Greece, confirms this when reflecting on how she deals with television:

> 'You have to choose because in the media you see everything, you can receive a lot of information that is garbage. Then you need a criterion, a critical spirit to take what you need. That's how I do it: I take what I need. I sift through the information and take only what remains.'

Activists rely less on television news, newspaper articles, and social media posts than they do on their personal contacts if they want to understand whether a news item is truly relevant in comparison to others and – even more importantly – if it can be trusted. Personal contacts are therefore important in activities that allow activists not only to filter but also to order the large amount of data that they regularly come into contact with. These personal contacts may certainly involve direct interactions, as Eulalia, another anti-corruption activist from Greece, explains:

> 'If I find something interesting [on television] I will use my phone to call my colleagues or to call journalists that might be involved, call people that I can ask ... what is going on ... I see [it] on television and I look for it to see if any journalists have written about it in a journalistic kind of online media and writing so that I can post it also.'

In this case, watching the news on television is not enough; Delphina uses her personal and trusted contacts in the world of media professionals to check not just if something happened for real, but – especially – if it happened the way in which it was explained on television. As we have also seen earlier, in Greece there is a mixed interpretation of legacy media, which activists struggle to trust completely even if they assign an importance to them. Constructing a trusting relationship with specific journalists, then, is a way to order the data that activists receive from other media.

In any case, activists also consider other types of personal relationships useful to gather information that is crucial for their daily political work. Eustratios (a grassroots unionist from Greece), Daniela (an Italian anti-corruption activist), and Miguel (a Spanish unionist in the field of media workers) all highlight the importance of speaking with specific actors in a direct and unmediated way:

> 'I prefer to go there [to the workplace] and say "Stef, sit down, give me a picture, what are the people saying?" If I want to make the best decision, choose the best thing, I must first listen. If I have a face-to-face conversation, I can do a lot of things. With the phone, instead,

I have fewer possibilities to do my work in the best way. I prefer face-to-face contact.'

'The great problem, the great challenge of an activist organization, is that it is external to the decision-making centers, to the centers of power. Its access to information is therefore limited. If you become a campaigner within a party, you have more access to information. You know when discussions on a law proposal are scheduled. This way, you can, for example, intervene in the legislation phase, not just in the amendment phase. [You can] intervene in a transparent way. As an activist organization, we face the challenge of accessing information. The more we cultivate relationships with those who can give us this information, the better we can do our job.'

'I get the information I need face-to-face. Starting early in the morning here in my office, there are meetings that I hold periodically with people who work here with me, from the Documentation Center, the Training Center, [people] with whom we meet almost once a week. [We have] different kinds of meetings. Up to [a] few minutes ago, for example, I was in a meeting with an association of lawyers.'

When discussing the relevance of trusted personal contacts, the three activists do not refer to the direct need of validating information that is already circulating in the public space. Rather, they are considering the impact, on their daily grassroots political work, of data that would remain unknown to them were it not for the personal relationships they have managed to build with key figures in the policy world. In this way, filtering activities in relation to the data stream are performed somewhat upstream. All three activists, in fact, decided to distance themselves – to various degrees – from the vast amount of data that various types of media would have provided them, and instead devoted their attention to face-to-face interactions, over time cultivating stable and trusting relationships with various types of political actors, both inside and outside their movement networks.

In these particular cases, the practice of information gathering acquires a peculiar meaning, connecting the activists' daily work to their potential allies. Thus, Eustratios considers his ability to make sound decisions concerning the workplace of which he is a union reference; Daniela, instead, reflects on her organization's ability to shape the lawmaking process; Miguel speaks of incessant face-to-face meetings in order not to miss potential pieces of information coming from different and heterogeneous media, political figures, and even social actors. In all three cases, the activists reveal yet another nuance of the practice of information gathering: while media may well be relevant when activists need to understand the official viewpoints of other political actors, they are less so when what is at stake is information that is not usually shared and spread publicly. In this case, face-to-face communication plays an extremely relevant role in filtering the most needed information, leaving aside the noise that other political actors make through their disintermediated use of media. Additionally, it is clear that these activists exploit the multiple temporalities that characterize the production and diffusion of data in the data stream; they rely on the slow pace of face-to-face contacts either to interpret or to bypass those data that are delivered at a much faster pace through social media platforms and other digital media.

While in the case of Eulalia and the other activists we are dealing with direct interactions that happen through phone calls or even face-to-face meetings, yet another media service is employed in the practice of filtering information. When it comes to social media platforms like Facebook and Twitter, activists often complain about the noise caused by the relentless flow of data in their profiles. Many of them have told us that it is simply impossible to make sense of all the data they receive by reading their feeds on social media. In this case, filtering the abundant data that activists gather in the data stream becomes an even more relevant practice. Beyond simply filtering information through the use of hashtags, activists already put in place filters when selecting the actors they decide to follow on Twitter, as Agata explains:

> 'Social media are important not only for what we communicate through them, but for the information we get from them. See what people say on Twitter, see what the positions of parliamentarians are … you often have to go and find them on Twitter. We use Twitter to map, so much so that when we make a selection of stakeholders, even just journalists, their Twitter profile is crucial. Stakeholder mapping would be much more difficult to do because it would be difficult to go and retrieve what this or that political subject has said without Twitter.'

According to Agata, this careful selection is necessary to get an idea of what relevant actors are saying about the topics that interest them at the national level; elected MPs, but also other stakeholders and journalists, share their viewpoints through Twitter, and in this way activists can have access to their public declarations live, without waiting for a journalistic account on this. All this is possible only because the accounts of the activists' organizations on Twitter have been set up to avoid noise and decrease the risk of information overload. The role that the specific digital platform plays in the practice of information gathering is therefore not irrelevant. On the contrary, when activists decide to strategically exploit some of the affordances of these platforms, thus interacting with them on a material level as well, they succeed in exercising their agency over the data stream in a more effective way.

Conclusion

In this chapter, we have presented and discussed the practice of information gathering, which seems to be of primary importance to the Italian, Greek, and Spanish activists we interviewed. Part of their daily work as activists is devoted precisely to the numerous activities through which they search for, process, and transform various types of data into information that is relevant to them. From this point of view, we have shown that there is not one single type of media through which activists perform such activities. On the contrary, while it is acknowledged that social media platforms are relevant in this sense, legacy media also continue to play an important role when activists want to get informed about something. Activists engage in the practice of information gathering through digital media, but most of the time a Twitter profile on a smartphone is just not enough. Information seems to be everywhere, and activists know this. For this reason, they value face-to-face contacts as much as those happening online. Likewise, they may listen to the radio news first thing in the morning, but then they complement this activity with a quick look at the print press during the day and a glimpse of television news before having dinner. In so doing, they are immersed in an ongoing data stream where the news of the day lives side by side with tweets by politicians and other stakeholders, followers' comments on posts published on the activists' Facebook profiles, and accounts gathered through face-to-face encounters with collaborators, journalists, and other experts.

Nonetheless, in this chapter, we have also argued that there is a division of labor between legacy media and digital media. Activists resort to the former in order to access news items that describe what is going on in terms of specific subject matters, offer in-depth commentaries, and – in the case of talk shows and similar programmes – present the official viewpoints of more institutional actors. With regard to the latter, activists consider social media platforms not just as news sources that anticipate legacy media news, but – more importantly – as sources of information in the broadest sense possible. In fact, social media are relevant to activists because they allow them to understand the political debate within the movement networks that they adhere to. Activists follow the profiles and pages of fellow activists on Facebook, Twitter, and other social media platforms. They watch what they share and read what they say, using this content as data through which to reconstruct the public debate outside the sphere of institutional politics. At the same time, social media platforms serve as a way for activists to connect with all those people who already are or may become their supporters, engaging in their future protest or advocacy campaigns. In this case, it is not only what these people say that matters to activists, but also how they interact with the social profiles of the activists' movement organizations and other digital media through which the latter distribute their content, such as websites run directly by activists on behalf of their movement organizations. In other words, activists sometimes also perform data analytics related to the meta-data produced by the people who come into contact with them, especially in the case of social media platforms.

However, in this chapter, we have also shown that engaging in data analytics is an uncommon activity. Activists undoubtedly try to leverage algorithms and data analytics techniques to learn more about their audiences, but they do so episodically and mostly rudimentarily. For this reason, it seems difficult to speak about the existence of a wide-ranging algorithmic literacy in Southern European movement organizations. There might certainly be exceptions, but among the broad range of activists whom we interviewed for our research only those from movement organizations in Spain seem to be more at ease with algorithms as a means of enhancing the practice of information gathering. In short, if it is true that Spanish activists are perhaps the only ones to have gained an awareness of the power and usefulness of both algorithms and data analytics to perform, at best, the practice of information gathering, they share with Italian and Greek activists the fact that all are still very far from handling these tools professionally. When reflecting on algorithms, though, it is also interesting to note that activists produce knowledge about the way their different audiences think and act by combining algorithms with other activities that are not algorithm-based. In this chapter, we have thus begun to address one of the recurring themes of this book: the need to examine activists' use of and encounter with algorithms in their practices by contextualizing them within the diverse set of other activities in which digital media are used alongside non-digital media.

Another relevant point that we have made in this chapter is related to the data stream in its overall complexity, concerning both the challenges of searching for the right data to then produce information and the agency that activists exercise over the data stream, using some of its qualities in their favour. We have thus described the activists' construction of different temporalities within the data stream. In some cases, the data reach the activists extremely fast, other times just fast, and on other occasions at a slower pace. This difference is due precisely to the use of different types of media – digital and otherwise – for the activities that activists perform to find the required information. The materiality of the media intertwines almost imperceptibly with the activists' perceptions of different times in the data stream. However, the coexistence of different timelines, some subject to strong accelerations while others are characterized by a very slow pace, seems to play into the hands of the activists. The slower pace of data collected through face-to-face interactions allows activists to better interpret the data that arrive at a very high speed – or to avoid them by moving beyond these data.

Finally, we have observed that activists often find themselves dealing not only with data that come in at high speeds but also with very abundant data.

For clarity, we are not talking about big data in the classic sense: we are talking about large masses of data in the most diverse formats that activists often struggle to manage. These include, for example, newspaper articles and television newscasts, the comments under the latest Facebook post, and the Twitter threads related to the activities of the movement organization with which the activists collaborate. Being disparate from one another, these data are too many for activists to handle in a useful way. The abundance of data thus risks not translating into relevant information. However, in this chapter we have shown how activists are able, or at least try, to exercise some form of agency over this overabundant data stream. More precisely, we have argued that the practice of information gathering heavily depends on activists' ability to filter the data they receive.

Activists do this in many ways, often privileging their long experience in grassroots politics, which allows them precisely to evaluate and sort the data that create contacts. However, they also do so by using their personal contacts to understand what information is actually worth considering and what can be safely ignored. If, on the one hand, an almost artisanal approach to the use of algorithms can be attributed to activists in Italy, Greece, and Spain, on the other hand, they show that they have developed a sophisticated use of face-to-face interactions to exercise their agency over the data stream. In the course of this book, we will see more often how, in a world characterized by the strong interconnection between digitalization and datafication, activists assign a central role to face-to-face interactions with various kinds of actors.

3

The Multiple Patterns Towards Visibility During Latency Stages

It is a Thursday afternoon in September. The following day, we will be traveling from Florence to Milan to interview a young project manager of a movement organization that fights against corruption in Italy. We have already booked our train tickets, but we suddenly need to change our plans. Daniela, the activist we want to interview, has sent us an email to tell us that she is no longer available; she has just received an invitation from a morning television show on RAI1.[1] She apologizes, adding that when activists receive an invitation like this, they cannot say no, especially when the interview is aired on the television programme with the highest peak viewership in the morning. At the end of the email, she proposes to meet in Rome a couple of hours after her television interview. We change our plans accordingly and join Daniela in Rome the next day. As soon as we meet with her, she again apologizes. She says she has never postponed an interview, nor has she ever changed the interview location with only a few hours of notice. We tell Daniela there is nothing to be sorry about, and we start our interview.

Unsurprisingly, the first topic we cover is the relationship that her movement organization has with Italy's main television programmes. The organization usually has no access to them and this is a problem, according to Daniela, because these programmes can easily attract a large part of the Italian television audience. In so doing, they contribute to building the political agenda of the whole country and heavily influence how people speak about a variety of public issues. Thus, if you are a member of a movement organization with limited access to television, it makes perfect sense to suddenly postpone an interview that you have been asked to give if it is only for an academic research project.

As the interview unfolds, it becomes apparent that most of the daily choices of Daniela's movement organization converge toward one main aim: spreading its message on corruption fast and in a way that it reaches as many people as possible. Television, newspapers, weeklies, radio programmes, news websites, social media platforms, text messages, and instant messaging apps are part of her organization's strategy to make different audiences aware of its values, activities, and achievements. In other words, Daniela and her movement organization put complete visibility at the centre of their strategy, exploiting all available communication channels. No option is left aside because her movement organization's aim is "becoming a point of reference for whoever would like to engage in the struggle against corruption: for this reason, we must answer to whatever input we receive", Daniela explains. Hence, she could easily agree to be interviewed for media outlets that are neither tied to her anti-corruption struggles nor entrusted with the mission of giving information on politics. However, among all the available media, television has allowed Daniela's movement organization to achieve a goal that would have been difficult to accomplish through a post on a social media platform, regardless of their popularity. It is television – especially that specific television programme aired at 8 am on an ordinary workday – that allows Daniela to speak to millions of viewers at the same time, informing them of her organization's anti-corruption stance thanks to a brief interview. Daniela explains that the same results could not have been achieved if she had been interviewed for the print press or in a radio show, let alone for an article published on her movement organization's website or in its newsletter; even the events that her movement organization arranges across Italy as part of its anti-corruption campaigns would not have sufficed.

Like many other activists we interviewed, Daniela has a cross-media and cross-platform understanding of the whole media environment in which she operates. She indeed acknowledges the current role of television in attracting millions of viewers thanks to a brief interview, but she also knows that television alone is not enough to gain visibility. Therefore, even when Daniela succeeds in the difficult task of obtaining television coverage, this specific media exposure does not fulfil her quest for visibility. In times of latency, she needs to devote particular attention to other forms of visibility, digital media being constantly on her mind. According to Daniela, the large number of people that her organization is able to reach through digital platforms allows her and her fellow activists to gain the attention of more powerful political actors in a relatively short amount of time. This is not a secondary aspect for her, because the time of institutional politics rarely matches that of grassroots politics – and timing, as activists know very well, is all but a secondary and irrelevant factor in politics.

The interview we conducted with Daniela and the insights that she shared with us highlight important aspects of the practice of gaining visibility, also in terms of how activists exercise their agency over the data stream in order to be noticed among a variety of other political actors during latency stages, that is, when they are not in the streets. On the one hand, through their interactions with legacy media and the professionals that work in them, activists engage with the data stream in an attempt to become trusted producers of information and, accordingly, of the data that sustain the production of news and other content types in television programmes, radio broadcasts, and newspapers articles. On the other hand, activists engage in the autonomous production of data about themselves and their activities, often 'cooking' – so to say – those data in ways that render them appealing to journalists and other audiences. They do so through social media platforms, hence entering into contact with another data sequence in the data stream, but in some cases also through the creation of their own media. The teleoaffective structure that guides the practice of gaining visibility seems to revolve around the willingness to become a data source from which various types of media professionals and audiences can then deduct what the activists' movement organizations are, what they are doing at the political level, and why they deserve their attention. As we will see, knowing how to do this, in terms of both a practical and general understanding of the practice of gaining visibility, differs from country to country, especially when it comes to the activists' interactions with legacy media. What the activists in Italy, Greece, and Spain have in common, though, are the challenges that they must face when attempting to become data sources and – in this way – address the data stream from a proactive position.

This chapter discusses these challenges and reflects on how activists and their movement organizations can exercise a certain degree of agency when they interact with both legacy media and social media in an attempt to become visible beyond the smaller activists' circles that already know them. We will first reflect on the important role that legacy media still play today for the activists in the three countries under investigation. Although the possibility for an activist's disintermediation from journalists through digital media is rather large in the present day, movement organizations continue to consider television, radio, and newspapers as particularly important to reach the broad public in times of latency. Next, we will discuss the trade-offs that activists need to deal with to become valuable data sources for legacy media journalists: adaptation to the logic of legacy media is not without costs and activists face many dilemmas. For this reason, some activists decide not to adapt, resorting to other ways of making themselves visible to their audiences. On the one hand, they use social media platforms. Although these are important in all three countries that we considered, in this chapter we will show how activists do not use them in the same way. On the other hand, we will see that activists – despite heavily relying on social media platforms – have not completely abandoned alternative media that they can manage independently and in their own time, away from both a legacy and social media logic. In general, the chapter reveals that activists curate their visibility to various types of audiences by strategically navigating the data stream and exercising their agency towards it, for instance taking advantage of its heterogenous nature. Before addressing these points, in the following section we will offer a definition of the practice of gaining visibility that today seems to play an important role for activists even when they are not involved in street protests.

The practice of gaining visibility

Visibility has always been a precious resource for activist organizations, especially in times of protest. Indeed, early studies on social movements' outcomes links the success of movement organizations to their ability to be recognized as legitimate political actors by their protest target and, more in general, policy makers (Gamson, 1975). To be recognized as a legitimate actor means, first, to be noticed and, even more so, to be noticed as the activists want to be. Along this line, the ability of activists to correctly frame what they want to achieve and the actions that lead to such achievements are both extremely relevant to determine the capacity of movement organizations to bring about change (Cress and Snow, 2000). In short, activists organize and come together to say something to someone else; to reach this goal, they need to be heard and seen. Since this accomplishment is central for social movement actors, they continuously engage in a wide array of activities to make themselves visible. The most straightforward of such activities is the act of going out in the streets to protest. In so doing, activists make themselves visible as claiming subjects and, through the performance of protest, they also link themselves to the object of their claims (Tilly, 2006: 35). Such performances can take many shapes: from signing an online petition to organizing a wild strike in factories. Activists plan them in a way that enables them to gain the attention not just of those audiences who physically attend the performance, sharing the protesters' same time and space, but also of those who are not there at the exact moment in which the protests unfold. In other words, throughout the history of social movements, activists have always constructed such performances in order to gain the mainstream media's attention and, in so doing, become visible beyond the limited physical boundaries of the performance setting (Gitlin, 1980; Ryan, 1991). From this viewpoint, organizing a protest is one of the many activities that activists and their movement organizations engage in to obtain visibility.

Nevertheless, it is not the only one. Speaking with a journalist during a demonstration or organizing a press conference before the start of a campaign are two further examples of the many relevant activities that activists perform to increase the visibility for themselves and their protests in mainstream media (Sobieraj, 2011; Mattoni, 2012). Additionally, activists have always employed other media to speak about their protest in a more direct way. For instance, they have created and managed alternative, radical, and autonomous media

(Downing, 2001; Atton, 2002; Lievrouw, 2011), ranging from free radios to street televisions, from posters and flyers to alternative informational websites.

In short, activists and their movement organizations continuously engage in a wide array of activities that revolve around their need to become visible and make their presence a stable one for the various audiences they need to interact with to reach their objectives. We consider these actions part of the broader practice of gaining visibility, which we define as all those activities that activists engage in when trying to be recognized as valuable political actors by different types of audiences, including their political opponents, political targets, dispersed bystanders and potential supporters who do not belong to the activists' social movement milieu. In the next section, we start unpacking the practice of gaining visibility by focusing on activists' interactions with legacy media.

Legacy media as challenging spaces for visibility

While websites, social media platforms, instant messaging apps, and other types of digital media have acquired a growing significance for the visibility of movement organizations in the past two decades, legacy media like newspapers and weeklies, radio, and television still play an important role for activists. This happens both during protests, as some studies on the subject matter also indicate (Sobieraj, 2011; Lee and Chan, 2018), and in the quiet times of politics, as we argue in this chapter. Interestingly, not just television counts for activists, but also radio and newspapers. As we will show in this section, activists highly value the ability of these legacy media to give their movement organizations visibility, also in times of latency. In some cases, they consider them even more useful than digital media, as becomes evident from the talk we had with Abril:

> 'We did not realize, a few years ago, that having your own website and your own social network is all very well, but if you do not appear on television, in the newspaper, ... on the radio, in the end nobody knows you, [so] you are very isolated. We are looking for notoriety and maximum impact.'

While Abril mentions using various types of legacy media, activists do not assign the same role to all of them. Rather, they see different affordances in them, also with regard to the kind of audiences that they could reach through them.

Television, for instance, seems to be valued most for its ability to reach large numbers of people. If Petro, a Greek activist, could make one of his wishes come true, he would certainly ask for his own TV station, because television remains the most important medium as far as addressing the general public goes. If you want to address the widest public possible, television is still the medium to use. If you ask any member of a union in Greece, they would say the same. We need to be heard by as many people as possible.

Television coverage is central for Petro, even if his movement organization communicates its members' claims and activities through a website, a Facebook page, a web forum, or in public events and meetings focusing on their issues of interest. The reason that such relevance is given to television is its ability – according to Petro – to reach broad audiences. Many of our interviewees touched upon this aspect, including Daniela at the opening of this chapter: activists in the three countries seem to attribute to television (especially generalist television) the ability to communicate its content with immediacy to a wide audience. In this sense, activists evoke the logic of numbers to which they often refer during mobilization phases (della Porta and Diani, 2020). During protests, movement organizations seek to engage a large amount of protest participants in order to become visible in the eyes of the (often few) institutional political actors to whom they direct their questions. During stages of latency, instead, the same movement organizations try to exploit appearances on television to reach a large number of viewers; this is certainly an undifferentiated group of people but nevertheless a useful one precisely because of its vastness.

Other than television, radio programmes and newscasts also emerged as particularly important. There are specific moments in which grassroots actors even prefer radio to television coverage, and this is also linked to the affordances of radio, a medium that traditionally revolves around the voice. According to Simona, this in turn leads "radio journalists [to] care more about contents. They have a higher level of professionalization. They care less about your appearance and more about your ability as a communicator". Radio offers activists another advantage: it is much more accessible, as we will also see later in this chapter. Although activists spend part of their time trying to get radio coverage and also enjoy participating in radio shows, they are conscious of the limits of this medium. Thus, the number of people they communicate with during a radio interview cannot be compared to that reached through television.[2] Also, according to activists, visibility obtained through radio programmes rarely triggers offline participation in terms of new activists joining the forces of a movement organization. Abril confirms this when she compares her appearances on television, the radio, and the print press in Spain.

> 'The radio does call us more but we have little availability to do interviews because they take away our operating time, and because we have noticed that they do not translate into an increase of members, of prominence. Both the press and television do: every time we go to a talk show we gain two or three new members.'

So far, we have reflected on the role of radio and television, but in this last excerpt Abril also gives value to another legacy media: print press. In fact, activists believe that printed newspapers or weeklies are still able to affect both media and political agendas. The reason for this is to be found not so much in the number of readers they can reach through the press. Rather, activists in the three countries greatly appreciate newspapers because of their legacy and the long history that characterizes many of them. For activists, then, receiving media coverage from a national newspaper is an important sign of recognition. No matter how many readers eventually get to know you through a newspaper article, having a story about your movement organization published in the print press is already an achievement in itself. Additionally, activists also acknowledge the variety of newspapers and value the local dimension of many of these. At the more pragmatic level, activists indeed know – because they have experienced this many times firsthand – that local newspapers are much more willing and able to publish media content that activists provide, such as press releases, but also detailed reports on specific topics or social media updates.

If activists do not value television, radio, and newspapers in an equal way, their understanding of legacy media in the three countries also varies. More precisely, if we consider the role of print press from a comparative perspective, Greek activists attribute a more prominent function to this mass medium in the process of acquiring visibility as opposed to their Italian and Spanish counterparts. It is mainly in Greece that most activists still see newspapers as the media able to affect a national media and political agenda. Thus, they believe that an interview in the main national Greek newspaper can give their communicative effort the best possible outcome. One of the Greek activists we interviewed, Eustratios, even said the following:

> 'I want my movement organization to have its own, proper newspaper. We cannot do that since it is a matter of money; this will cost a lot of money … Having a newspaper is important. If you go in a hotel where the people are having their siesta, [or] they are eating, [then] it is important if you can give them your newspaper.'

In short, living amid digitalization and datafication, activists in Italy, Greece, and Spain – while being surrounded by digital media of all kinds – do not forget legacy media, which they include in their repertoire of communication. Television, radio, and newspapers are not media of the past: they are firmly rooted in the practice of gaining visibility that activists perform even in times of latency. At the same time, activists acknowledge the fact that legacy media bring along significant challenges, mostly related to the close connection between institutional political actors and legacy media in Italy, Greece, and Spain. The attempt to obtain this kind of visibility through legacy media in times of latency may be even harder when activists and their movement organizations do not engage in any kind of mobilization. Without the disruptive power of protest actions, newspapers, radios, and television programmes prefer to engage less with movement organizations and more with institutional political actors, which represent more stable news sources. Unless activists set up a highly newsworthy series of events, legacy media tend to turn their gaze elsewhere. This is also a result of the strong ties between legacy media and political parties – or other types of political, institutional actors – that traditionally characterize Southern European countries: the latter influence the former according to a process of political parallelism (Hallin and Mancini, 2004). Activists in the three countries under examination consider legacy media to be strongly influenced by various types of political and financial actors; in the interviews, they provided concrete examples of this phenomenon, also related to their own experiences as activists trying to draw the attention of mainstream media. Hence, they consider news media organizations not so much a neutral space, but proper political actors whose legitimation through media coverage becomes even more relevant for activists. This is why activists in Greece, Italy, and Spain greatly value mainstream media and, despite the low probability that they effectively obtain media coverage, display a variety of activities to reach these media in an attempt to be heard and seen by the broad audiences that such media are able to reach. This is important also beyond the organization of protests, when the activists' daily political work unfolds as usual.

In sum, while activists attribute an important role to legacy media when performing the practice of gaining visibility, they also acknowledge that they need to face and overcome certain constraints. To do so, they seek to change their movement organizations from simple news sources to valuable data sources for legacy media. As we will explain in the following section, though, becoming a data source brings along many dilemmas for activists.

The dilemma of becoming a data source for legacy media

While activists usually organize protests that resonate with the news-making value of the print press or television broadcasting during mobilizations, they need to do something different when they are not protesting in the street. They still employ the strategy of adaptation to mainstream media (Rucht, 2004) in moments of latency, but their activities are tailored to the features that characterize legacy media, rather than to the qualities of the collective actions they organize. Activists exercise their agency over legacy media by producing knowledge of how they function. Indeed, all our interviewees know how legacy media work in their respective countries and are conscious of some of the difficulties that they need to face when seeking to obtain coverage during stages of latency. In the case of the Southern European movement organizations that we investigated, activists engage in a twofold strategic adaptation.

On the one hand, adaptation is linked to the exogenous features of legacy media and their connections with other institutional political actors. Activists adapt to legacy media considering them political actors, rather than as a neutral space of discussion. This means that when activists establish strong and long-lasting connections with journalists, the chances of becoming relevant data sources increase; as a consequence, it is easier for activists' movement organizations to become visible also when they are not in their mobilization stage. In other words, activists try to exploit the political parallelism and turn it to their benefit, seeking the right contacts with journalists who work in those legacy media that may be ideologically nearer to their positions, but also simply nurturing connections with individual journalists who work as freelancers and might cover their movement organization activities also in times of latency. This process becomes easier when activists already have ties with the world of journalism. As we will discuss in more detail in Chapter 6, when activists have a privileged relationship with journalists, gaining visibility requires less demanding efforts.

On the other hand, adaptation is linked to an endogenous characteristic of legacy media, namely the growing and widespread precariousness of information professionals – including journalists – who are employed in them (Deuze, 2007). In this regard, activists know that time is a precious resource in newsrooms, especially for precarious journalists, who are increasing in legacy media of all kinds. Given also her past as a journalist, Emilia, for instance, knows that providing the right type of data, packaged in a format that resonates with journalistic needs, can greatly increase her movement organization's ability to get media coverage, especially during stages of latency when activists do not make the news by filling the streets with hundreds of thousands of protesters. According to Emilia, precarious journalists suffer from a lack of resources that renders them more inclined than full-time, permanent journalists to favour "news items that are already cooked". This is why she and her movement organization 'cook' the data they have in order to make them appealing to journalists and, more importantly, ready to be used, as Emilia explains:

'[K]nowing the journalists, who need to have everything ready, for the press, I prepare a report, for example, which is 150 pages long. I prepare a five-page synopsis so that it reaches the journalists, and in those five pages they have everything they needs, and if they want to go deeper they do. ... So you build it up a little bit. In fact, we are working more and more on that because, unfortunately, most of them do a copy-and-paste [of what we supply to them].'

In some cases, activists exploit certain affordances of digital media to make the journalists' work even easier, such as instant messaging platforms to create direct contact with journalists to whom activists send various types of data, sometimes aggregated in the form of information that can easily be included in the journalistic accounts. An emblematic example is Miranda's use of instant messaging apps, like WhatsApp, to produce a continuous sequence of data about her movement organization's activities that she then sends to her journalist contacts without waiting for a request to be interviewed for a radio programme or the print press. She proactively releases data about what her movement organization is doing, how, and why, putting them together into consistent stories that already resemble pieces of radio news, as she describes in detail in this interview excerpt:

'Another thing I do with WhatsApp [is that] I have this ... there are two kinds: I have the press and I have the radio. In the press, I give news. But on radios I give audios ... Something happens and I say "hi, this is me, today, and I will talk about this", and I make my statement. They like it very much and then I say "I will send an audio with my statements on these points: this, this, and that". They see the text and if they find it interesting they listen to it and they take the part of the audio that is relevant to them and put it in the news. So the people who work on the radio, they told me "really, this is great, because then I don't have to call you, I don't have to ask you anything, you already give it to me and when I am preparing the news, I take the cut and I put it". They say that this WhatsApp audio is even better than if I talk on the smartphone, because ... this is not a mobile system: these are data. They download it, they take the cut they need, it and they use it.'

According to Miranda, WhatsApp audios can render the journalist's job easier and, in turn, increase the chance of obtaining visibility in their news programmes. Instant messaging apps, then, become central digital devices in the practice of gaining visibility as they allow activists to interact with journalists directly, sending them already cooked data in a format that is appealing to journalists who work with an unstable schedule, frequently across more than one newsroom, to make a living despite their precarious working conditions.

Becoming a data source also comes with trade-offs for activists. In some cases, journalists working for news media organizations make clear requests to activists, offering visibility in exchange for stereotyped characters to be used in television programmes, as Simona explains:

> 'It works like this: TV journalists call us saying: "hello, we have our show tomorrow. We need a temporary employee, possibly a young new mum, because we have to talk about precarity and fake VAT workers". I used to joke about making a lot of money if we set up an agency offering uncool characters for television. That is what they want from us.'

Simona jokes about these types of requests that render her movement organization a supplier of stereotypical workers who can speak about precarity. However, through her joke, she points out a relevant aspect of the relationship between movement organizations and legacy media. When the former manage to become trusted data sources thanks to their adaptation strategies, the latter interact with them from a different viewpoint, considering them less as political actors and more as on-demand content providers. This is a risk that activists run when adapting to legacy media: their political role is to some extent put in the background as the front stage is meant for individuals who somehow stand for the vulnerable groups that activists support. Gaining visibility of such vulnerable groups through the intervention of emblematic characters (for example the precarious working mother, the victim of corruption crimes) may of course be a positive aspect also for the movement organization that supplies them to legacy media. However, the risk is that movement organizations, their messages, and political activities at the collective level remain unseen and that the audiences of legacy media consequently fail to recognize them.

Although legacy media adaptation strategies are quite widespread in all the countries that we considered, it must be pointed out that Greek activists are less inclined to use them than others. Almost all of the Greek activists we interviewed reject the logic behind a media system in which journalists and their news outlets have close ties to institutional political actors. Such a rejection implies – among other things – that they refuse to cultivate contacts with journalists and, more generally, do not strategically adapt to what legacy media want them to be in order to better represent them on television, radio, and in newspapers. At the same time, this means that Greek activists may in some cases decide to conquer their own media spaces through direct action in the editorial offices of newspapers, as Kosta told us:

> 'When we do … big events, like the strike that we had last week, we go and do like a small protest squat at radio stations, where we say our word directly. Last time we had prepared our statement in [the form of an] audio and we went to one radio station where we could do it

and put it on the programme. Something like: "we are going to hear some people from the union". We went there with our recording and we said "it's like this, something between a protest and a squat, a small invasion". And in a second radio station, there was a big conflict, they didn't want to do it, so they said "we are going to call the police", or something like that. And our assembly had chosen that we won't go very far with the violence, so we didn't do it finally.'

Gaining visibility through direct action, as described by Kosta, is not a common activity among the Greek activists we interviewed. However, it represents an interesting exception that underscores what other studies on the topic already pointed out: while adaptation to the media logic is certainly common among activists, this is not the only strategy that they imagine and practice. Even in times when legacy media played an even more central role in covering political events and public protests than they do today, activists could choose to reject their logic of newsworthiness, obtaining media coverage according to their rules and not those of the journalists, or even creating their own communication channels (Rucht, 2004; Mattoni, 2012). This last option remains particularly central to the practice of gaining visibility even today, although nowadays the choice lies not so much in building alternative media through which to spread one's ideas, but in trying to exploit the possibility of disintermediation offered by social media platforms, as we will explain in the next section.

I do social media ergo sum

When seeking visibility, activists and their movement organizations try to become relevant data sources. However, they may also attempt to obtain recognition in other ways, mostly through digital media producing data for and disseminating them through social media platforms, mostly Facebook and Twitter.

When they include social media platforms in the practice of gaining visibility, activists do this from the perspective of the general understanding that one social media platform is more efficient in reaching the general public than another. Such understanding does not necessarily reflect the actual relevance of social media platforms in terms of their ability to reach broad audiences. The activists we interviewed do not seem to care about the actual use of Facebook or Twitter among the general population of their respective countries. However, as we have mentioned earlier, they develop a general understanding that seems to be driven more by intuition and based on their personal experiences of the social media platforms they interact with. Interestingly, these general understandings are not the same in Italy, Greece, and Spain.

Unsurprisingly, almost all activists in the three countries assign a relevant role to social media platforms in the process of becoming visible. When we interviewed Delphina, a labor unionist based in Greece, she paraphrased the famous Cartesian motto *cogito ergo sum* to summarize the importance of social media for her movement organization: "[W]e have reached a point now where the cogito ergo sum has turned into Facebook ergo sum." Far from being an isolated position, Delphina's general understanding of social media is shared by most of the activists we interviewed in Greece, Italy and Spain. Despite some exceptions, social media platforms appear to be essential in the practice of gaining visibility for Southern European activists. However, even if activists tend to combine different social media platforms, we noticed that activists in all three countries develop a distinct general understanding of which social media platforms are more valuable for them and a practical understanding of how to use them. This awareness is subsequently reflected in the actions that they undertake to manage their social media profiles and pages.

In Italy and Greece, activists consider Facebook the most efficient social media platform to gain visibility beyond the smaller circles of their supporters. It is not surprising that activists in both countries affirm that they produce data mostly to be published on this social media platform, as the following Italian activist noticed when reflecting on the types of communication that she engaged with for her movement organization: "[C]onsidering all kinds of communication together, not just video communication, the main one is Facebook" (Davide). This general understanding is so relevant that some activists even go a step further: they equate efficient communication with Facebook communication, as this member of an anti-corruption movement organization suggests when he says that "[c]ommunication means that I publish a post on Facebook. In my experience, there is nothing more effective". It is also for this reason that activists employ Facebook for their grassroots political engagement even when they use their own private profiles. As a consequence, the activity of posting on Facebook is not a private matter but a political one. As Riccardo, an activist who works in a prominent civil society organization fighting against corruption in Italy, explains, "for me, Facebook is work. For me, Facebook is important for the positioning of the association also through social media".

Facebook, in short, is relevant for the positioning of activists' movement organizations in the broader social movement milieu, building bridges with social movement actors. However, this positioning does not happen through the engagement in public debates within the social media platform, or, at least, it is not the primary function that the activists we interviewed attribute to Facebook. In fact, they consider this social media platform not more than a window through which to show who they are and what they do. The data that they produce through Facebook are meant to convey a stance about the movement organization itself and its daily political work.

Activists tend not to take advantage of the social media platform as an online space to develop a debate between the activist organization and its diverse audiences. They ignore the interactive affordances that Facebook offers and mostly employ their accounts – especially the pages of their movement organizations – as channels in which to broadcast messages following a one-to-many pattern of communication that they manage in a top-down fashion. Although Facebook may be, at least in principle, a social media platform that also supports interactions with their audiences, activists do not value this possibility. This is what Simona and Kosmas explained to us in this regard:

> 'In my view, our Facebook page is not a place for debating. This happens only sporadically and about little things. A real debate occurs on a wide level and on Facebook more in general, but not on our Facebook page.'

> 'On Facebook sometimes we have enough shares of a post, and that's engagement, but we don't have too many comments. They absorb the information but usually they don't interact. This is not bad because we don't want to debate, we want to inform and if someone wants some clarifications we answer him or her, but I don't want to debate, I don't like this.'

In short, the general understanding of Facebook among activists in Italy and Greece is that of a social media platform where they can be seen. The practical understanding of the kind of actions that activists should undertake is consistent with this interpretation: affordances that would trigger and nurture a debate about the movement organizations, their choices, and their strategies are not interesting for activists. They do not use them, and this is a deliberate choice that is not linked to any lack of digital skills.

Conversely, in Spain, we encountered a different type of general understanding, according to which Twitter is the most important social media platform that activists have to reach people. Indeed, as Ruben points out, activists see Twitter as: "A more serious social media platform where issues are not as cruel and trivial as the famous cat videos on Facebook. Twitter audiences care about other kinds of issues. That's why we communicate much more on Twitter."

This quote is emblematic of a distinction that almost all activists we interviewed in Spain made between Facebook, considered a place that is not for politics in the first place, and Twitter, where audiences are more open to receiving political messages about certain contentious issues, as the following extract from Ruben underlines:

> 'Political conversations on Facebook are horrible because noise, noise, noise, noise enters and you cannot get to any point of substance.

Facebook cannot change electoral behaviour. It cannot change people's opinions. Everything is totally false and nothing more than publicity for Facebook. Facebook is a dead social media in which people do not interact; you barely have any interactions. There is a severe crisis of interaction going on. However, interactions still occur on Twitter.'

Interestingly, in the case of Spanish activists, the interactive potential of social media platforms is still at the centre of their general understanding, although they interpret this potential in a different way than their Greek and Italian counterparts: while the latter use Facebook seeking to avoid interactions, the former use Twitter because it allows them to interact with their audiences to a greater extent than Facebook, where debates are considered noisy and rude. Consistently, Spanish activists view Facebook as a social media platform that is no longer central for general conversations and more politically inclined debates. Twitter, on the contrary, is the place where people talk about politics; this feature, in turn, renders it the social media platform where activists want to become more visible. That said, it is also worth noting that some of the Spanish activists we interviewed know the primary limits of Twitter, their preferred social media platform, up to the point that some of them have even decided to stop tweeting, as Abril told us:

'We've stopped using Twitter, because we've seen that this choice has no repercussions, that nothing happens, that Twitter is of little importance because its target audience is not ours. Twitter's target audience is under 25 years old, without any degree or working in politics and media, but [it is] not the general public. So we obviously already reach politicians through other channels and, at the same time, we do not reach the general audience through Twitter.'

It is, then, crucial not to overestimate the role of Twitter even in Spain. If compared with activists in Italy and Greece, there is no doubt that Spanish activists strongly rely on this digital platform as well, although they do so according to a much more professional approach to digital media, very often coupled with a parallel awareness of the strength and power of algorithms.

The differences between the general understanding of Facebook and Twitter in the three countries are profound. Despite some exceptions, for Spanish activists, Twitter is the social media platform that attracts the right type of audience and allows for a particular communication style, which values civil interactions that focus on political issues. Vice versa, Italian and Greek activists consider Facebook a trendy digital environment where the majority of people hang out: one in which you want to be to produce and disseminate your data. Such a general understanding does not match the actual diffusion of the two platforms in the three countries, where no significant differences arise: around

70 per cent of Greek, Italian, and Spanish citizens who are online use Facebook, while this percentage stops at 20 per cent in the case of Twitter (Newman et al, 2019). However, the difference between activists' general understanding of social media in the framework of gaining visibility and the actual diffusion of Facebook and Twitter in the three countries is not relevant. What counts is that when activists consider one social media platform relevant to become visible this has consequences for how they ingrain it in their actions, as we have discussed earlier. There are, however, other ways through which activists seek to become visible, beyond social media platforms: as we will see in the next section, they engage in the creation of alternative media.

Gaining visibility through alternative media

As we have already stated in the introduction, activists and the movement organizations they belong to often link their visibility to media other than legacy media. Indeed, in the previous section, we have shed light on how activists engage with social media platforms that have been developed by commercial companies. These platforms cannot be considered alternative digital media in the strict sense (Treré, 2018), although the kind of content that activists share on platforms like Facebook or Twitter may of course present alternative political viewpoints. However, activists do not control them and the logic of visibility that they promote, which is mostly tied to commercial aims (Poell and Van Dijck, 2015; Hutchinson, 2021). Other than using these social media platforms, activists in Greece, Italy, and Spain also rely on alternative, radical, and autonomous media (Downing, 2001; Atton, 2002) to gain visibility. Those that emerged as particularly relevant in our analysis include independent websites; banners, posters, flyers, and leaflets; and communications via fax. While the latter cannot be conceived as alternative media in the full sense of the word, we consider these forms of communicative interactions a valuable way for activists to produce data sequences that escape the social media logic.

Alternative, radical, and autonomous media have often played an important role in the practice of gaining visibility. Without going back in time too much, we could mention the case of the independent informational website Indymedia, which was particularly relevant in sustaining and accounting for the protests of the global justice movement that developed in the late 1990s in Seattle, to then quickly spread across the world (Kidd, 2003; Juris, 2005). Additionally, our investigation revealed that this type of media is important to sustain activists' organizations during moments of latency, when people are not in the streets and activists are not planning protests. While being of a different kind, alternative, radical, and autonomous media become the window through which activist organizations can let their voice be heard even in these quiet moments, sharing their worldview beyond the narrow circle of their members to involve other audiences that are not necessarily connected to the core organizers of the protests.

In fact, the activists we interviewed also spoke at length about the media – and the related technologies – that they control in an autonomous manner. Independent websites, for instance, are often used in the practice of gaining visibility; activists perform several activities aimed at the creation of their independent websites also when they do not mobilize in the streets. More specifically, there is a general understanding of independent websites as a static digital space, where static does not necessarily have a negative connotation: in a world of quick information diffusion, where the data stream might have a very fast pace, having a space where data can flow at a controlled pace may become a relevant feature – perhaps even a luxury. Furthermore, independent websites also offer a digital space in which activists can proclaim who they are and what they do without having to tackle the temporal limitations of social media platforms. For instance, when activists manage their own independent websites and the content they publish on them, the visibility that they develop stretches well beyond the fast pace of Twitter feeds, WhatsApp chats, and other digital media platforms that work in an accelerated way. Furthermore, they can ensure visibility that lasts longer and gives a temporal depth to their organization's identity, so that it does not remain trapped in an eternal present made up of continuous statements that change hour by hour, when not faster. The Greek activist Delphina aptly summarizes the clash between social media platforms and the affordances of independent websites when it comes to visibility:

> '[In social media platforms] you cannot upload a text that no one reads. It does not make any sense. You can do this on your website, because if someone wants to have information on your organization, they visit your website, and you can find everything there. You have to be shorter and more attractive on Facebook.'

The data stream that surrounds grassroots politics and the related daily practices that activists perform once again reveals its heterogeneity: the slow and somehow self-reflective digital space that independent websites represent for activists seems to clash with the overall accelerated production of data in which the same activists participate when they produce content for the social media platforms that they also employ every day. The abundance that characterizes the data flows in an age that is at the crossroad between digitalization and datafication inevitably generates these differences at the level of the practice of gaining visibility. While the teleoaffective structure remains similar, the activities performed to sustain the visibility of movement organizations may greatly vary. In this regard, it is interesting to note the renewed role of alternative media. If in the late 1990s Indymedia was the main digital place for activists to quickly disseminate information related to their protest activities, today movement organizations promote their visibility in a more fragmented way, each on their website. The independent websites of movement organizations are, indeed, digital spaces where activists can better represent their daily efforts in an attempt to acquire more visibility for their demands without reducing the substance of their claims. For instance, Fabio told us: "The website is a fundamental component, because the website raises the level of the public debate that you try to affect. It does so by producing updates, information, news, and content. It would be a real problem if it were not there." The Spanish activist Abril, instead, observed that "the website we have serves the purpose of showing that we exist". According to Abril, the website has an important function for her movement organization because it gives it a sort of quality certificate. It not only shows that her movement organization exists; it also provides a kind of authority, professionalism, and reliability that other digital media platforms, like Facebook, are not always able to deliver on their own.

However, not all activists appreciate the slow pace of independent websites. According to some, alternative media are no longer useful exactly because they are not consistent with the acceleration and ubiquity that characterize the current diffusion of information. For this reason, a more stable digital space risks becoming so static in the delivery of its content that it somehow clashes with a form of visibility based on a constantly changing flow of information. Adrian has very straightforward ideas on this point: "[W]e have a website, which is static. There is a blog on the website, but we don't really write anything there. A long time ago, we reached the conclusion that it's not ... it doesn't work." In short, some movement organizations decide not to engage in the practice of gaining visibility through activities that include the creation of independent websites: they no longer see the advantage of developing this type of alternative media because they consider it to be out of tune with the overall rhythm that characterizes the present-day flow of information.

While in some cases the practice of gaining visibility rests on a broad combination of activities that keep together older and newer media technologies, in other cases this combination seeks to escape the heterogeneity of the data stream, simplifying its features and somehow reducing it to a more homogeneous way of understanding the spaces and times that characterize it. Once again, the type of media technology that activists decide to engage in is deeply tied to a general understanding of what visibility must be given to grassroots activism in the present. The differences related to what visibility means and how activists should achieve it are also striking when it comes to Greece. The Greek activists we interviewed indicated other types of media technologies as being relevant in the practice of gaining visibility. Most of these are situated outside the spectrum of digital media: older media technologies, like paper or cloth, still play an important role when it comes to seeking visibility for Greek movement organizations; flyers, leaflets, and posters are also very common in Greece. Conversely, these traditional devices no longer seem to exist in Italy, at least within the movement organizations that we investigated. As suggested by an Italian activist, Simona: "[W]e no longer use paper-based forms of communication: leaflets, posters, business cards printed for years and now stored somewhere, unused. No one reads them anymore." Spain situates itself in the middle. Flyers, leaflets, and posters are not used as regularly as they are in Greece, but they nevertheless remain part of the practice of gaining visibility, as the following example from Julia demonstrates: "We have a very cool pamphlet: it is like a caricature. We sneak into hotels as if we were customers, and we put our pamphlet in bathrooms as well as strategic places to make them visible for security cameras, so that workers join us in our assemblies."

What distinguishes the Greek case in this more frequent and massive use of flyers, leaflets, and posters is a geopolitical and demographic factor: half of the Greek population lives in Athens. Almost all political and economic centres are in Athens. Although the Italian and Spanish capitals attract a significant amount of political power, it happens less than in Greece. This unique trait of the three Mediterranean countries pushes Greek activists to also rely on low-tech media in their practice of gaining visibility. Since movement organizations have to haunt a limited territory, it makes more sense to spend their money and time on putting up posters in public spaces or crowding the capital's main streets with their own leaflets and flyers. Political power is far more dispersed in Italy and Spain, where the population is also more spread out across several medium-sized cities, which discourages Italian and Spanish activists from using those visibility strategies employed by their Greek counterparts.

In the case of the Italian activists, another interesting yet marginal media technology turned out to play a more central role in past waves of protest: the fax. In this case, too, we are not speaking about a common activity in the framework of the practice of gaining visibility. However, the use of the fax is indicative of the activists' ability to go beyond the usual activities, introduce changes into their everyday political work, and be creative when seeking visibility and, accordingly, the recognition of other political actors. Indeed, practices may be frequent and consistent over time, but they are not fixed: they could change through the incremental transformation of certain activities or more abruptly and depending on the circumstances in which activists find themselves. While a certain practical and general understanding remains stable, the need to face otherwise unsurmountable obstacles can lead to unexpected activities, or even to activities that were at the centre of the practice of gaining visibility in the past, like the use of the fax. This is the case of an Italian movement organization that sought to become visible to policy makers, as Simona explains:

> 'We discovered that if you send emails to the various addresses of the Senate and the House, which end up in the spam folder, then it all gets clogged up and you end up there. But if you send a fax, whoever is on the other end is institutionally required to protocol it because it is an official communication in some way. So we bought one of those services that let you fax online, we spent 50 euros as an association and we invited everyone to log on and send a fax. People would actually just log on to our site, click, fill in their name, and sign up. We clogged them up with faxes. Within 2 hours, we sent them 50 euros worth of faxes, while the committee was in a meeting, until they picked up the phone, called us, and asked us to stop. They told us they understood and called us back.'

Activists strategically used an older technology (fax) to make their claims visible to the institutional actors they wanted to relate with, then employed newer media-related services such as their website, newsletters, and social media accounts to involve their networks in this fax bombing strategy, all the while taking the street with a few dozen of their members to obtain a face-to-face meeting with legislative actors. This case of Italian freelancers casts light on the combination of different media technologies, and their related affordances, that are embedded in the practice of gaining visibility. It may require activists to merge different data flows, such as face-to-face and digital interactions, also including media technologies – like the fax – that no longer exist for most activists even if they are still normatively anchored within the organizational and bureaucratic practices of public institutions. The activists' practical understanding of how the fax works in such a specific context, in which they wanted to gain visibility, was indeed key to reaching their objective.

Conclusion

In this chapter, we have discussed the practice of gaining visibility. We have explained what it means, for activists, to engage in the data stream to become noticed and recognized when no protests are going on and the public's attention is caught by other issues. Social movement studies usually consider visibility a precious resource when there is a mobilization happening and people are protesting. When activists succeed in either bringing people to the streets or involving them in online actions to claim their demands, they also want such protests to be seen and heard. For this reason, organizing a protest and then trying to have that protest covered by the mainstream press as well as in social media platforms is an important part of the practice of gaining visibility. However, as emerged from the interviews that we conducted with activists in Greece, Italy, and Spain, activists and their movement organizations have continuous attention to the visibility of their movement organizations beyond moments of protest. Indeed, our research proves that the practice of gaining visibility is crucial for activists also when it does not entail making claims in the context of a specific mobilization. Activists do not wait for the next protest to acquire visibility; they want various types of audiences to watch, recognize, and legitimate them also when they are not mobilizing, hence allowing them to enter a state of permanent visibility. This attitude is consistent with what happens in the realm of institutional politics, where political leaders and their parties are constantly engaged in electoral campaigns even when these are not happening (Joathan and Lilleker, 2020), also as a result of the use of social media platforms (Elmer et al, 2014). Similarly, it recalls the overall practice of presencing – that is, of sustaining a public presence – that Nick Couldry (2012) more generally associates with what people do in social media platforms, as we have mentioned earlier in this chapter. However, elsewhere in this chapter, we have seen that activists do much more than establish a public presence on Facebook or Twitter: they sustain their visibility in times of latency across a whole range of media, including mainstream and alternative media. From this viewpoint, we could say that the logic of presencing that is strictly linked to social media platforms nowadays goes beyond these digital media services to permeate the whole practice of gaining visibility.

When performed in times of latency, this practice does not involve the organization of protests that can attract the attention of legacy media and provide materials for social media content. In this chapter, we have shown that the practice of gaining visibility in times of latency requires activists to make more subtle interventions in the data stream, crediting themselves as legitimate and reliable data sources in the eyes of various audiences – in particular news professionals, like journalists. We have illustrated that there is no such thing as a single type of visibility. On the contrary, activists attempt to gain visibility through various types of digital and non-digital media, hence developing a transmedia visibility strategy that is tailored to societies with a higher quantity of information and more extensive audiences that such information could reach; these audiences are less controllable because political actors cannot foresee what and when they will receive this information, and with what consequences for their visibility (Thompson, 2005). Furthermore, since each media technology shapes visibility in a specific way (Thompson, 2005), in this chapter we have described the different paths that activists follow when engaging in the practice of gaining visibility through the use of both digital and non-digital media.

From this perspective, it is clear that activists are confronted with a heterogeneous data stream even in their daily attempts to gain visibility. We have shown how, in a world where digitization and datafication have partly changed the way activists communicate, legacy media are still very important in Southern Europe. Activists consider it relevant to receive media coverage from television, radio, and print media even when their movement organizations are not engaged in public protests. There are undoubtedly differences between the three main legacy media: television is important because it helps you to reach a wide audience, the radio because it allows you to publish your messages more accurately, and print media because it has political prestige in the eyes of activists. Either way, all three remain a strong point of reference, even if activists often struggle to convey their point of view in this type of media. The reason for this is that – as we have shown – legacy media in Greece, Italy, and Spain are not neutral spaces but resemble more proper political actors. In addition, the journalists who are employed in them are usually precarious and forced to work under conditions that do not benefit the quality of journalistic work. These are two major obstacles that activists have to face when trying to voice their demands within these media types.

To overcome these impediments, Greek, Italian, and Spanish activists seek not so much to make their movement organizations newsworthy in the context of their political work. Rather, they try to become stable and reliable sources for journalists; intervening directly in the data stream by producing data that journalists will be interested in is a way of adapting to legacy media in which journalists are hard-pressed by their precarious working conditions and the newspapers they work for are often closely tied to the political and economic elites of the three countries. It is not an easy job for activists, but in all three countries, they manage to adapt to both legacy media and the data stream as a whole.

In addition to legacy media, social media platforms are also in a prominent position. In this chapter, we have shown that these are now firmly inserted in the communication repertoire of activists, who try to exploit them as much as possible precisely to obtain ordinary visibility based on the regular and constant publication of content, even in phases of latency. Using these platforms to talk about themselves and publish data on the activities of their movement organizations is often seen as a routine activity, not necessarily linked to moments of protest. Through social media platforms, activists are visible all the time, day after day. However, we have demonstrated that the social media platform of preference changes depending on the country one is looking at: activists attribute a precise role to each social media platform they use, associating it with particular categories of users and content. Thus, if Facebook is the reference point for Greek and Italian activists, Twitter has a more prominent role in Spain as far as the practice of gaining visibility is concerned.

Social media platforms are not all activists have at their disposal beyond mainstream media to become visible in times of latency. In this chapter we have shown that they use alternative media also relying on the employment of more low-tech devices, which allow people to produce data about their movement organizations more gradually, even integrating them into physical places beyond the mediation of digital media. In this way, activists can reach people they would not reach through their Facebook profiles, making themselves visible in the streets of their cities or during meetings with politicians. Alternative media space then can be seen as rivulets of the data stream. While they are probably not widespread, they are of crucial importance for activists, as they give them back control of portions of the data stream, thus making them autonomous agents of their own visibility, independent of both the political ties of legacy media and the commercial interests of social media platforms. Again, these are rivulets of data in the context of a broader data stream, in which the search for an activist agency – as we have shown in this chapter – requires a considerable effort.

Overall, it is clear that activists' agency towards the data stream concerning the practice of gaining visibility relies on their ability to move from one platform to another, from one medium to another, as they seek visibility among different types of audiences. This ability to move along the data stream and interact with different data entry points – each characterized by a different set of services and digital devices – is very important for activists. In this regard, we have demonstrated that activists exercise an agency over the data stream by removing themselves from the production of certain data sequences that nowadays seem more popular than others, like those related to social media platforms. They partially do this by adapting, more generally, to one of the principal aspects of the data stream: its heterogeneity. These activists embrace the fact that they can interact with different sequences of data without excluding one or the other and, indeed, combining them. By contrast, other activists decide to somehow reject this heterogeneity by focusing on data sequences that tend to be more marginal, but which allow activists to regain the slow time of politics even in their visibility practices. Activists do this when they decide to employ alternative media, such as personal websites or digital radios, posters, face-to-face encounters, or apparently archaic media-related activities such as fax bombing.

In the next chapter, we will continue to discuss the practice of gaining visibility and the agency it entails by considering another aspect of the data stream: when activists engage with social media platforms, they have to deal with a highly relevant non-human entity, the algorithm, which further complicates the practice of gaining visibility.

4

Algorithmic Visibility and Activists' Management of Reputation

Enrique earns a living as a social worker in Barcelona. He is one of the leading members of a movement organization fighting for basic income, in which he has various roles, including the management of some of its social media accounts, such as Twitter. He seems to be a proficient social media user who knows very well how to interact with all kinds of digital media, including social media platforms. While talking with Enrique, we discovered that he has never done any social media management training. Rather, he has learned how to engage in social media by himself, reading books. Although he posts content on social media, he told us that he finds it difficult to understand how such content then spreads online. Talking about Twitter, for instance, he said the following: "When I publish something, and there are 25 retweets, I say 'wow!' When there are four retweets I say 'Four? Why only four of them?' The tweet I posted hasn't been disseminated that much and I don't quite understand the mechanics of it." The same difficulties also apply to other digital media content that he produces and its ability to spread online: "Sometimes it is difficult for me to understand why [online content] is or is not disseminated. There are articles that have a lot of diffusion and articles that don't and you don't know why: sometimes it's the title, sometimes it's the topic." In short, Enrique does not know the rules according to which some digital media content spreads and other content does not. Such rules challenge him because they remain opaque, both when he produces and seeks to diffuse social media content online and when, instead, he looks for relevant data that he needs to acquire for his movement organization. In other words, he does not fully grasp how the algorithms that regulate the online dissemination of data work.

However, this lack of knowledge only disturbs him to a certain point. What he seems to care about most is his movement organization's ability to get a good reputation, not necessarily online. He wants it to be respected and considered serious, reliable, knowledgeable, and esteemed. There are various strategies that Enrique and his movement organization employ to meet this objective, but according to him, algorithms play a very marginal role in these. This is why his organization does not invest any money in sponsors for social media posts or a professional social media manager who could help increase its online visibility. Although they would not have the necessary resources, the interview with Enrique revealed that his movement organization would not have done it in any case. That said, a good reputation – as Enrique knows well – is very difficult to achieve and, even more importantly, to maintain. Building a solid, positive reputation does not end with the careful management of the movement organization's social media accounts, its news coverage on legacy media, and so forth. It exceeds all this because it is also linked to what the most renowned members of the organization publish in their personal social media profiles, hence forcing them to constantly and carefully consider what to share and what not to share, also at the individual level of their political activities.

Our interview with Enrique was very telling, because it suggested that activists may not always care about algorithms, despite living in a society that is deeply shaped by them. Rather, as it will become clear in this chapter, while algorithms seem to play an important role in the shaping of a movement organization's visibility, activists frequently engage in algorithms in a nuanced way and in combination with other digital and non-digital media. Indeed, activists do not seem to consider the algorithmic management alone as a decisive element in the process of making them visible outside the social movement milieu.

Regardless of the level of personal awareness of algorithms and the intention to master them, there is no doubt that activists nowadays operate in a society in which yet another layer of mediation comes into play owing to the algorithms, which play an important role in the data stream within and beyond social media platforms. In this regard, some scholars point to the increased importance of 'algorithmic visibility' (Magalhães and Yu, 2017; Treré and Bonini, 2022) and the vain attempts of various types of actors – including journalists (Bucher, 2012), cultural workers (Petre et al, 2019), online gamers (Willson and Kinder-Kurlanda, 2021), and fashion and beauty bloggers (Bishop, 2019) – to manage it without knowing the algorithms they are dealing with.

In recent years, the growing literature on algorithms and social movements has demonstrated that activists easily manage to use their knowledge to refine their repertoire of communication when they are aware of their functioning, power, and effects. In his work on analytic activism, for instance, David Karpf casts light on large movement organizations' recourse to 'a cluster of technologies that allow organizations to monitor online sentiment, test and refine communications, and quantify opinion and engagement' (2017: 11);

this allows activists to exploit big data and the related algorithms as leverage to foster their campaigning activities. At the same time, the algorithmic influence on visibility can even become an object of contention for activists. For instance, the activist Johanna Burai denounced the racial bias in Google Image search results through an awareness campaign targeting legacy media in Sweden, in 2015 (Velkova and Kaun, 2021). Activists may also exercise their agency over algorithms in a more collective fashion, coordinating their interaction with social media platforms to increase their visibility online, as in the case of the Spanish 15-M mobilizations in 2011 (Treré et al, 2017). However, if in some cases activists take advantage of algorithms, in other cases they fail to do so (Milan, 2015; Galis and Neumayer, 2016; Treré, 2018). In these situations, activists either develop negative and distorted 'algorithmic imaginaries' (Bucher, 2017), thus distancing themselves from digital media, or decide to turn to legacy media and other digital media in which algorithms play a limited role, if any. Nevertheless, even when activists convincingly decide to take algorithmic visibility seriously, this does not result in an automatic ability to obtain what they want. Gaining visibility through algorithms is anything but a smooth ride.

In this chapter, we will examine how activists deal with algorithms that intertwine with the practice of gaining visibility. We will first discuss how such a non-human element, which often remains opaque and difficult to understand, presents a significant challenge to the activists' management of their online content. After having unpacked this challenge, we will consider three ways in which activists and their movement organizations engage in the practice of gaining visibility, also – albeit not exclusively – to go beyond the structural constraints that algorithms impose on them. We will first focus on the importance of building a good reputation, which goes beyond the visibility obtained in one specific media outlet. This allows activists to become independent from algorithms and present themselves as a trusted and visible collective actor whose information is reliable and valuable. While developing and maintaining a good reputation may be a draining activity in the practice of gaining visibility, this is not the only difficult aspect that activists have to deal with when facing algorithms. In this regard, we will discuss the strong individualization at work within social media platforms. Visibility, in this case, is not just connected to the social media profiles of movement organizations; activists also have personal profiles, which they often use to support their grassroots political work and increase the visibility of their movement organizations. We will show how activists look for a balance between their social media profiles and those of their movement organizations. In the last section of the chapter, we will address another relevant topic related to the practice of gaining visibility, namely the material side of digital media that activists employ on a daily basis to make their grassroots political work visible.

We argue that, although the mobile dimension of some media devices allows activists to deal with immediacy better, they only truly succeed in delivering their communicative production at a high-quality level through desktop computers and professional software. In the conclusion, we will summarize and elaborate on some of the challenges that activists must face when dealing with algorithms that intertwine with the practice of gaining visibility.

The constraints of algorithmic visibility

When activists use social media, they also expose themselves and their movement organizations to the algorithms that regulate social media platforms. In the simple act of publishing posts on social media, activists allow algorithms determine the potential of their content to gain visibility. Indeed, algorithms 'do not merely enable information flows, but actively intervene and shape those very flows' (Gran et al, 2020: 13). The recourse to social media platforms to spread information about the activities of their movement organizations is, of course, one of the ways in which activists encounter the algorithmic regulation of the posts they produce. In this regard, activists may suppose how algorithms work and attempt to sustain certain kinds of interactions within different platforms. Nevertheless, they do this based only on *what they think they know* about social media platforms. This is not an easy task for activists because 'algorithm awareness is better understood as a meta-skill', a kind of skill that is undoubtedly very useful, since it can also 'improve other digital skills' (Gran et al, 2020: 13), yet it is difficult to acquire. Algorithms are very complex artifacts, and becoming familiar with them is neither an automatic nor an accessible operation (Bucher, 2018). In a way, the practice of gaining visibility meets and merges with algorithms in the data stream indirectly, when activists speculate about the functioning of an algorithm and then behave accordingly. Hence, how activists imagine algorithms has a direct effect on how they shape their strategies for visibility in social media. However, with few exceptions, the findings on this topic suggest that activists rarely possess a deep knowledge of how algorithms work (Treré, 2018) and how to develop their algorithmic skills to increase the visibility of online content (Klawitter and Hargittai, 2018). Consequently, they are seldom able to take advantage of algorithms, preferring other strategies when communicating on the Internet, where activists might enter into action to 'emancipate individuals from media cultures and structures imposed by the system they attempt to resist' (Galis and Neumayer, 2016: 12). Most of the time, activists can, at best, guess how algorithms work, hoping to get as close as possible to their complex and intricate mechanisms of functioning. This happens because activists perceive algorithms as something that is 'blackboxed', since they are 'created in environments that are not open to scrutiny and their source code is hidden inside impenetrable executable files' (Kitchin, 2017: 7).

Nevertheless, some activists we interviewed for our study still manage to correctly guess how algorithms work and they do so through a process of reverse-engineering (Kitchin, 2017): looking at the outputs that algorithms create in the data stream, they then figure out which rules these algorithms follow. Even when it is more difficult to cope with them, activists are in a position to develop a close awareness of how algorithms work by observing the outcomes of their communicative actions within different digital platforms. In other words, they learn by doing. Based on this never-ending learning process, activists shape their communicative strategies in such a way as to face the algorithmic manipulation of online content. The awareness of how algorithms work therefore has a substantial effect on the practice of gaining visibility in that it might push an activist to publish specific content, as Kosmas explained when evaluating how his movement organization employs Facebook:

> 'Actually, we are preparing more video content and we believe that this will be more challenging for the people [if they want to] engage with us [on Facebook]. I think that when you post an article or some data, maybe this is not the appropriate stuff for someone to comment on … I think that using video will encourage engagement.'

Publishing audio-visual content is one of the strategies that activists employ to increase their visibility through engagement. This reasoning also reveals a clear idea about what the algorithms of a social media platform like Facebook value more, that is, images instead of just written texts, as becomes evident when looking at how social media users behave when they are engaging with the official accounts of political actors (Ceccobelli et al, 2020). Along the same lines, David – a Spanish trade union activist operating within different labor sectors – explained to us:

> 'People basically watch us (on the website) between 9 am and noon, the highest peak is between 9 am and noon and then between 1 and 2 pm. We know that those are the times when we have to put in more news because we have studied the range in which people watch us.'

In this case, activists employ data analytics to better understand what their audiences do with the content they publish, in this case within their organization's official website. Hence, they react by fine-tuning activities like publishing new media content to perform the practice of gaining visibility more efficiently.

Beyond reverse-engineering, activists sometimes decide to trust the social media platforms that they use by exploiting some of the paid services offered on the platforms. For instance, some organizations invest money to sponsor their content on Facebook, although this is not very common among the activists we interviewed. They may do so to reach a specific target audience with whom they want to communicate and engage. In this case, activists essentially try to exploit algorithms to fuel the data stream with their pieces of information. Based on the amount of money that they may invest, algorithms replicate specific content that activists produce for a social media platform, like Facebook. Once payment is made to the private owner(s) of a digital platform, an algorithm activates an extra sequence of data for whoever is paying. The word 'extra' is not used by chance here: to sponsor one's own social media content implies having the platform's assurance that the content will reach a minimum number of people. This certainty is nothing more than an additional sequence of data regarding the content that is algorithmically created by the social media platform. Activists decide to control the magnitude and intensity of this sequence of data depending on how much money they invest in their sponsored content in a given amount of time. Luca points this out when reflecting on the relevance of Facebook for his movement organization:

'You have free Facebook, but if we had the money, considering our needs and what we logically want to convey, Facebook, more than anything else, is the most suitable tool. And so, if we had more money maybe we would develop that [because] if you want to convey your message, nowadays [you do] a sponsored post on Facebook and you reach a lot of people.'

However, movement organizations usually do not have the material resources to generate these additional data sequences around their content. In fact, our interviewees told us that they only rarely sponsored social media content. Even in these sporadic cases, though, spending money to boost the visibility of their movement organizations does not represent a recurrent activity in the practice of gaining visibility. Indeed, even those activists whose movement organizations would have the money to buy either a sporadic or even a daily sponsorship of their posts on social media platforms are not supportive of doing so. Rather, they prefer to use their money to fulfil other communicative and organizational needs, for several reasons. One is the idea that the efficient use of social media – perhaps even managed by a professional – can give activists online and offline visibility without them needing to sponsor their content on social media platforms, as Miranda explained: "We never got public money from the State. Never. And we don't need it. You make your webpage, you go on Twitter, you also go on some online forums, Facebook, and then you do it. If you don't have Internet, then you need money to deliver the information."

In Miranda's words, the "Internet" replaces the amount of money she may decide to invest in social media ads. She believes that there is no need to pay private companies to take advantage of digital media. Rather, knowing how to use them and then strategically produce and disseminate content accordingly is what her movement organization needs to master at best. Yet, even when we asked our interviewees if they would have invested money to sponsor their content on social media platforms if their movement organizations could have afforded it, some of the activists strongly rejected the idea of paying a private company to spread their political messages online. Ivan, for instance, told us that "even if we had the money, we wouldn't spend it on sponsoring Facebook posts". A few others, instead, declared that they would accept paid sponsorship on social media platforms to increase the visibility of their movement organization, as Jorge stressed: "I would like to have 300,000 more euros than I have in my budget, because €300,000 make a difference for me. Because then I can buy ads on Facebook, then I can make much more important people come to Barcelona."

In sum, we could argue that the Southern European activists we interviewed struggle to proficiently manage their algorithmic visibility. On the one hand, they have to face a highly competitive digital environment in which they rarely succeed in making their messages reach the screens of that significant number of people they want to communicate with during a mobilization, but especially on those days when nothing extraordinary happens in politics. It is precisely when their banners and megaphones are stored away in secret wardrobes that they need algorithms to 'support' and fuel their political fights the most. However, our interviews with activists in all three countries clearly denote that they are not able to get algorithms on their side because of their inability to generate the kind of content that algorithms reward by making them circulate more within that component of the data stream that algorithms constantly produce. On the other hand, there is no doubt that the lack of a significant amount of money may hinder their ability to exploit algorithmic visibility, one ever more based on and rooted in recurrent, paid ads (Kreiss and McGregor, 2018) – something most movement organizations are not able to afford but also tend to refuse even when they have the necessary resources.

Since adaptation to algorithmic visibility does not pay off or is out of the activists' economic reach, playing with or bypassing algorithms may represent two plausible options. In other words, activists engage in the practice of gaining visibility seeking not to subject themselves to the rules of algorithms. In this regard, building a reputable image is one path they strive to follow. However, much depends on the activists' will and ability to invest in reputation-building activities; a good reputation is both hard to accomplish and hold on to, as the next section will demonstrate.

The construction of visibility through reputation

Algorithms certainly play a role in the capability of movement organizations to make their voice heard by citizens. There is, in fact, a deep-rooted connection between the extent to which algorithms intertwine with the activists' daily struggle for visibility and their ability to gain a good and long-lasting reputation, as recent studies on digital media and organizational reputation demonstrate (Etter et al, 2019). As we have explained in the previous section, having algorithmic skills, particularly in the sense of being aware of the hidden procedures of algorithms, could provide activists with a competitive advantage when engaging in visibility actions on digital media.

However, the attempt to fully grasp how algorithms work in social media platforms does not always translate into direct activities that can take advantage of the effects of algorithms. In this regard, a telling example is that of an Italian movement organization involved in data production and analysis of the legislative productivity of MPs at the national level. While interviewing one of their leading members, we noticed a certain competence in digital communication, including in-depth thinking about the functioning of algorithms and the related data sequences that they generate and affect. The members of this movement organization are well aware of the importance of engaging in the click fight on social media platforms – for example through click baiting strategies – to spread their digital content effectively. Notwithstanding these strong incentives to adapt to algorithms to gain visibility more efficiently, this organization opted for another approach to social media. As stated by Giovanni, one of its founders,

> '[O]ur aim is to obtain institutional changes that can make us progress on the issue of transparency and participation, or at least encourage a structured debate on these issues. We don't participate in the click fight, though; like I need 10,000 clicks on an article, it's not like that for us. So this is a very important element in our social strategy. That means trying to bring in a certain style of communication, deliberately choosing to exclude an audience that could also give you satisfaction.'

This style of communication via social media responds to a precise need: building and maintaining a positive reputation across all media environments. Giovanni further stressed this point by arguing that the visibility of his movement organization does not depend on the use of one specific digital media outlet, but on the overall attempt to become visible by working on the organization's reputation.

> 'Since the availability of information that anyone can access through social networks, services, the web, search engines, and so on is growing, there is a need to identify sources that one considers reliable. So it is no longer a matter of "where did you read this thing? On the internet, on Facebook?" but rather a matter of "who told you?" That specific activist organization told you, and it doesn't matter if it did so on its website, blog, or Facebook profile.'

A reputation based on credibility is therefore a precious resource. Indeed, in some instances it is the credibility of a movement, much more than the specific cause it is struggling for, that help increasing the support of the public opinion (Leizerov, 2000). However, activists need time, patience, and the right communicative and organizational choices to achieve it. Furthermore, a good reputation transcends a single media outlet or a specific social media platform, since it is associated with one's name and even logo, as studies in marketing research also point out (Cretu and Brodie, 2007). The construction of a good reputation is related to the role of trust, which is of course particularly important in the current digital media environment, as has emerged from studies in the field of journalism (Splendore and Curini, 2020) and, more broadly speaking, political communication (Enli, 2015). Trust is akin to starlight in the night of the data stream, crowded with an incessant flow of content that comes from various sources beyond movement organizations and activists. It enables a movement organization and its activists to stand out, with their content shining more than others in the data stream as a result. This is why trust is a vital resource for activists and collective organizations in general (Mayer et al, 1995). In a way, it is as if Giovanni's movement organization decided to play with algorithms, trying to take advantage of their logic. It is precisely the awareness of how algorithms work that pushes Giovanni to employ strategies apparently at odds with what the algorithms would seem to demand, favour, and encourage. This is, in fact, what happens when one tries to gain visibility through reputation: to be able to somehow defeat the unpredictable and ever-changing logic of algorithmic visibility. The reason behind this choice is straightforward: when citizens see online content that comes from sources that they trust, they will devote much more attention to it regardless of the presence of other online content (Stroud, 2010; Sunstein, 2017). In other words, if someone 'does not trust the information it receives from a source, it will not pay attention to it' (Johnson and Kaye, 2010: 58). Thanks to a good reputation algorithmic visibility might therefore increase, for example when algorithms recognize that social media users begin to pay more attention to a presumed residual online content in the data stream, hence making such online content increasingly visible to other users as well.

Reputation therefore functions as a spark. It is an activator, which progressively – sometimes also exponentially – creates a growing surge of interest. This process occurs in different steps. First, reputation amplifies a movement organization's visibility thanks to the trust that an initial group of social media users has in the organization and its online content (Molaei, 2015). Hence, this initial group of loyal individuals has the power to trigger a multiplier effect that exposes more and more individuals to the activists' messages, values, and even recognizable faces. However, this is not a never-ending process; at a certain point, the trust that individuals assign to a certain movement organization stops this surge of interest from growing. This happens as a result of a phenomenon that scholarly literature defines as a filter bubble or echo chamber, namely the formation of groups of individuals who mutually strengthen their personal beliefs and convictions but without being able either to influence those of other individuals outside their groups or even to encounter ideas or opinions differing from their deepest credence within digital environments (Quattrociocchi et al, 2016).

That said, thanks to the expanding literature on filter bubbles and echo chambers, we now know that these popular metaphors of isolated information environments may misrepresent how citizens relate to what they believe in and trust (Dubois and Blank, 2018). Citizens easily go 'outside the bubble' (Vaccari and Valeriani, 2021) owing to several factors, with algorithms still playing a role. Here, we refer to the practice of sponsoring specific content on social media, as we have pointed out in the previous section. Paid content is a piece of information that enters into a filter bubble. There is, then, a constant tension between the data that people trust and *want to relate to* and the data that algorithms *impose* on them, such as the paid ones. However, the latter may not be well received, because they are detached from the power of interpersonal trust (Lazarsfeldt et al, 1944), as the next section will discuss.

At the same time, it is beyond doubt that in terms of simple diffusion (that is the entry into an individual's media diet) paid content spreads online thanks to algorithms that beat reputations. Yet, reputation has an inner power that algorithms lack: it goes deeper and draws people's attention. It stops them from scrolling and attracts their attention by preventing them from considering a piece of information undifferentiated from and identical to others. To be even more explicit, while individuals avoid paid content 'as much as possible' (Lilley et al, 2012: 89), they behave precisely the other way around when they encounter pieces of information from trustworthy sources. Movement organizations that can politically afford not to pay social media platforms to spread their messages beyond the narrow set of their current members and sympathizers are precisely those that can develop a visibility strategy capable of bypassing algorithms in order to 'beat' them, as the aforementioned case of Giovanni demonstrates.

Trust and reputation can also activate another effect: cross-media outcomes. They trigger visibility in those legacy media that activists fight hard to get coverage in. Reputation very often derives from the way in which movement organizations build their communication in digital environments. It depends on those daily communicative choices that shape an aura of trust and reliability (Etter et al, 2019). Activists are well aware of this further function of reputation, and this leads them not only to develop a better ability to connect with lay citizens within digital media spaces but also to gain visibility on legacy media. Two activists, Alvaro from Spain and Riccardo from Italy, made this point very clear during their interviews.

> 'Of course, if you want to communicate outwardly, and the great tool we have – which is the Internet – to a certain extent democratizes the power to send your message, the only way to get your message across is through conventional media. And in order to appear in the conventional media, you have to build up a reputation on the Internet, in the digital media, and that makes you end up appearing in the traditional media.'

> 'In general, journalists look for you. I think that some of the content that I propose would never have had the same echo if another movement organization had proposed it. There is a reputational capital tied to a story that, on the one hand, maybe facilitates you in a sort of automatic manner, but on the other hand also credits you for your merits.'

The activists also realize how important it is to manage visibility in legacy media carefully in order not to *lose* their reputation. Since reputation is one of the most precious resources they can rely on, losing it or simply seeing it diminish would be a serious blow for them. In this regard, legacy media can be a double-edged sword. If a good exposition in legacy media drives a good reputation (Evans, 2016), a bad exposition on television or in the printed press can severely harm a movement organization's reputation. It can also occur in different ways. An Italian activist fighting against organized crime in Southern Italy recalled one specific example in which the story of an activist covered incorrectly in a national newspaper upset the life of this activist, who had to escape to a foreign country and take on a new identity because of the public visibility they had obtained in a legacy media outlet, as Salvatore told us:

> '[This person] was presented as a prominent figure in the fight against organized crime. Such a portrayal in a national newspaper was read as a

sign of self-promotion by the people who lived in the neighbourhood where this person was active. So this person was then in serious trouble, and after a while, they had to leave the city; they moved abroad and left everything behind.'

After this negative experience, Salvatore decided to limit the exposure of his movement organization in legacy media only in those cases in which he was almost entirely sure not to harm anyone, including his organization's reputation. In particular, this mistake taught him that when movement organizations are willing to get media coverage in legacy media, it is "better to have media coverage only once, but in a correct way, than five to six times in an incorrect manner".

In addition to cross-media effects, reputation and trust also trigger cross-practice effects. This is the case of movement organizations that manage to activate new relevant connections (see the next chapter) thanks to the reputation they have built through online activities. Here, the logic at work is fairly simple: numbers matter. Although we know that 'popularity online does not automatically translate to popularity offline' (Benney, 2011: 13), numbers still have the power to open doors that would otherwise remain closed. As Daniela, the activist with whom we opened the previous chapter, clarified, "[T]he numbers are behind us: we have more than 200,000 likes on Facebook. Over the years, we have reached 1 million unique signatures on our petitions. It's something that opens doors: it's a knock-knock at the politician's door."

This is a clear example of how the digital affects other domains, such as face-to-face interactions with prominent political figures and media actors. Efficient strategies of gaining visibility within digital environments allow activists to build a reputational status that subsequently makes them feel more at ease with mass media coverage but also is useful for other practices: in this case, that of establishing connections. It is worth noting that face-to-face interactions, too, can increase online numbers and thus open doors as well. Likewise, movement organizations can acquire political relevance through successful street demonstrations or public meetings. This is the so-called logic of numbers that social movements often rely on to present themselves in public as legitimate political actors, precisely because of their ability to mobilize large numbers of participants in their protests (Tilly, 2002; della Porta and Diani, 2020). Daniela's case therefore tells us that activists can adopt various strategies to achieve their goals, such as engaging large numbers of people, both online and offline, to support their movement organization also in a time of latency so that they can enter the otherwise closed arena of institutional politics.

Moreover, political actors often achieve high levels of trust, credibility, and reputation through a continuous and proficient combination of online and offline relationship-building practices, thanks also to the role of individual activists (Bennett, 2005). In this regard, an activist's reputation plays the same role as the reliability of their movement organization. This aspect brings us to another strategy that movement organizations employ to become visible: managing the individual dimension of activism. Their efforts at this level are aimed not only at the protection of the reputation of individual activists, but also at the connection of their individual reputation with the movement organizations in which they carry out their daily political engagement, as we will illustrate in the following section.

The individualization of visibility in social media platforms

Social media platforms have one salient characteristic: they are personal media, primarily designed to connect individuals rather than collective actors. This feature can amplify the voices of individual activists, overshadowing the collective work of signification of movement organizations (Barassi and Fenton, 2011). Since activists know this characteristic of social media very well, most of them actively employ their personal social media profiles to spread those messages published on the official accounts of their movement organizations. When they do so, they believe that the personal visibility acquired on different digital platforms over the years could help their movement organization to meet its political goals. However, personal visibility obtained through a Facebook page or a profile on Twitter or Instagram is not devoid of negative effects when it comes to politics, in particular at the level of grassroots movements; the latter often lack those protections that are guaranteed when one belongs to an institution or a strong, deep-rooted political party. At times, when activists expose themselves too much this could produce unwanted outcomes, very often leading to self-censorship precisely in digital media (Lupien, 2020) so as to avoid lawsuits and all kinds of threats – from anonymous individuals online but also state actors (Lupien et al, 2021). As in the case of visibility obtained through legacy media, personal exposure on social media can also take the form of a double-edged sword.

On the one hand, personal digital accounts are much more effective in creating strong and permanent bonds between a source and its followers, positively affecting the communicative potential of personal communication. Existing literature tells us that citizens tend to trust other individuals much more than collective organizations (Hardin, 2002; Cook et al, 2005). This happens as a result of multiple factors; the main driving forces are ongoing processes of individualization (Inglehart, 1997) and distrust (Norris, 2011) rooted in modernization (Bauman, 2012). On the other hand, a collective organization protects its members. The social media account of a collective actor does not imply personal exposure: it is a logo, a flag, an impersonal name that speaks, but not an individual activist with a recognizable face. This is exactly what Gianluca experienced in his political activism for an Italian movement organization:

> 'My movement organization also works a lot like that. When the Minister of Labor said the shit about young people going abroad, that it's better to lose them than to keep them, and you make a graphic image of [his] face and we share it as a movement organization and everybody shares that, I don't have to share it myself. It's a collective political entity that wrote it and I share it: one, it has more impact; two, it puts me less at risk, as an individual, of being seen as the one who makes the personal attack, of being targeted because all collective identities, every collective entity is also built to ensure a minimum level of anonymity for those who are part of it and who can then convey strong messages without exposing themselves too much.'

Hiding behind a collective organization's identity is not the only way to communicate one's ideas without being personally involved. Social media platforms allow for the creation of fake profiles with no or few possibilities to disclose the real identities behind them (Krombholz et al; 2012; Romanov et al, 2017). At times, the leading members of a collective organization may not have the freedom to express certain extreme and even uncivil opinions. They hence use fake social media profiles to express critical comments while at the same protecting both themselves and the movement organization they are part of. Martino, who is a member of an Italian trade union, frequently uses a fake social media profile precisely for this reason. He explained this choice in the following terms:

> 'I have a fake account that I use to troll. I can't afford to troll using my real profile: it is not right. Even if I were trolling as a person, it would still be perceived as if it was my union doing it. And trolling is something a union would not do, even if this happens through the personal profiles of its members.'

Other than hiding behind an organization or a fake account, activists have another strategy for defending both themselves and the collective actors they are part of and represent. Usually, this strategy takes the form of self-censorship (Chen, 2018), as the case of Jorge, a Spanish activist who works for a political foundation fighting for more decent working conditions, demonstrates.

> 'I have to be cautious with my use of public social media. I mean, I criticize a lot of people in social media, and I express my opinions

strongly, it's not like I'm always very careful with what I say, but maybe sometimes I would like to speak more openly about certain topics and I may say "no", because it could be misinterpreted. My opinion could be mixed up or confused with the opinion of the Foundation.'

Whatever the reasons behind the choice to communicate carefully in social media may be, activists rarely decide to just get rid of a personal account. They value their exposure in social media and this consideration leads them to actively spread the messages coming from their movement organization. However, we also recorded cases in which activists decided, instead, to completely detach their personal accounts from their political engagement, as Davide, an Italian activist indicated: "[M]y personal profile doesn't play a role in my work, I don't use it at all." Nevertheless, our interviewees tend to see personal social media profiles as front lines and recurrent amplifiers of movement organizations' political fights, as the case of Emilia demonstrates.

> 'I use my personal profile often, in fact, let's say that 90 per cent of my Facebook profile is used to share the things that my grassroots movement does. I don't do it daily because of time issues and a thousand other things. But if you see my Facebook page it is all my grassroots movement stuff. Because I have many contacts, I accept all friend requests, I have almost 2,000 contacts and so, for me, it is the channel that I use the most when I want to spread important news.'

By using personal accounts to perform the practice of gaining visibility, activists also experience those dynamics of deconstructing boundaries that we will also discuss in Chapter 5, devoted to the practice of political organizing. In particular, the boundaries that usually separate their private, political, and work activities (when activists are not employees of a movement organization) are easily broken when they engage in digital data sequences. A concrete example is that of Eulalia, who is very straightforward about this subject matter.

> 'Yes, that kills me. On Facebook and Instagram, who are my friends and who are not, and where is the overlap? Because your friends also want to see what you're doing and that is the overlap I'm exhausted by. I just want to post a holiday picture on my private Facebook, but then I have 4,000 people following me because of the website, and I'm not going to post that [because] I have to keep it professional. It blurs the lines between professional and private.'

In producing digital data sequences through their personal accounts, every day, activists make accurate decisions on what to publish and what not. The greater their responsibility and public visibility within their movement organization, the higher the precautions they seem to take when managing their personal digital profiles. Every single piece of data they publish into their personal account can, in a way, be linked to their political identity as activists, depriving them of the freedom of publishing whatever they want to, such as mundane content. "I don't have a completely private Facebook profile anymore", Riccardo told us, "[and] people know that for my movement organization I'm the one who talks about these things. In general, I never express completely personal opinions on the Facebook channel because I know that I have responsibilities on behalf of an association". Domenico, instead, reveals that "on Instagram, I publish more personal photos, but I never publish anything about my family". This attitude emerges from several interviews we conducted in all three countries under examination.

Finally, it is worth mentioning a positive effect of personal profiles being strategically included in the practice of gaining visibility. Having at least two profiles – one personal and the other political – is common among activists, who exploit them in synergic strategies. One example is that of Luca, whose personal accounts and those of other members of his movement organization and their close friends played a crucial role in disseminating their messages and political fights:

> '[T]o increase awareness of the association, we made a video in which I gave an account of what we had obtained. We had done a campaign in which members and friends of members each posted a picture on Facebook with the words "our movement organization is" [followed by their explanation of what we were], and in a week's time we got 300 likes on the page.'

From this perspective, the practice of visibility rests on the coordinated efforts of many individuals, and not just on the collective actions of a movement organization. For instance, Ivan explains how the role of each activist in the movement organization contributes to increasing the visibility of the content they publish to be able to intervene in the data stream more proactively: "Of course, this is how we do it. We post it there, then we send a message to the team saying 'look, this is the post, start sharing', … you know, because if you have a lot of shares, what you post becomes more prominent." Therefore, echoing what Stefania Milan (2015) observes about visibility dynamics in protests that revolve around social media platforms, visibility in latency stages rests on the coordinated efforts of both collective and individual actors, with individual members of movement organizations playing a role that is at least equal to, when not more important than, the role of the movement organization as a whole.

Facing the immediacy of algorithmic visibility through materiality

In addition to building the reputation of their movement organizations and carefully managing their profiles on social media platforms, activists deploy a third strategy when it comes to managing algorithmic visibility, which uses the very materiality of digital media. As we have already illustrated in previous chapters, looking at materiality helps us to understand the relationship between activists and the digital data sequences within the data stream they engage with. This is particularly important when activists are not taking the streets, because the role of materiality does not diminish during more ordinary political times. Yet, literature on social movements has not devoted much attention to the function of smartphones, laptops, and other technological devices beyond massive protest events. Conversely, several studies discuss the extent to which activists manage to employ different mobile tools and services in times of mobilization. For instance, cell phones had a relevant role in spreading information via text messages during a terrorist attack that affected the city of Madrid in 2004, which was followed by a popular uprising owing to government misinformation about this tragic event (Castells, 2009). When cell phones evolved into smartphones – or other forms of 'wearable technologies' – as a result of the incorporation of Internet connectivity, mobile devices increasingly fine-tuned their ability to co-trigger, co-enable, and continue protest events thanks to those digital environments (for example social media) that better match both the communicative and the organizational needs of activists as they take the streets and mobilize (Gerbaudo, 2012). Reflecting on the affordances of mobile media, Schrock (2015) isolates four of them: portability, availability, locationality, and multimediality. These and other affordances, practices, and cultures related to the mobile dimension of devices – such as smartphones and tablets – have been identified as fundamental for the origins and success of new social movements in Western societies and beyond (Howard and Hussain, 2013; Monterde and Postill, 2014). What remains in the dark is, then, the role of mobile devices and the new affordances that they enable when activists leave the streets but still fight on a daily basis to achieve their political goals.

In this regard, our interviews reveal that, during the latency stages of politics, visibility is not mainly achieved with the help of mobile devices such as smartphones or tablets, but through laptops or desktop computers. This happens because activists deem the former unable to provide the same quality as the latter when it comes to the media content that they want to produce. Agata, an Italian activist working in the communication department of an anti-corruption movement organization, describes those differences in these terms:

> 'I use my desktop computer for some things and my smartphone for other things. If I have to choose between the two, I opt for my desktop computer because I can do certain things only with that. There are things you cannot do with the smartphone, such as graphic work.'

In other words, different devices fulfil different functions. Here, there is a tension between quality and immediacy, which rarely co-occur. When activists use a smartphone or a tablet, they can easily deal with immediacy, for example by publishing live on a social media account a picture taken or a video recorded on these mobile devices. Even when using the most expensive and professional smartphone or tablet, the professional quality of a picture or a video taken or recorded through this device will never be the same as that achieved with professional cameras and editing software. Different devices are therefore needed to obtain a higher quality. At the same time, professional cameras and editing software on a desktop computer cannot deal with immediacy: they demand time. Being stuck in the data stream, activists cannot always wait for hours, or even a few minutes, to publish specific content on a social media outlet or release a press note.

As we have also observed in other chapters, the data stream benefits from an accelerated tempo in which the immediacy of activist actions plays a prominent role. This is especially true when we consider certain types of digital media, including instant messaging services, but also social media platforms and their algorithms, which process the large amount of data produced by their users, including activists, in real time. This immediacy is therefore also linked to the possibility of obtaining a certain degree of visibility in social media platforms. It is an immediate – sometimes even temporary – level of visibility that activists do not fully control precisely because of the opaque and constantly changing operation of the algorithms. However, activists know how to overcome this limitation, seeking to increase the possibility that their movement organizations are noticed, become recognizable, and gain legitimacy. They do so, again, through the creation of content thanks to the professional software that they use on their laptops and desktop computers and which they then try to spread quickly on social media platforms.

It is no coincidence that some activists we interviewed told us they get very angry when they struggle to access the Internet. Daniela, for example, admitted that it is very frustrating for her to have to deal with a slow Internet connection, as it prevents her from quickly receiving all those videos that the other activists working with her produce when they are in the field, being engaged in various types of collective actions. There are, in fact, very long videos whose quality can be improved through the use of professional software, which can even reduce their duration to the most salient points of the events being reported. Transforming low-quality into high-quality videos in terms of both form and content is important to ensure that the data being disseminated through social media platforms are not lost in the data stream; if that happens, they risk going unnoticed. They will be diluted, dispersed, and overtopped by more professional pieces of information. For example, Daniela may want to mark these videos with a logo to make them more attributable to her organization or to edit and condense them into a 90-second content piece. However, this is not always possible. When we asked what media-related aspect would make her life as an activist easier, she answered:

> 'I would always like a faster Internet connection. We use video a lot. The thing that sets me off is that if I have a cameraman do a shoot, and then the editors are in another city, they either see each other physically or it takes them a very long time to send each other the materials they need to create a proper video through the Internet.'

It is not easy for activists to balance quality and immediacy. Technological limitations play a significant role in this regard. Some can be overcome, some cannot. There are no universal solutions for movement organizations in different countries. Activists engage in a constant process of learning and adaptation driven by their skills, organizational structure, but also material issues; if they work in a territory without broadband or fiber connection, this could severely affect their practice of gaining visibility, as the extract from Daniela's interview demonstrates.

Along with its technological limitations, the material dimension within the practice of gaining visibility may also imply an opportunity for activists. The technological advancements made in the past decades have enabled digital media devices and services to enter the daily lives of both media and political actors. Laptops, tablets, and smartphones – and the related WhatsApp or Facebook notifications, phone calls, and Zoom calls – do not remain locked in an office until it is time to call it a day. These devices, services, and communicative actions come home along with the journalists, parliamentarians, and activists. They follow them while they work out in a gym, take their children to the movies, or drink a cocktail with friends after having closed the office of their movement organization (when it has one). This ubiquity of communicative actions, services, and devices involves each of the four practices analysed in our book, including that of gaining visibility.

However, it is precisely this ubiquity of mobile media and their inherent culture of instantaneity and constant connectivity that enables activists to react immediately – regardless of their whereabouts – the moment an event suddenly occurs. Recalling Michael Schudson's concept of 'monitorial citizens' (1998), we could say that mobile media are those technologies that allow activists to always have the situation under control and behave accordingly in real time when some emergence demands them to do so. The fact that they prefer other technological devices, such as laptops, when performing the practice of gaining visibility during ordinary times of politics does not downgrade the mobile dimension of materiality. Portable technologies are always in their pockets in case they need to choose immediacy – like the quick need to take a picture and send it to other activists – over quality.

Conclusion

In this chapter, we have shed light on how activists deal with algorithms that sustain social media platforms in their quest for visibility. In addition to showing that algorithms are 'blackboxes' that activists seldom fully understand, we have demonstrated that Southern European activists need economic resources to manage algorithmic visibility when communicating so intensively in corporate social media. While some of the activists we interviewed occasionally invest their money in the sponsorship of content on social media platforms, this is not the most widespread activity that we detected in the three countries under examination. The way in which social media platforms function seems to push grassroots politics toward a greater economic commitment, hence favouring visibility-related dynamics that are more common in the Anglo-American world, where the potential for media coverage is closely linked to the availability of money to invest in it (Mancini and Swanson, 1996). This is not surprising given that social media platforms such as Facebook and Twitter were born in the United States; here the link between economic resources and visibility is particularly strong, as demonstrated by the famous expression "money equals speech", used in the US Supreme Court's ruling[1] of 2010, which kicked off the widespread deployment of super PACs throughout the country (Briffault, 2012).

However, as we have pointed out throughout this chapter, the use of economic resources to bend the algorithms governing social media platforms to one's will is not widespread in Italy, Greece, and Spain. Activists reject – to some extent – the logic of 'money equals speech' that seems to prevail in certain Anglo-American countries. While in the case of other practices – and that of gaining visibility more generally – we found discrepancies between the three countries, these differences almost disappear when it comes to visibility and algorithms. Italian, Greek, and Spanish activists have a similar approach to the algorithms that govern social media platforms and many of the online services they use. It seems as if the lack of homogeneity in the inclusion of digital media into their practices relates more to those specific technological affordances that are immediately perceived by activists, such as the possibility of reposting certain content or following certain profiles. When it comes to algorithms, the general functioning of which is less easily comprehensible to activists, and their potential in terms of gaining visibility, there is greater homogeneity between activists in the three countries.

Activists in all three countries face algorithms by trying to go beyond them. They do so through the exploitation of other data sequences that are not algorithmically regulated in the data stream. In particular, we have discussed three different strategies. First, activists can try to bypass the limits thanks to reputation-building activities. By appearing reliable and credible, they can make the content that they publish on digital media much more visible, rather than being dispersed within the data stream. A reputable image allows them to play with and then beat corporate algorithms because their good reputation makes their digital content visible on the screens of lay citizens even without the help of paid ads. Moreover, a good reputation acquired online also has cross-media power in that it can lead to coverage in those legacy media that activists struggle to get through to, such as television. Hence, it is precisely thanks to their good reputation that activists manage to gain visibility not just online, but also in older media like television broadcasting.

Furthermore, activists also rely on the personal exposure of individual activists, rather than that of movement organizations as a whole. Personal digital profiles have a strong capacity for diffusion, which can be even more efficient than that of collective actors. Nonetheless, the employment of personal profiles for political purposes can also imply serious threats to individual activists. Collective digital profiles can make activists feel much freer to express specific political views in order to protect themselves and their loved ones, especially in the case of a personal over-exposure to thorny issues, such as labor policies and corruption. This chapter has shown that activists have to manage their personal accounts on digital media carefully so that they don't risk repercussions on a personal level or get their movement organization in trouble. In doing so, the chapter has emphasized the tension between the individual and collective levels of political engagement that affects all activists who participate in politics through their movement organizations. In fact, individualized political participation is not only present in the realm of so-called connective action (Bennett and Segerberg, 2013), but also in more traditional forms of political participation, which draw on a collective actions within shared spaces and times.

Finally, activists differentiate between digital media depending on the material aspects of the used devices and services. In so doing, they seek the right balance between the quality of the data sequences that they produce and the need to create and spread them immediately. Quality and immediacy do not always go hand in hand. Moreover, they are closely linked to one or more technological devices: a single device can rarely combine both. If a smartphone can quickly deal with immediacy, it might well fall short in satisfying activists' need for quality. At the same time, software installed on a laptop can enable the production of different communicative products of high quality, like a video or a picture. Nevertheless, this type of content demands time as activists need to edit it, and it is therefore at odds with immediacy. Although activists in this everlasting tension between quality and immediacy tend to prefer quality, in most cases, they are aware of the trade-offs implied by this choice. They believe that too much emphasis on immediacy will make them lose those quality traits that are so vital that they cannot hinder their reputation.

To conclude, in this chapter we have shown how activists deploy at least three different strategies to deal with the difficulties generated by the algorithmic visibility that they face on a daily basis, especially when they are not engaged in protests that manage to involve large numbers of people. These strategies highlight some of the important issues that activists have to deal with in the present day, including the management of their visibility through the construction of a good reputation, online but not only; the need to reconcile the collective representation of the activists' political demands with their individual participation through online personal profiles; and, finally, the attempt to balance the need for quality content – aimed at entering good data in the data stream – with the speed that characterizes the media platforms. The immediacy in the creation and reception of data is precisely one of the issues that activists must also address in the daily organization of their movement organizations' political work, as we will see in the next chapter.

5

The Accelerated Times of Activists' Organizational Work

During his interview, Eustratios revealed to us that he has several passions, including photography and technology. Even though he does not consider himself a geek, he is an early adopter of technological innovations: he was among the first Greek citizens to have created a website in Greece. When it comes to his personal hobbies, digital media are an important part of his lifestyle; he cannot live without his smartphone, uses his laptop extensively, and regularly connects to Facebook. Eustratios is a leading member of a Greek trade union that is particularly active in defending labor rights, and which often organizes large workers' protests in the country. When he and his fellow unionists have to organize an activity, like a national strike, a sudden local demonstration, or a small internal meeting, they use different organizational strategies involving various types of digital and non-digital media, even if they do not give them the same importance:

> 'The phone, first of all. If I want to tell them that they should be in Athens tomorrow or the day after tomorrow, or next week, I will make a phone call to tell them. Otherwise, the easiest way is [via] email. We use a lot of emails. Email is our primary tool, because via email you can attach a lot of things, everything: a picture, a speech, whatever.'

However, when we asked Eustratios about other forms of communication, such as a Facebook or WhatsApp group, he told us that his trade union organization cannot rely on them. The risk of sharing sensitive information through these digital platforms is too high for him and the other unionists he works with. They fear that third parties can gain access to their names and the opinions they post on these digital platforms, threatening their freedom and putting other members of the trade union at risk. Although Eustratios is very familiar with these digital platforms, he is strongly opposed to using them to coordinate the work of his trade union organization. Eustratios added another point: he and the other trade unionists do not need a Facebook group or a WhatsApp chat to better coordinate their daily political work.

Their organizational structure allows any kind of information to spread fast, widely, and efficiently without the support of social media platforms. According to Eustratios, the most fundamental thing is that his movement organization "works as a pyramid" and has a vertical organizational structure. In such a situation, Eustratios adds, "the crucial role is not played by the tool you use, the platform, [or] the communication. The crucial factor is the structure of the organization". According to Eustratios, the vertical organizational structure of his movement organization allows for fairly seamless communication that goes from the leaders of the organization to the other activists who are engaged in the trade union. Since the organizational structure is already there and appears to be a solid one, social media platforms would not make a great difference to Eustratios.

Although his position at the top of the pyramid gives Eustratios full control over the communication flow within the trade union, being in this position also has some negative effects. For instance, Eustratios's activities within his movement organization never stop. He is available day and night: his fellow activists can reach him anytime, anywhere. He complains that he has no free time and no space to hide, but he also makes clear that it cannot be otherwise. Even during his leisure time, when he is not supposed to be involved in the trade union's activities, Eustratios says that "if I do not have a smartphone with me, I feel as if I were naked".

Eustratios's story resonates with what other Greek, Italian, and Spanish activists told us about the role of digital media in the daily activities that sustain the political engagement of their respective movement organizations. On the one hand, there is widespread use of the smartphone – often paired with instant messaging platforms – that enables a fast circulation of information within movement organizations; on the other hand, the interviewees stressed the importance of face-to-face contacts and hence the centrality of non-mediated interpersonal communication.

This chapter explores what it means, for activists, to find the right balance between the use of smartphones, instant messaging platforms, phone calls, and face-to-face exchanges to coordinate the workflow of their respective organizations. More specifically, we will discuss two sides of the data stream within the practice of political organizing, and how they can work both in parallel and in combination with one another: one side being highly digitalized side and the other predominantly revolving around face-to-face interactions. We will demonstrate that for activists to be able to exercise their agency they need to manage these two sides of the data stream and combine them in sustainable ways. More specifically, we will reflect on the challenges that activists face and the strategies they develop to tackle them. First, though, we will define the practice of political organizing and describe what it means for activists, independently from their use of digital media.

The practice of political organizing

Organizing is a crucial feature of grassroots political engagement. Although we often read in the news that the latest protest erupted spontaneously from a group of angry people, studies on social movements almost always contradict a similar public representation of mobilizations. Indeed, protests do not develop suddenly, out of nowhere. They might be the result of meticulous preparation by movement organizations, hence revolving around the work of cohesive collective actors. Or they might be the outcome of a long process of individual activists' political engagement, hence revolving around the commitment of individuals who work side by side, sometimes using social media platforms in a scattered yet effective way. Frequently, they are both. In any case, they are always rooted in some sort of 'mobilizing structures' (McAdam et al, 1996).

Such organizational structures bring together collective and individual actors in various 'modes of coordination' that are related to decisions about the allocation of resources as well as to the construction and maintenance of organizational boundaries (Diani, 2015). Although different in many respects, each of these modes of coordination requires activists to make a number of decisions about the daily activities of grassroots politics. When people are protesting in the streets, the organization of collective action can happen quickly and may include the myriads of organizational activities that render a massive demonstration possible. Among other things, activists seek to understand how to interact with the other collective actors that are part of the social movement, how to allocate the – usually scarce – resources that they can rely on to sustain their protests, but also what to do in case of sudden repression of the protest. However, activists and their movement organizations also need to coordinate the workflow of their grassroots political engagement when they are not organizing mobilizations. During these moments, some of the pressing requirements include developing effective ways of making decisions together, on a routine basis, and making sure that these decisions are then implemented in the movement organization. Furthermore, activists within the same movement organization seek to understand not only how they can work together notwithstanding the severe time constraints under which they all work, but also how their movement organization can collaborate with others that are interested in the same contentious issue.

Hence, the organizational dimension of social movements revolves around two different moments: the time of protest and the time in which mobilizations are not taking place. At the same time, there are two different yet strictly connected levels to take into account. On the one hand, when we examine social movements and movement networks, we can see how various movement organizations coordinate their work together. In this sense, social movements are 'interorganizational fields' (Klandermans, 1992) to be studied from a relational perspective that considers how coordination among various types of movement organizations and other collective actors that support them is possible. On the other hand, when we focus on movement organizations and their activities, we can discern intraorganizational dynamics, according to which activists within the same movement organization coordinate their efforts to reach their common goals.

Although the activities that support the coordination of a movement organization's daily political work can take different shapes and timings, as we have shown earlier, they all revolve around the same practice. We call it the practice of political organizing, which refers to the vast array of coordinated activities aimed at allocating resources, making decisions together, and distributing tasks that activists perform to achieve the political goals of their movement organization, hence rendering collective action possible and effective. Thus defined, the practice of political organizing is present in each type of collective actor, whatever their structure, culture, and aims are. Whether being an established government-sponsored trade union or an emergent and unfunded activists' collective, each type of collective actor that is involved in grassroots politics must deal with specific tasks related to their organizational structures processes. These tasks might be achieved in many ways: via personal and direct interaction, through face-to-face meetings, and through the mediation of communication technologies.

Among the existing studies on the way digital media intertwine with the organizational dimension of collective actors in the realm of politics, there is a wealth of literature that focuses on the digitalization of our societies to redefine specific concepts and processes, such as organizational structure (Bimber, 2003; Davis et al, 2005), organizational culture (Tatarchevskiy, 2011), or the emergence of new organizational types and their hybridization with older and more traditional ones (Chadwick, 2007). The diffusion of digital media has had a distinct and profound impact on the organizational patterns that sustained the most recent waves of mobilizations. On this matter, some scholars spoke about the emergence of 'networked social movements' in the early 2000s, defined as a new species of social movement that massively employed digital media as opposed to those that developed in past cycles of contention (Castells, 2015). Similarly, after the spread of social media platforms in the early 2010s, other scholars proposed a novel theory of connective action, based on the assumption that social media platforms deeply changed the organizational patterns of protest campaigns and mobilizations (Bennett and Segerberg, 2013). Yet other scholars underlined how social media platforms whose role was notable in the pro-democracy protests that occurred in Tunisia, Egypt, Turkey, and other countries across the world between 2010 and 2011 also brought with them some relevant organizational fragilities (Tufekci, 2017).

Whether they are overly optimistic or adopt a more cautious approach, these and other studies advance the idea that the increased use of digital media changed the interorganizational dynamics that characterize social movements (Kavada, 2013; Dencik and Wilkin, 2018), putting a stronger emphasis on the efforts of individual actors and bringing to the fore new types of fragilities related to mobilizations (Bennet and Segerberg, 2013; Tufekci, 2017). In other words, they emphasize the capacity of digital media to shape social movements and movement organizations, in particular when activists are in the streets, engaged in massive mobilizations or – at the very least – busy promoting their protest campaigns.

To offer a more encompassing picture of the role that digital media, in all their mutability, have in the practice of political organizing, in this chapter we will shift the focus to those moments in which activists are not in the streets and their movement organizations are not engaged in any specific protest campaign. In other words, we look at how the daily logistics of movement organizations intertwine with digital media and, in so doing, pose new challenges to everyday grassroots politics. As in the other chapters, we will not focus on one specific type of digital media, but we will compare and discuss the activists' employment of many forms of digital and non-digital communication to support their logistics. In so doing, we look at how activists perform their organizational activities through the lenses of the data stream. More precisely, while in the next chapter we will touch on some interorganizational aspects related to the practice of sustaining meaningful connections within, but also outside, the social movement milieu, in this chapter we focus on the intraorganizational dynamics of movement organizations. We start in the next section considering how two different sides of the data stream play a role in the practice of political organizing.

The organization of daily political work between the two sides of the data stream

The data stream that activists deal with in their practice of political organizing is continuous, without any significant interruption, especially when they employ their smartphones in combination with instant messaging platforms. If we compare the three countries, the smartphone turns out to be a relevant cornerstone: Greek, Italian, and Spanish activists alike rely on it to perform many of their daily actions to support the coordination of their political engagement. Often equipped with many types of applications, the smartphone is a highly versatile device that allows activists to be constantly connected to fellow activists and their political work.

The chat we had with Miranda before interviewing her is telling in this regard, as it revealed a shared understanding among activists in the three countries. Miranda is the founder of a small activist association in Spain that works on transparency, broadly speaking. We met her in her organization's headquarters, where she explained that smartphones are extremely important in the daily coordination of her workflow. More precisely, she added that it is the combination of WhatsApp with smartphones that works particularly well. At that point, one of her fellow activists – who was listening to our conversation – intervened and said that "WhatsApp is part of the organization", like an additional activist participating in the movement organization rather than a simple communication tool. In fact, it is through the instant messaging platform that Miranda and her fellow activists coordinate their grassroots political work: there, their movement organization is divided into chat groups, each representing a specific branch of their movement organization. WhatsApp helps her and her fellow activists to solve daily organizational tasks very quickly and far more easily than they would do with other tools. It is like a permanent assembly, her fellow activist adds, which never stops and is always evolving.

WhatsApp and other instant messaging platforms are pervasive in the organizational practices of contemporary activism, to the extent that some scholars point to the emergence of mobilizations that are entirely coordinated through WhatsApp, which therefore proves to be self-sufficient leverage for activists to organize their protests (Milan and Barbosa, 2020). However, our research gives a more nuanced picture of instant messaging apps and portable devices, which are relevant for activists but never exclusively and not necessarily to the same degree in each country. Despite having a common function, smartphones are nevertheless used differently and according to three diverse configurations, in which some of the device's functions are more prominently used, while others take a secondary role. In Greece, activists spoke about their smartphones as a device used mainly to make phone calls and send emails; in Italy, activists employ this device to communicate, individually, through the instant messaging platform WhatsApp, and to make phone calls; in Spain, finally, activists refer to the smartphone almost as a synonym of instant messaging platforms such as WhatsApp and Telegram, which are used more for group communication than for one-to-one interactions. Additionally, while in Greece the smartphone is combined with laptops for the purpose of sending emails, in Italy and Spain activists mostly integrate it with face-to-face meetings.

In sum, activists refer to both smartphones and laptops as relevant devices to support activities related to political organizing practices, which are complemented by face-to-face interactions during meetings with fellow activists. Activists therefore deal with two sides of the data stream: on the one hand, the fact that it is deeply tied to the process of digitalization; on the other hand, the fact that it relies instead on face-to-face interactions among activists.

Activists often experience the two sides of the data stream in combination and see them as complementary in terms of allowing them to reach the overall objective of keeping things moving and achieving goals within activists' collectives, associations, and organizations. When considering the data stream that activists have to deal with, then, we can identify a certain degree of hybridity between the digital communication that happens on the smartphone and the non-digital interactions that occur during face-to-face meetings. In fact, whether used alone or in combination with one another, the data that support the daily organization of political work are both written and spoken, digital and non-digital. From this viewpoint, the data stream is prominently multimodal. Consequently, the practice of political organizing simultaneously takes place within a space that is neither only the space of face-to-face meetings nor simply the space of WhatsApp group chats.

While this fluid connection between digital and non-digital, offline and online communications characterizes the practice of political organizing in the three countries under examination, differences emerge when we look more specifically at the types of devices and services that seem to be more relevant to activists to perform this practice. Again, we did not find just one type of media that dominates the scene; activists employ more than one device (for example a smartphone or a laptop) and service (for example a social media app or an informational website). This is hardly surprising, since one of the consequences of using digital media for grassroots politics has been that of enhancing the media hybridity that activists deal with; they constantly combine online and offline, older and newer, independent and corporate communication technologies (Treré, 2018) in a multifaceted repertoire of communication that supports not only the activists' image beyond their immediate circles, but also those interactions that serve to keep the movement organizations they belong to alive (Mattoni, 2012).

While such combinations of different types of media devices, services, and actions are potentially infinite, specific clusters give a specific nuance to the hybridity we found in the practice of political organizing, which is different from the one we detected when considering other types of practices. This means that neither this hybridity nor the role that digital media play in shaping the practice of political organizing is ever the same; they change depending on where activists are and what they are doing. More importantly, such hybridity opens up new opportunities for activists and at the same time poses relevant challenges to them. In short, to understand how activists perform the practice of political organizing, we need to consider not the presence – or absence – of hybridity, but its configuration and consequences. The remainder of this chapter focuses on these consequences, which frequently come in the form of challenges for movement organizations, and how activists face them, hence exercising their agency over the data stream.

The accelerated times of the data stream

As already noted earlier, to manage the organization of their daily political engagement, activists frequently find themselves immersed in a data stream that is deeply tied to a wide range of digital media. These include smartphones and other types of mobile devices, which play an important role in the practice of political organizing, especially in Italy and Spain.

A good example in this regard is the experience of David, a 40-something employee of a Spanish national trade union. He has spent much of his life working as a unionist and taking care of various issues within his union, but in the past couple of years, he has focused his attention on the communicative side of unionism. He always brings along both his smartphone and tablet. The smartphone is extremely useful when traveling, by bus, across the city in which he lives; especially when the bus is crowded, it is difficult to work on his tablet. By contrast, the tablet – thanks to its wider screen – is much more useful when he takes a lunch break and finds himself eating alone. Next, in his office, David also has a computer. This means that he conducts his work as a unionist by constantly switching from one device to another, also depending on the physical environment in which he is located when he is working, be it a bus, a restaurant, or his office. However, David stresses that these devices are not the same; the types of software and applications that they are equipped with may be similar but play different roles. For instance, when he speaks about the daily coordination activities that he carries out within his trade union, he makes a clear distinction between the smartphone and the computer. David uses both, but the former gives him immediacy, rapidity, and the ability to confront certain organizational needs in an almost automatic manner. The latter, on the contrary, allows him to do things with a bit more reflection and take an occasional break, giving him a calmer pace in his political engagement.

The need to slow down points precisely to the fast, accelerated rhythms of the data stream, which activists experience in a quite direct way when supporting the daily political activities of their movement organizations. Especially when digital media are being used, activists in Italy, Greece, and Spain continuously produce and consume data, primarily through their smartphones but also thanks to other digital and non-digital devices. They do so at a high speed and therefore perceive their daily grassroots political work as being deeply embedded in the immediacy of a present that proceeds quickly and frequently accelerates, as the following interview extracts by Stefano, Miguel, and Ivan illustrate:

> 'If I made a proposal via a mailing list, [or] if I sent a flyer, I had to wait 24 hours to send it to print, because there was this thing that everyone had a look at the email within 24 hours, and so everyone could have a say in it. Now everything is much more immediate: they do not wait

24 hours, because in the meantime we are all always connected. And it is a tool that gives you immediacy, but it requires you to follow it much more constantly.'

'For example, to make a statement in the past, we had to organize ourselves via email. But I'm talking about 5 years ago. Today, WhatsApp is immediate. Now [we use] only WhatsApp. Because before, you had to send the email, wait for someone to see it, then have someone reply to you … and sometimes 24 hours would pass for something that was "an immediate need". WhatsApp has made our work a lot easier.'

'My feeling is that Internet just creates more time and more space for me, first to do something, then to do it faster and to be able to communicate easier with other people. Then I can do it for free, which is a very important thing. You can absolutely do it for free. And third, you can imagine, in previous years, being without Internet, how much time you spent on covering distances. You had to meet someone to discuss [something]. You had to [go and] find him or you had to call him. You were not able to do a conference call, so to say, or a conference meeting with 10 to 20 different people. You had to approach them or you had to make 20 calls. It basically saves you time and you can dedicate the extra time for your own purposes.'

The activists point to the ability to access data that allow them to perform specific tasks immediately and to get quick feedback on the task that they have just performed. While the majority of the activists we interviewed spoke about the immediacy of digital media, especially when considering smartphones and instant messaging platforms, it is also true that some activists linked the idea of immediacy to other media devices and services. This is the case of text messages sent via mobile phone as opposed to phone calls. The following example relates to Greece, as Eustratios explains:

'We received the information from the parliament at around 6.30 in the evening. … In such [a] few hours we had to make a huge effort to inform everyone, and the best way was that I make a phone call to my trade union here in Athens. … Because of the Erdogan visit, the mobile phones did not work properly, so what do you do then? You must move quickly; you must do something else. Using text messages was the fastest way, and within 30 minutes all our branches were informed about the protests that were going to happen the day after. The text message was a 15-second thing. I did it in 15 seconds and I informed 5,000 people.'

According to Eustratios, then, it is not just the media device or service in itself that gives a certain quality to the data stream that activists have to manage; rather, what counts is how a certain media device can spread information and how activists think it can do this. In other words, the combination of material and perceived affordances (Siles and Boczkowski, 2012) of the media device allows activists to deal with a data stream that enables them "to move quickly" as Eustratios put it, in specific circumstances.

In general, activists have the perception that there is an accelerated time frame in politics. In particular, the use of digital media seems to bring along a sense of immediate efficacy regarding the activists' organizing efforts. Moreover, this accelerated tempo of politics, in which every decision must be made quickly even during latency phases, goes hand in hand with the creation of a strong sense of connectedness among activists within their movement organizations. Always being in contact through various, especially digital, media channels certainly strengthen the sense of connection with – if not belonging to – a movement organization. However, constant connectivity through digital media comes at a price. In addition to dealing with the acceleration of time in politics, activists face the dissolution of boundaries between various spheres of their lives, as we will explain in the next section.

The data stream and the dissolution of context boundaries

Activists not only experience the accelerated time of politics, as mentioned earlier, but they also often fully immerse themselves in their daily work as activists. The data stream that activists contribute to creating through smartphones and various media services never stops, nor does their engagement in the data that they and their fellow activists create. This became clear to us when Stefano explained his engagement with digital media. Some years ago, Stefano was the spokesperson for a relevant trade union in Italy. Equipped with his smartphone, he was always available; he would constantly check his smartphone to see if anything had happened that required his intervention, regardless of where he was and what he was doing. Always connected, Stefano was not even able to watch a whole movie without checking his smartphone, because he always had to be available in case someone might need him. When he thinks about his life as an activist before the smartphone arrived, he confesses that it was more peaceful; once outside the office, he would no longer be available, and he was therefore done for the day.

As we have pointed out earlier, the interconnection between digital media and the practice of political organizing is strong in each of the three examined countries. Beyond facilitating the logistics of activists' daily political work, the immersion in a data stream that is deeply tied to the use of digital media also sets in motion the deconstruction of the so-called boundaries that characterize activists' lives. Although many of the people we interviewed acknowledge that a life devoted to activism often forces one to put everything else aside, many also underlined that the presence of digital media contributes to further blurring the lines between political, family, work, and leisure activities, among other things. These lines, which may already be perceived as being thin when one regularly engages with activism and with the intensity that this kind of engagement requires, seem to become even thinner when the data stream related to digital media comes into play. The immediacy granted by the use of WhatsApp on the smartphone may, then, turn into the trap of constantly being connected to the sphere of politics and political engagement, as these emblematic extracts from interviews with David and Eustratios respectively suggest:

> 'One thing is a disgrace: the smartphone ties you down for 24 hours, social networks and emails tie you down, Tweets always do, and the smartphone always accompanies me until late at night, and that includes WhatsApp, email, networks … That flows all day, every day, including on weekends, because some companies do not close.'

> 'I am connected 24 hours a day. You cannot disconnect yourself, of course not. Something may happen … I still have memories from the time before smartphones. I think my life was better. Maybe it sounds a bit romantic. I have never been against technology: I am a gadget guy. But I think my life was better; I had more time to spend with my friends. But I don't know how it was for trade unionists: I think it was worse without a smartphone because now it is easier for me to find my colleagues wherever they are. And if it is something urgent, I can find them. Before, it was impossible. My personal life is worse, but for my political work it is much better.'

In the interviewees' experience, digital media – and the smartphone more specifically – can introduce political engagement into spaces and times that were once entirely devoted to other activities, such as spending time with friends and family. What the activists told us recalls the process of 'context collapse', when social media platforms converge a broad range of audiences into the same context: the social media profiles that social media users create for themselves (Marwick and boyd, 2011). Furthermore, not just present but also future contexts may converge, because content producers in social media platforms cannot know in advance exactly where and when their content might be reproduced (Wesch, 2009). For general social media platform users, dealing with context collapse means crafting their social media presence and identity by following different strategies to face – or not to face – the dissolution of boundaries between the different social worlds that they inhabit (Marwick and boyd, 2011). For specific categories of social media users, a presentation in public that transcends the divisions between private and public life can indeed be particularly important yet difficult to manage. This is the case, for instance, when politicians want to convey a sense of authenticity to voters (Hoffman and Suphan, 2017; Ceccobelli and Di Gregorio, 2022), or when activists strive to strengthen their emotional connection with supporters and sympathizers (Kavada and Treré, 2020).

However, the process of context collapse is not only related to the public presentation of the self on social media platforms. The activists we spoke with in Greece, Italy, and Spain told us about a deeper process that goes beyond social media platforms, like Facebook and Twitter, and does not only concern how activists present themselves in public. It is a process in which activists experience the intricate interconnections between the various roles that they play in their lives beyond their engagement in politics, and mostly through the use of instant messaging platforms. Activists might use WhatsApp while they are at work, to organize the next big assembly of their movement organizations, or take part in a harsh political discussion in a chat group while preparing dinner for their children at home. This is not simply a case of context collapse, but rather a process of dissolving the boundaries between the different social situations in which activists perform their practices. The responsibility for this situation lies not just with one social media platform, but rather with the continuous data stream that allows them to interact with a wide array of digital media, especially when they combine smartphones with instant messaging platforms.

Many of the activists we interviewed vividly remember a time in which they were already politically active but did not use any digital media, because these did not exist. Consequently, they recall how the practice of political organizing was conducted then and compare it to what it has become today. Their stories did not necessarily give a negative connotation to digital media; as the interview extracts reported earlier also reveal, smartphones make it possible for many actions to be performed more efficiently than in the past, and at precisely the right time. However, they can also be interpreted as stories about boundaries becoming more blurred among different types of practices: thus, that pertaining to the political sphere finds its way among – even briefly interweaving with – practices that belong more to the sphere of leisure and affect. Suffice to think of specific services like instant messaging platforms, as Adrian, an activist from Spain, explains when speaking about his work for an activist association:

'The worst thing, for me, is that you have your friends writing to you about social stuff using the same tool that you use for work, which is Telegram or WhatsApp. So, you use WhatsApp to tell your mum or your brother something, but then you get a message from a group you are part of, about something that needs to be answered straight away, and you answer it. You end up working everywhere: you work in the street when you are walking home; you work at home when you are cooking; and you work before you go to sleep and when you wake up in the morning.'

The use of smartphones coupled with instant messaging platforms contributes to dissolving the boundaries between political engagement and everything else that activists may be doing, including walking home.

Some digital media connect practices that would otherwise remain separate, such as cooking dinner, watching movies, or taking care of children – at least in the lives of the activists we interviewed. There is, then, a combination of purely mundane practices and more politically oriented practices. While it is undoubtedly true that being politically engaged in grassroots politics is time-consuming and could become an all-inclusive experience, our interviewees point out that the presence of digital media greatly contributes to the transformation of the practices that sustain activism into all-encompassing practices that infiltrate other types of practices. The activists' accounts of the dissolution of boundaries demonstrate that digital media can function not only as connectors of people (for example by linking an activist to fellow activists, supporters, and audiences) but also as anchors of the many practices that we encounter in our societies. From this viewpoint, activists deal with a data stream that pertains to many types of activities that they perform not just as activists, but also in many other capacities.

Slow down and interrupt the data stream

The previous two sections have cast light on two relevant aspects of the data stream that activists deal with when performing the practice of political organizing: first, its accelerated pace and the resulting immediacy of all those activities that make up the practice of political organizing; second, its ability to connect different types of social worlds and roles that activists have beyond their engagement in grassroots politics. In this section, we argue that activists do not passively deal with these two aspects. Rather, they actively engage in such a data stream through the combined use of smartphones and instant messaging platforms. Furthermore, activists try to organize their grassroots political work through sophisticated employment of other types of digital media that can reduce the fast pace at which information flows within and outside their movement organizations and, to some extent, also interrupt the data stream; in this way, they can more easily separate the information that they encounter through digital media of all kinds.

One aspect that stands out when we consider the immediacy that activists experience while organizing their grassroots political work is the incompleteness of information that usually accompanies the fast dissemination of messages among activists. When thinking about the use of text messages to inform their union members, for instance, Eustratios points out that:

> 'In a text message, you cannot get all the information. How can I say in a text message what the government is trying to do and why I voted for a strike? It is not easy. You can say [a] few things, but not the full story. That is the point.'

While text messages can reach thousands of people in a short period of time, they cannot tell the whole story. Indeed, activists cannot rely on the impact of immediacy alone; hence they decide to include more than one media device, or more than one media service, in their repertoire of communication. This is not just because different digital media allow them to communicate with fellow activists differently. The main reason for this inclusion of multiple devices or services is that activists need to cope with an aspect of the data stream that could offer relevant opportunities (that is to immediately act and react) while at the same time challenging the need to have exhaustive information when certain decisions should be taken.

Alvaro, for instance, explains that he and his Spanish movement organization usually complement Telegram by using a mailing list capable of slowing down the data stream, so that it becomes more manageable:

> 'Telegram is immediate: "Hey, they write to me from La Sexta to see if we can talk to them about this." On television they cannot wait for you, [if you don't answer quickly] they will look for someone else, so we turn to Telegram: "Send someone? Well, no, because they do not let us explain our political line, so, let them look for someone else." Nevertheless, even if you have made that decision our protocol is that it has to be transferred to the mailing list, which is the official thing. That's where everything has to happen, [where we keep] all the decisions, all the minutes of our meetings.'

Activists' use of digital media certainly revolves around the immediacy of Telegram and similar instant messaging platforms, like WhatsApp. To grasp their highly volatile content, though, activists need to slow down the data stream by using other types of media services – like mailing lists – that are still digital but allow for a slower pace of communication among activists when they have to discuss relevant topics for their organization and make such discussions available in a more stable space. The data stream that activists deal with could therefore accelerate very quickly. However, activists seem able to slow it down to the point of stopping it so that they can render relevant information more stable.

Another strategy that activists deploy in all three countries under examination aims at avoiding the merging of different social worlds in their daily use of smartphones and instant messaging platforms. To do so, they selectively employ certain media devices and services to perform practices that occur beyond the sphere of grassroots political engagement and others to support the practice of political organizing. Scholars have detected this selective employment in other types of social movements as well, for instance during the Hong Kong Umbrella Movement in 2014, activists employed the strategy of unfriending on Facebook to avoid the convergence of different social and political contexts in their social medial profiles (Zhu et al, 2017).

However, our study shows that activists face the dissolution of boundaries and deal with it even when people are not out in the streets participating in mass demonstrations that could polarize their political views. Furthermore, activists do not manage the dissolution of boundaries just on one specific social media platform; rather, they act upon a data stream that depends on the use of multiple digital media devices and services. They decide to differentiate the use of digital media to create internal boundaries in an otherwise cohesive data stream and keep their political life, which is more public, separate from their social roles – as friends, family members, or fellow workers. Additionally, some activists may decide not to use a certain device or service during specific times of the day, as becomes clear from these extracts of interviews with Adrian and Marta respectively:

> 'I think I'm learning to make better use of my smartphone. When we had meetings here, we used to look at our phones all the time and we established a rule, which is that "you are not allowed to watch your smartphone while we are in a meeting". This is a mechanism that we have established. And I try to do that myself when I am home, like during after-work hours, but it's not easy.'

> 'I have a personal policy: I stop reading and responding mainly to political messages and emails at 10 pm. I switch off the Internet connection because it is the only way not to receive messages, especially via the WhatsApp chat, that put particular pressure on me to make decisions or commitments regarding my political activity, I therefore switch off the Internet connection. Mainly WhatsApp; Telegram and Messenger in second place, more or less together. A large part of my organizational activity takes place via WhatsApp.'

Activists may therefore appropriate different media devices or services that they employ daily, with each of these acquiring a role that goes well beyond their communicative function (Silverstone et al, 1992). In the following extract, for instance, Gianluca, an activist from Italy, explains that he allows certain services on his laptop to break the boundaries between his working time and the time devoted to activism:

> 'I chat a lot more because with chatting, even while I am working, I answer you in a second, I talk to you, etcetera, whereas if you call me during the day, most times the answer is, "no, look, I will call you tonight". Also because I usually tend to go home on foot and then at half past 6, at 7 pm, when I go home and have three or four phone calls to make, I do them while I walk or cycle home, because then maybe I would waste less time calling, but I have the idea that I'm working and I don't want to lose half an hour on the phone, also because here you work with others, [there are] disturbances … so if I have to write a few lines in a chat I will write, but if I need to make a phone call, we can talk tonight, without rushing.'

The phone call is, instead, perceived as a more serious intrusion, and it therefore has a different role in the activist's organizational routines; placing it in the liminal space and time after leaving work and before arriving home, the phone call is an in-between action that protects the boundaries between two different spheres. Activists assume that making a phone call is an urgent, uncommon, and somewhat disturbing action both for their activist identity and in its blurring the boundaries of their personal life. A mutual negotiation constantly takes place between these two different levels and is inserted in an incessant personal and societal learning process, which extends across generations, social spheres, and practices. As research related to the mundane use of phone calls has also pointed out (Matassi et al, 2019), younger generations nowadays perceive the use of landlines to call people at home as something unnecessary and related to a somehow archaic media practice that is to be dismissed. The way in which people, including activists, evaluate the use of specific media technologies, such as landline versus smartphone calls, helps to explain their symbolic understanding of the data stream and how it, in turn, entangles with the general and practical understanding of how activists and their movement organizations can organize their daily political work.

The data stream amid surveillance, privacy, and the protection of communication

The previous section has shed light on activists' employment of older digital media services like mailing lists to slow down the data stream that they deal with through the use of smartphones coupled with instant messaging platforms. Also, it demonstrated that activists' practical understanding of different types of digital media may contribute to creating ruptures in the otherwise continuous data stream. These are not the only challenges that the data stream brings along when the data sequences that activists generate are rooted in digital media. The risk of being surveilled and the consequent need to increase their privacy is another relevant aspect that activists must consider, although this does not happen in the same way in the three countries. This section deals with this third challenge; it shows that it is relevant also when it concerns the day-to-day activities of the practice of political organizing and explains how activists and their movement organizations seek to face it.

Activists neither construct the smartphones they employ nor develop the applications that they use on them. Therefore, although activists see the emancipatory potential of the newest digital media, with their promises of immediate organizational accomplishments through relatively few resources, they also acknowledge the risk of oppressive forces of surveillance that operate on activists through those same digital media (Uldam, 2018). It must be said that this tension is not equally prominent for activists we interviewed in the three countries; it is very pronounced in Spain, vaguely present in Greece, and practically absent in Italy. The lack of awareness of the threat that social media platforms pose to activists' privacy is not altogether surprising. Other scholars have already pointed out that new generations of activists seem to care less about the technological infrastructures that allow them to communicate both among themselves and with the outside world (Milan, 2015). However, those activists who are concerned with surveillance develop a distinct feeling that digital media are generally subject to scrutiny by the opponents of social movements, oppressive powers, and police forces (Kazansky, 2021). As becomes clear from the following extracts of interviews with Rodrigo, Ruben, and Adrian respectively, this understanding of digital media applies transversally to older services, like email providers, and newer services, like instant messaging platforms:

> 'Right now, there is a problem and it's the fact that there are people who use Google Hangout, and then you have to use it as well. But there are certain things that I never speak about on Hangout. ... So it's no surprise that I now use Signal as the application for security issues; this is the application that we consider to be the most secure, and we don't do certain types of contacts with people if we can't use Signal or an encrypted email, that is, we ignore emails that are not encrypted.'

> 'During the last 5 years, we have provided quite a lot of training on safety and the privacy of communications ... for journalists, we have organized many workshops, we have provided a lot of training ... So

certain emails from these mailing lists go through PGP; our computers are encrypted, [and] the hard drives are encrypted.'

'We installed Signal last year, in the days before the referendum, which became very popular after 20 September, when the movement started to be very strong, and we were involved in that too. I mean, during those days there was a lot of paranoia about needing to install Signal and communicate through it. ... I think that a good lesson we also learned in 2011 is that if you really have to do something very sensitive, don't put it on any platform. And this has happened a couple of times, when we just say "well, let's meet".'

As these three extracts show, the activists' understanding of the most widespread digital media platforms as a means of surveillance leads them to develop plausible alternatives, namely the employment of platforms that are considered safe, as well as security and safety measures, like the use of passwords and encrypted emails. At the same time, they tend to consider face-to-face interactions the safest possible way to organize things together, as Eustratios, an activist from Greece explains:

'When we organize a strike or a fight, there is some information that is very very private, and we do not want the hotel or factory owners to steal it and know our plans. [Using Skype] could be an easy and cheaper way than everyone meeting here in Athens. For many [activist] organizations ... to bring them here to Athens is very expensive, but for us, it is the safest way, safer than a Skype call.'

The recourse to face-to-face interactions also seems to depend on the type of contentious issues that activists are dealing with. Among the activists we interviewed, those involved in anti-corruption organizations explained that they are much more dependent upon direct communication when organizing their daily political engagement. The reason for this dependence lies in the fact that these organizations may need to manage very sensitive information, such as secret documents or the personal details of their informants, which requires them to identify precise strategies to protect such delicate information. Some of that information cannot escape the closed circle of those who manage an entire organization that is active in the fight against corruption. The only way to be sure that one is not subjected to any leaks is to rely on direct forms of communication, in particular when very sensitive information is at stake. In these cases, even a phone call or WhatsApp message in an individual or group chat is not perceived as safe. This is mainly why anti-corruption activists organize their work much more through face-to-face meetings with co-workers and collaborators than those involved in grassroots organizations focusing on labor issues do.

As stated earlier, strong differences across the three Southern European countries emerge when it comes to digital security and the fear of surveillance. Furthermore, our in-depth analysis of the type of movement organizations and the contentious issues they act upon confirms the thesis that Spain is the only country where activists develop a set of best strategies to protect their sensitive information within a digital environment. Italy identifies as a country in which anti-corruption activists are not as careful as their Spanish counterparts when it comes to protecting themselves, their sources, and sensitive information from the potential intrusion of third parties into their organizational, mediated practices. Again, this difference may depend on the background of many of the Spanish activists we interviewed for our research: their roots are in the 15-M movement that developed in 2011 and that is, in turn, strictly linked to the widespread political hacker subculture of the country (Treré et al, 2017).

The luxury of face-to-face communication

The previous section has demonstrated that activists may opt out of digital media to counter the risk of surveillance and increase the privacy of their communication also during their daily grassroots political activities. To do this, they resort to in-person, face-to-face exchanges of data, especially when they need to organize more sensitive activities, for example in the field of anti-corruption fights. However, not everyone can afford to speak in person to other activists within their movement organization. While in principle many of the activists we interviewed in the three countries consider face-to-face interactions relevant in supporting the practice of political organizing, in the daily unfolding of their movement organizations' activities this is seldom easy to achieve.

Marta's account of her political engagement as a trade unionist is exemplary in this regard. She is an Italian activist engaged in many civil society organizations, including a branch of a traditional trade union and a progressive activist association with members from all over Italy. She also works as a researcher on a fixed-term contract, dividing her time between her precarious academic job and her political engagement. When it comes to the meetings of her activist association, Marta and her fellow activists do not have the time or the money to be physically present in the same place. Each of them has multiple activist affiliations and often also a fragmented working life that forces them to jump from one temporary contract to another; if they all wanted to meet in the same place to make important decisions together, that meeting would never happen. At the same time, Marta and her fellow activists believe that speaking in each other's presence is vital to keep the association's activities going and to provide a general framework of coordination that is shared by everyone within the association. For this reason, in 2016, Marta's association began to employ TeamSpeak, a VoIP software application created to enable live communication among the team members of online multiplayer games. For Marta's association, TeamSpeak is a low-cost solution that allows its members to meet online. Indeed, the fact that TeamSpeak came with a free server license responded to the needs of the association, which depended on limited material resources and whose members were sensitive to surveillance issues.

This emblematic example demonstrates that it is also important to look at the type of movement organization that activists are involved in to understand how they deal with the data stream in the framework of the practice of political organizing. This aspect seems particularly relevant when we compare funded and structured civil society organizations to unfunded and unstructured ones. It is mostly structured grassroots organizations, which can economically support their members, include physical meetings in their most common daily practices of political organizing. They are different from the looser grassroots organizations in their ability to combine the two sides of the data stream that rest on digital media and face-to-face interactions, respectively. The rituality of these daily, physical face-to-face meetings with co-workers and collaborators must not be underestimated. Of course, movement organizations that cannot afford to rent an office or pay some of their members a basic salary do not collapse. However, according to our interviewees, the ability to meet face-to-face matters a great deal, as Gianluca, an activist from a loose grassroots organization also underlines:

> 'Most of my political engagement happens in a mediated form. This is something I have reflected on many times, as I don't like it. I really miss the physical dimension of militancy. All political interactions are also based on a relational mechanism, which is also emotional ... of being together and feeling good about being together. Very frequently, the meetings are really difficult because you have to reflect deeply on things, you have to discuss things, and it may be that you have to argue [with your fellow activists]. Without the element of being physically together, of thinking that it is good to be together, everything becomes more difficult and frustrating, and I see myself sitting alone in front of my computer screen for a 3-hour meeting, and that is not good.'

Although activists do not need physical encounters to keep their daily political work going, the lack of direct contact with other leading members can have negative effects as well. For instance, when Marta recalled her frequent use of TeamSpeak in her activist association, she said that:

'[i]t was something that happened three times a week; meetings started at 6 pm and ended at midnight. We also had an internal chat where we exchanged documents and decided on opinions and policy. After a while, I completely disappeared from those meetings because they were a black hole.'

Marta highlights the risk that participation in a collective organization may become less pleasant and somewhat frustrating, which can lead to an effective and concrete detachment in the long term. More generally, not having face-to-face meetings and assemblies could also weaken the activists' ability to fully experience the deep power dynamics that unfold in movement organizations, thus limiting the operative capacities of a managing team that would act in a far more effective and rapid manner if there were more frequent and constant face-to-face meetings involving all its members.

Conclusion

In this chapter, we have explained that, within the activists' practice of political organizing, the data stream rests primarily on the sequences of data generated through digital media and – perhaps more surprisingly – on those generated through face-to-face encounters between activists. In so doing, we have offered some important insights into the extent to which digital media and physical encounters affect the daily routine of movement organizations. We have demonstrated that, as with other practices discussed in this book, activists rely on a wider array of digital and non-digital media to organize their political work. In short, we have shown that Southern European activists are unable to even think about organizing their political work at the grassroots level without employing a wide heterogeneous ensemble of media-related devices, services, and actions, most of them well ingrained in digital media.

Next, we have discussed the three main challenges that activists in Italy, Greece, and Spain face every day when dealing with the data stream. First, we reflected on the acceleration of the time of politics, which allows activists to immediately make decisions and assign tasks within their movement organizations; at the same time, though, it forces them to tackle the lack of time for political reflection and collective sharing. Activists' political commitment is marked by a deep sense of the immediacy of communication that comes precisely with the heterogeneous data stream that they relate to. While they certainly value this immediacy, as it allows them to react quickly to the pressing and incessant demands for intervention in the different tasks involved in the practice of political organizing, they also fear it. Later in the chapter, we have highlighted how activists cope with the dissolution of boundaries between the sphere of their political activity and other spheres of action during their daily lives. Since the data stream is perpetual and pervasive, activists are dragged – so to speak – into endless political activities that can envelop even those moments of life that are unrelated to the activists' political engagement. The ubiquitous and perpetual traits of the data stream also imply a total immersion in an incessant, daily political activity that eventually takes their political engagement to spaces and times that were once entirely devoted to other non-political and mundane activities. Finally, we have pointed out that the production and dissemination of data by activists take place in a data stream over which they have almost no control because the digital media that they tend to use are owned by commercial companies. Moreover, the risk that these digital media are used as a means of surveillance is always present.

Activists address these challenges by exercising a level of agency over the data stream, and they do so in three ways. First, they seek to slow down the data stream by including digital media in their organizing activities that involve slower communication; precisely because of this, they become important for activists, who thus regain the slow time of politics that they otherwise seem to have lost. Differentiation in the use of digital media is another way to manage the challenge of dissolving the boundaries that activists belong to. By intervening in the data stream, activists seek to divide it into more manageable data sequences, making it more discontinuous than it actually is. Finally, activists resort to less digitally mediated forms of interaction, up to and including face-to-face interactions, to protect themselves from the potential risks of surveillance and the consequent breach of privacy. However, as we have shown in the chapter, activists also value face-to-face interactions for other reasons and seek to engage in them as frequently as possible.

Overall, the chapter has revealed that unmediated forms of communication strongly characterize the practice of political organizing; this implies that a mediatization process is taking place but without eliminating face-to-face meetings, whereas physical exchanges refrain from using any kind of mediated filters. In other words, activists still meet in person. They do it as often as they can; they need and love to do so. As our interviewees pointed out, sharing opinions while sitting around a real table is not an archaic and unnecessary ritual for them when organizing the flow of their political activities. Rather, it still embodies values of transparency and efficiency. Moreover, it is perceived as a pleasant activity, despite also being a luxury that is more accessible to funded and structured movement organizations.

The acceleration of political time, the dissolution of the boundaries between political and non-political activities, and the surveillance of political activities are three topics that emerged strongly in the interviews we conducted in Italy, Greece, and Spain. Yet, in this chapter, we have also shown that the data stream and the challenges it introduces are not experienced in the same way in the three countries, especially regarding the issue of online privacy and security. In addition to the reasons behind these differences that we have mentioned in the previous pages, it must be noted that the practice of political organizing is affected differently by the mediatization process depending on the country at stake. In other words, mediatization is present in all three countries but not in the same way: the activists' experience of it seems to be stronger in some countries than it is in others. Following this line of reasoning, throughout the chapter, we have also noted the importance of both the political issue that a movement organization deals with and the resources it can count on when exercising – or not – its agency over the data stream. For instance, we have described how Italian, Greek, and Spanish activists behave differently when it comes to securing their internal communication; only the latter tried to prevent unwelcome guests from entering their communicative flows. In this regard, what emerges from our interviews is the reliance on face-to-face encounters, in particular, among one of the two types of interviewees we spoke to: those who, on a daily basis, manage very sensitive information on behalf of anti-corruption organizations. Again, as we have noted in other chapters of this book, what emerges from our research is the fact that mediatization cannot be understood as a process that homogeneously influences social movements and movement organizations. Even when it comes to the day-to-day organization of one's political activity, mediatization – whether considered in terms of digitalization or datafication – is experienced and addressed in different ways even within the same country. In the next chapter, we will describe a similar situation regarding another important practice for activists: sustaining connections that are relevant to a movement organization's political activity.

6

The Creation of Connections Between Activists and Their Audiences

Miranda is a leading member of a movement organization that works on transparency and accountability in Spain. We interviewed her in the organization's meeting room. Together with members of her staff, she welcomed us very warmly. It was immediately clear that she knew how to connect with people and make them feel at ease in a meeting, a simple conversation or even through online communication. We had already sensed this ability when we received her email reply to our proposal to interview her for our research project. When we met her in person, our initial impression was confirmed. It was clear to us that Miranda considered establishing a connection with people a core aspect of her work as an activist. During our conversation, she meticulously described how she relates to different media and political actors, ranging from journalists via elected officials to people not already connected to her movement organization. Moreover, we noted a distinct ability to shift from digital to analog media. As she said during the interview, she needs to craft different ways of communicating depending on the type of actor she has to deal with to better support the aims of her movement organization. Miranda, then, is also very active on those social media platforms where she thinks political, media, and economic actors develop a relationship of mutual trust (Molyneux and Mourão, 2019). However, not all social media platforms are equally important in this respect:

> 'I don't like this Messenger [service] of Facebook, because 5,000 people can send you messages at the same time ... sometimes ... this is ok, but look ... I look at it, I check it. I don't answer, but I check it. And what happens? People send you things like ... noise. Yes, it's noise. This is like noise, that's right, noise. When they say "feliz navidad", or sometimes ... And there's another group that sends you a merry

Christmas wish or another group that writes "please put a like on my website" or something. Noise, noise, noise.'

Miranda spent much time discussing how she manages the continuous flow of information that people produce when they contact her and her movement organization for a variety of purposes, whether it's asking for information on political activities or simply cheering her up. The interview thus reveals how relevant the activists' ability to manage the fragile balance between different forms of communication is when seeking to connect with various types of actors, ranging from fellow activists with whom they wish to collaborate to the diverse and dispersed set of people who activists would like to render more aware concerning specific social and political issues. In some cases, a face-to-face meeting is the only way to create a lasting bond through which activists can then start collaborations on the issues they care about. In other cases, a simple message through WhatsApp or Facebook Messenger, or even an SMS can represent the best choice to keep strategic connections alive. While extremely relevant to sustain their daily grassroots political work over time, nurturing all the connections that Miranda and her movement organization have built over several years of activism is not an easy task. The reason for this also lies in the fact that, as mentioned earlier, activists need to build relationships with different types of actors. Nowadays, much more so than in the past, activists can rely on a wide variety of ways and means to do this in addition to the more traditional face-to-face meetings.

In this chapter, we will explain how activists appropriate multiple types of digital media and the related technologies to build and nurture their connections with institutional political actors, people who might support their movement organizations, and the community that gathers around their movement organizations. We will discuss the very strategies that activists deploy in the practice of establishing and curating connections by considering three different types of actors that are particularly important for movement organizations: other movement organizations with whom to build broader coalitions and other – collective and individual – actors who might support those coalitions, including political parties and policy makers; the supporters who sustain the movement organization in various forms while not formally being part of it; bystanders, that is, all those people who have sporadic and sometimes casual contacts with the movement organization but who may nevertheless become more active supporters in the future, participating in mobilizations and other initiatives. These three types of actors vary not only according to their degree of involvement in the movement organization, but also – as we will see later in the chapter – in terms of how activists choose to interact and create various types of relationships with them. We will show that face-to-face interactions are considered central primarily to engage with audiences who are closest to a movement organization and the vast array of institutional actors that activists need to engage with, but that instant messaging services are equally important, though often difficult to manage. In addition, we will discuss how activists maintain a relationship with more distant actors by distinguishing between activities taking place behind the scenes and those carried out in public, for example through interactions with comments on content posted on a social media platform. We argue that, in order to keep connections with this diverse set of individual and collective actors alive, activists must navigate a data stream in which various types of data sequences are encountered, each with its own distinctive features. To conclude, we will reflect on an aspect that strongly emerged in our investigation: the greater importance that activists give to written versus oral communication when having mediated interactions with their audiences. First, though, we will explain how important connections are for activists and define the practice of sustaining connections.

The practice of sustaining connections

Grassroots politics is a deeply relational social phenomenon: activists do not act alone, and social movements 'emerge out of repeated and patterned interactions between multiple actors' (Diani and Mische, 2015: 306). Furthermore, activists and their movement organizations engage in sustained interactions with other types of individual and collective actors outside the social movement milieu, including potential protest participants, distant supporters, and bystanders, but also with news media actors like journalists and institutional political actors like policy makers. In this regard, actors who sustain the process of claims-making in contentious politics typically 'consist of networks deploying partially shared histories, cultures, and collective connections with other actors' (Tilly, 2005: 61). Additionally, we can look at social movements as processes that happen in a number of arenas where various players, including activists and their movement organizations, engage in strategic interactions to achieve their goals (Jasper and Duyvendak, 2015).

Interactions are important for activists and their movement organizations for at least two reasons. On the one hand, transforming interactions into more durable social relationships may empower movement organizations' ability to operate successfully also in the long term. For instance, the establishment of stable relations with a journalist can increase the likelihood that the activists' protests are represented in news media in a more timely and accurate way. On the other hand, taking care of casual interactions is also important in the short term, although perhaps in a less obvious way. Thus, interacting online with potential supporters, or even with harsh denigrators, can have an impact on how activists construct the public identities of their movement organizations and, in turn, on the extent to which they can succeed in mobilizing people.

In short, the careful management of interactions with other actors is vital for activists who are part of a network of relationships that they nurture and sustain, and who attempt to change it over time also depending on their objectives. In her research, Ann Mische (2008) illustrates how important communicative practices were for the careful crafting of relationships among different movement organizations in Brazil from 1977 to 1996. Relation building formed a relevant part of the Brazilian activists' work, involving several types of activities that ranged from the recruitment of new members to the coordination of joint collective actions (Mische, 2008: 50). Similarly, in our analysis, the practice of sustaining connections emerged as one of the most relevant activities that activists in Greece, Italy, and Spain perform in times of latency. More specifically, activists spoke extensively of the way they build relationships with a broad range of actors during their daily grassroots political work, going well beyond interactions with other fellow activists. With this aspect in mind, we define the practice of sustaining connections as one that includes all those activities that allow activists to manage their interactions with the aim of establishing and nurturing social relationships with a wide range of individual and collective actors in the political, media, and social realms.

Social movement scholars usually focus on the relevance of networks of social relationships for movement organizations and activists; they emphasize the relationship between social network density and the activists' ability to recruit other members, organize contentious collective actions, and spread their discourses and protests (Krinsky and Crossley, 2014). In this chapter, instead, we will demonstrate how activists construct these networks without focusing too much on their shape and consequences. In other words, we will see how relationships between activists and other actors develop from the activists' viewpoint by considering the types of activities they engage in to support the practice of sustaining connections. In doing so we will choose a specific angle, that is, we will look at the role that digital media and the related technologies play in the making of connections, their sustainment over time, and the challenges that they could pose to activists.

Face-to-face interactions that sustain movement organizations and their coalitions

Movement organizations rarely act alone. In fact, they often build coalitions that gather different movement organizations committed to a common goal. In addition, they seek the support of allies who can help them in their mobilizations, for example by taking the activists' demands to the heart of political decision-making. Weaving the web of these relationships is a laborious task that cannot be done shortly before a mobilization; it unfolds in the quiet time when activists are not mobilizing. When it comes to building and maintaining relationships with other actors that are close to movement organizations, our interviewees seem to converge on one activity in particular: meeting in the same physical space, hence face-to-face, with activists belonging to other movement organizations, but also with politicians who could plead their cases in the arena of institutional politics, thus becoming valuable allies, hence recurring to the 'inside-lobbying' (Kriesi et al, 2007) activities that complement the use of public protest to issue their demands. Isidoros, for instance, considers the face-to-face dimension of communication the cornerstone of the practice of sustaining connections. He describes his understanding of how to interact with other activists using a straightforward and clear statement: "[P]hysical contact is the best way to have strong relations with people." More than any of the other practices that we have discussed in this book, that of sustaining meaningful connections has at its core the body, interpreted as a means through which activists – in this case – establish and sustain new social ties with other actors. Practice theories have always given the body a prominent role: it is through the body that people perform practices (see Bourdieu, 1990; Schatzki, 1996). In the case of the practice of sustaining meaningful connections with other actors, both individual and collective ones, activists emphasize not so much the importance of the body itself, but rather the indispensable proximity of bodies in the same physical space. In other words, it is about putting back at the centre of the practice those activities that include relationships mediated only through one's body, which then becomes a medium in itself, and not through devices, such as digital media. Without denying the usefulness of the latter *tout court*, activists have a general understanding of face-to-face relationships as being key to generating those bonds of trust that can create strong, lasting, and important connections capable of sustaining their daily political work.

This is the case of Giovanni, a precarious worker and leading member of an Italian movement organization that mobilizes people on the issue of basic income. While he would know how to connect with people through digital media and various types of communication technologies, Giovanni usually does not do this. The reason he gives for this is that "I am in this truly twentieth century. For me, public space means seeing other faces: to be in the same place, to share the same environment, having the chance to go and meet people." According to Giovanni, the public space should not revolve around digital media. Although he does not deny the existence of social media platforms and instant messaging apps, he considers face-to-face encounters a moment of recreation and diversion. When Giovanni needs to touch base with someone he already knows or someone new, he prefers to make a quick phone call and schedule a lunch meeting rather than interact with a screen. Occasionally, this happens even with only 30 minutes' notice. Giovanni enjoys the time devoted to his political commitment most when having lunch with another activist, journalist, or policy maker; in these face-to-face occasions, he relaxes, even forgets personal and work-related concerns, and thus emotionally sustains his activist's identity. It is also thanks to these enjoyable moments in his activism that he decides not to give up his political commitment after a harsh argument with fellow activists or a painful political disappointment.

Like Giovanni, many of the activists we interviewed have a basic understanding of how to perform the practice of sustaining connections, which puts at the centre the physical encounters between activists and other actors as well as the teleoaffective structure that sustains it, namely the positive emotions linked to meeting and chatting with people coupled with the goal of gaining their trust. Furthermore, such a general understanding is consistently combined with the explicit rule according to which activists have to meet people face-to-face because this is the only way to develop a direct and lasting connection with other actors, avoid misunderstanding, and – once again – construct trusty relationships. In other words, technologically mediated communications fail to offer activists an acceptable alternative to physically meeting and talking to another human being in terms of the depth of the social relationship taking place. Even phone calls appear to be less important, as Mauro, an Italian activist involved in the fight against precarious work, explains: "[T]he basic goal of phone calls is to establish a clearly virtual connection at a given moment that later, if it wasn't already there before, turns into a real connection. The phone call has no comparison whatsoever to a real, social relationship." Interestingly, in Mauro's words, "reality" equals the face-to-face interactions where two or more bodies are simultaneously present: that is the only way to develop a "real social relationship". In an age that is so deeply shaped by digital media, face-to-face interactions remain something activists cannot do without.

In short, the activists' attempts to focus the practice of sustaining connections on the physical proximity of activists' and other actors' bodies could also be linked to a broader understanding of how digital media interfere with the creation of sound relationships between individuals. This findings on the relevance of face-to-face meetings is in line with the results on other forms of political participation, including those on lobbying activities for which face-to-face interactions – ranging from official meetings in policy makers' offices via quick coffee breaks in the palaces of power to fancy lunches and dinners outside (paid) working hours – have strategic and pivotal importance to build trust among political actors, even in a time so pervasively shaped by digital media (Nothhalft, 2017).

Despite the relevance of face-to-face interaction, for most of the activists we interviewed seeing each other in person and sharing the same physical space is often very difficult to achieve. In Chapter 5, devoted to the practice of political organizing, we have explained that face-to-face meetings with fellow activists from the same movement organization might be a real luxury.

This is even truer in the case of the relationship between activists and actors who position themselves outside their movement organization. In this case, activists are somehow forced to resort to digital media; consequently, the practice of establishing meaningful connections also intersects with those data sequences that pass through digital media, as we will explain in the next section on activists' connections with their supporters.

Three ways to nurture the connection with movement organizations' supporters

Movement organizations frequently act in coalition and are supported by allies who are often collective actors or their representatives. Another important role, however, is played by those who – in one form or another – belong to the movement organization, supporting it both in its phases of mobilization and when there are no protests. This is usually a dispersed crowd of supporters who are extremely important for the activists' movement organizations in the construction of the overall infrastructure of protest events and campaigns before they unfold. They can grant the necessary material resources to movement organizations and, perhaps even more importantly, serve to enhance both visibility and participation. Consequently, taking care of supporters is particularly relevant also in times of latency, and activists use very different strategies to do this.

More specifically, we have identified three strategies that activists employ when they seek to create, maintain, and nurture their connection with the dispersed, heterogeneous, and multifaceted crowd of supporters: the refusal to rely on mediations via digital media, focusing on face-to-face encounters to develop social relationships; the opposite choice to mold these connections with the crucial help of digital platforms; and a middle ground between these two strategies, which pays attention to face-to-face interactions but without excluding the use of digital media. The activists' choice to prefer one strategy to another, hence focusing on one data sequence rather than another, is not a neutral choice as we will see throughout this section. For instance, relying more on face-to-face meetings or quick messages on Facebook Messenger has consequences for the activists' ability to perform other important practices. As we have suggested in the previous section, selecting or discarding one among all the possible media technologies that activists can employ also contributes to shaping the public image of movement organizations.

Some movement organizations do not believe that digital media have the power to support their connections with supporters. According to the activists involved in these movement organizations, the digital can increase the risk of hindering these connections. Their practical understanding revolves around the idea that caring for fellow activists in the best possible way means meeting them in person, talking to them while being in the same physical space, and looking into each other's eyes. This is the only way to develop and then maintain a relationship of confidence and trust. This strategy is adopted by the Greek movement organizations close to the radical left and active in labor issues, in particular, and suggests that the collective dimension related to decision-making processes opposes the individualization often advanced by the most widespread digital media.

These movement organizations have a general understanding of digital media – and especially social media platforms – as forces that contribute to the spread of a highly individualized society in which collective worldviews are put in the background and risk disappearing (Atton, 2015), even if – at the dawn of the internet revolution – they were the more enthusiastic supporters of the technological innovation brought about by the digitalization of society (Tsagarousianou, 1999). The simple use of a digital environment such as Facebook is conceived as an unpleasant and somewhat forced choice that they would like to get rid of. However, such a general understanding of digital media, which is also very common in Greece even beyond the political borders of the national radical left (Katsikas and Gritzalis, 2017), does not prevent the Greek movement organizations from abandoning digital media as well as social media platforms. The reason for this is that they do not see effective alternatives that would allow them to reach their supporters and, along with them, large numbers of people who are not yet supporters in a short time and without further intermediations. As a result, these movement organizations have to deal with a constant and pressing tension between the necessity to connect with their supporters and the use of digital media that they consider dangerous for themselves and their movement organizations. To face such tensions, activists frequently engage with social media platforms by appropriating them in ways that go beyond some of their specific features, like the individualization of communication, as Ivan explains when illustrating how his movement organization manages its connections through Facebook:

> 'If you see an account on a Facebook page that replies to the comments it receives immediately, it means that [the movement organization managing that Facebook page] has not discussed its answer before posting it. But we are based on a ... you know, we have a different viewpoint on how we must express our opinions online. It has to be firstly discussed, decided, and then we can publish our answers because our Facebook page is not a personal profile. We cannot operate on the basis of a non-democratic decision. I know it's slow. But we cannot just use the page to comment as if we were an individual, because this makes it very personalized. And we do not want to have one person who makes the decision on how to comment on something. We

don't want to do that. If you want, you have your own profile, you do whatever [you want], but not in the name of everyone else.'

The slowness in responding to received comments is due to the tension between the use of a social media platform that tends to individualize and personalize collective actors, on the one hand, and the activists' willingness to be true to their collective nature even when deciding how to respond to comments they receive on Facebook, on the other. Although this slowness is perhaps unproductive in the context of social media platforms, which convey immediate reactions, activists thus manage to protect the internal decision-making mechanisms used to present themselves to the supporters who are closest to them. In this way, activists exert an agency over the accelerated times of social media platforms, hence resisting the imposition of a single, hegemonic time based on speed and continuous references to the present (Barassi, 2015b). This is a strategic choice that privileges the creation of connections outside digital media and which is, once again, dictated by a general understanding that leads to the perception of social media platforms as potentially dangerous to activists, their movement organizations' identity, and the activists' ability to connect with their supporters.

Contrary to the discussion elaborated earlier, most of the movement organizations that we considered rely on digital media and, in particular, social media platforms. In this case, the activists' general understanding leads them to perceive digital media as emancipatory forces that can strengthen the movement organizations that use them. Indeed, one of the activists we interviewed pointed to the role of social media as enablers of community-building activities (Lovejoy and Saxton, 2012); she argued that when activists interact – intentionally or not – with people on their profiles, they manage to make these people engage in the online communities that develop around their movement organizations, sometimes leading them to take action themselves, even offline, thus turning them into activists. This is the case of a Spanish movement organization that invests much of its energy in online communication to maintain a connection with its supporters on social media platforms, after which a positive spillover into the organization of events and mobilization campaigns takes place, and not necessarily online. When we asked Ruben, one of the activists of this movement organization, why they care so much about and spend so much time with their supporters online, this was the answer:

> '[F]or us that's what we have: we don't have television, we don't have big media, we don't have a classic one-way channel through which we can say something and have 40,000 people listen to us. We only have these communities, and these communities are made of this. So this ... means that anyone who retweets us, anybody who retweets a tweet

where we are mentioned in one of our accounts, we process it in some way. Because that's how it is ... Our account has 30,000 followers, but it's capable of quickly filling a theater with 10,000 people.'

This extract reveals the presence of a further bond across practices, in this case between the practice of sustaining connections and that of gaining visibility. Scrupulous attention to the practice of sustaining connections at the level of interacting with potential supporters in different digital environments can result in better opportunities to plan and organize successful events on the ground. The case of Ruben's movement organization proves that even digital communities with a noticeable but limited amount of digital users (30,000 Twitter followers) can be active communities if activists nurture the connections with their supporters in a careful way. These digital communities show that quantity does not always go hand in hand with quality. Instead, quality – in the sense of more substantial, stable, and deep connections – is much more capable of transforming online political participation into mass offline events.

Other movement organizations neither emphasize face-to-face interactions nor depend on social media platforms and other types of digital media to nurture the connections with their supporters. Rather, they rely on a wide array of digital and non-digital media, including instant messaging apps and phone calls. This third strategy starts from the activists' assumption that all forms of communication are relevant in the process of sustaining connections with the movement organizations' supporters, each in its own way and, therefore, complementary to the others. In fact, it is not uncommon for activists to combine various types of media to sustain and nurture interactions with the same person at different times. As Simona points out, "the direct face-to-face approach with people works well if it is closely connected to technology, because it allows you to bridge time gaps". In short, it is not a question of choosing between an activity centred on face-to-face interactions and one centred instead on the use of social platforms. According to Simona, they are all indispensable, even if at different moments, especially when it comes to supporters who are in contact with a movement organization through different channels at the same time.

In this section, we have discussed the three different strategies that activists deploy to strengthen their relationships with supporters. In general, all three strategies hint at the presence of a strong link with the symbolic aspect of the practice examined in this chapter. In fact, activists include or exclude digital media from activities aimed at building and maintaining a bond with their supporters depending also on the role that they assign to digital media. Moreover, this general understanding of what digital media are and what they can do may dovetail with what activists deem most appropriate for their movement organization. In some cases, it is more important for activists to keep the movement organization's internal, collective decision-making processes intact; in others, the movement organization also decides to exploit the participation, and decision-making procedure, of the individual activist in managing its communication with supporters in order to prioritize the immediacy of the relationship. Still, the movement organization may also focus on one – or at most two – social media platforms to ensure continued interaction with its supporters. In other cases, though, movement organizations consider the development of these interactions over a longer time frame, during which different types of media may come into play.

In the next section we will illustrate how different ways of performing the same practice coexist even when activists decide to take care of their relationships with all those people who are in no way linked to the movement organization, although they may in principle be interested in the issues it deals with.

Connecting with bystanders between public and private online interactions

Activists seek to maintain connections not only with people who already support movement organizations, but also with people who are part of a more diverse audience, potentially interested in the activists' issues but not necessarily connected to the activists' movement organization in any way. In this case, more than in those previously discussed, interactions predominantly take place through digital media. In particular, social media platforms such as Facebook and Twitter, where activists have their own – individual and collective – profiles, seem to be at the centre of the activists' activities. The practice of sustaining connections, then, assigns a place of primary importance to this type of digital media.

Our research revealed that the activities associated with this practice have a dual nature. Some of these conversations may potentially involve large audiences, for example when activists interact with other people through comments under a Facebook or Instagram post or replies and retweets on Twitter. However, not all communicative exchanges that activists engage with are visible and accessible to everyone: many are visible only to those people with whom activists are interacting. These activities happen away from public scrutiny. We are referring to text messages over the phone, internal chats within social media platforms, instant messaging apps, emails, and so forth. In short, if on the one hand, we have data sequences that are, at least in principle, visible to all those who visit social media platforms, on the other hand, we are dealing with data sequences that are not accessible to all and remain hidden precisely from those who do not interact with activists. In fact, the data stream has neither a predominantly public nor a completely private nature; this implies that activists sometimes manage the data stream before everyone's eyes, while other times they do so in the background of their daily political work.

In the context of a continued ping-pong movement between the public and private sides of politics, activists spend a significant amount of time engaging with their more distant potential supporters and people who are simply interested in the same contentious issue that activists also care about. The magnitude of these communicative exchanges is not fixed. Deciding to relate with an undefined and widespread variety of people, day after day, is the direct consequence of choices involving the communicative structure of a movement organization: using a social media platform like Facebook, which allows interactions among users; relying mostly on the organization's website to offer users an opportunity to comment on its content; making the organization's email address public – all are decisions that can either increase or decrease the points of contact between activists and the various actors with whom their movement organization interacts. At the same time, choosing one communication channel over another leads the movement organization to develop contacts with this or that type of actor. Finally, by making these choices, movement organizations play an active role in supporting the production of certain data sequences as opposed to others. When movement organizations choose to prioritize the production of data sequences that are characterized by high intensity, like those tied to social media platforms, they are next faced with the challenge of managing large amounts of data in the most effective way. This is a very important issue in the context of the practice of establishing meaningful connections with various types of actors, because the ability to manage these data is directly linked to the ability to interact fruitfully with other actors, external to the movement organization and its coalitions.

According to our research, there are three main ways in which activists deal with this challenge: they may decide to ignore the most intense data sequences, seek to address them in their entirety, or only deal with those they deem most relevant. A lot depends on the number of messages that they receive on different media-related services. Thus, a movement organization could receive inputs on one or more email accounts, on different social media platforms (for example Facebook, Twitter, or Instagram), and on instant messaging apps (for example WhatsApp or Telegram), to cite the most recurring services mentioned in the interviews. Furthermore, it may be contacted through both its collective account and the personal accounts of its members, hence generating the same tension between the voice of individual activists and that of the collective movement organization that we have seen in previous chapters. All these inputs produce data sequences that, compared to the movement organizations' ability to deal with them, are so intense in their volume and velocity that the activists' ability to perform the practice of sustaining connections decreases considerably. As we will see in the rest of this section, this situation occurs when activists perform this practice both in public – in front of large audiences – and through more private interactions that remain hidden from most people.

Sustaining connections through private interactions

The data sequences that activists deal with when engaging in private interactions with other actors have a twofold, and partially contradicting, nature. On the one hand, these messages generate a lot of "noise". As Miranda explained in the opening section of this chapter, this means that they are no more than persistent disturbing factors for movement organizations' activities. On the other hand, they allow activists to engage in deeper daily interactions with potential sympathizers, providing all the detailed, precise, and personalized information that they may demand. As Ivan said during his interview,

> 'We only receive messages on Facebook [through Messenger], we receive that. They are not public. We reply to them because they are related to what we do. They mostly need information: "How can I find you, what happened with this, do you have any news of that?" You know, this kind of stuff.'

This extract suggests that private chats on social media accounts demand concrete interventions that are handled with due care and attention. Together with social media chats and instant messaging apps, activists have to handle another relevant data sequence that seems to have strategic relevance for the movement organizations that we investigated in the three countries: that which revolves around the writing, reception, and answering of emails. Activists in Greece, Italy, and Spain all pointed to emails as one of the most significant means of interaction with other actors. Taking care of emails coming from potential sympathizers and bystanders is important to create new interactions and nurture existing ones. In turn, when activists rely on emails to perform the practice of gaining connection, they are also giving an image of availability and responsiveness, in contrast to those of prominent political or media figures who rarely answer the messages they receive through emails or social media platforms (Nothalft, 2017). The grassroots association of Simona – who is well aware of these dynamics – is very zealous and diligent in not leaving any email message unprocessed:

> 'If you email our president, she emails you back. That amazes a lot of people. It especially amazes politicians. If you write to me, I write back.

If you write to leading national trade unionists or call them, they do not answer you. It would never occur to us to do something like that.'

This is one of the main traits that distinguish activists from certain prominent political or media actors: being (almost) always accessible and giving feedback. However, this openness can also lead to difficulties. An overload of interaction demands, a strategic resource that activists could not rely on before the spread of digital media, may result in the activists being overwhelmed.

Furthermore, differences between the various digital services and devices may become less relevant when activists have to deal with large amounts of data. According to Adrian, the boundaries across different digital platforms can become more and more blurred, resulting in the activists' inability to distinguish between interactions that happen via email, social media chats, instant messaging apps, and so forth, as if they were all on the same level:

'I think what bothers me a lot of times are the different ways in which people communicate with you. So I have a lot of people write me an email and I don't answer immediately; it maybe takes me a day or so to answer, but then I see they have written to me through Messenger, on Facebook, because they find you on Facebook and they write exactly the same thing for Messenger, and if they got your cell phone they would write exactly the same thing through WhatsApp or something. ... I have to open my email, I have to check WhatsApp, I have to check Telegram, I have to check Messenger, which I had uninstalled from my cell phone but I have had to install it again because a lot of people write through Messenger or Facebook and it's a pain in the ass, because I really don't like the app.'

As with other practices that we have discussed in previous chapters, one feature of the data stream appears to be problematic for activists. It is its heterogeneity that may prevent activists and their movement organizations from placing one type of media service at the centre of the practice to obtain meaningful connections, creating difficulties in the management of interactions with bystanders. This, as we will see, affects not only the activists' private interactions with the other actors they relate to but also those occasions in which the practice of sustaining meaningful connections is performed in public.

Sustaining connections through public interactions

A significant part of the practice of sustaining connections takes place also in public. Activists interact with bystanders and potential sympathizers through the comment section below content that activists and movement organizations publish on social media platforms like Facebook, Twitter, and Instagram. However, the interactive features of the movement organizations' websites often also allow activists to take care of such interactions in public. In this regard, Salvatore offers an example of a movement organization that has developed a sustainable strategy for handling all inputs received via different digital services, including the front-stage side of politics. His strategy is based on immediacy and full responsiveness:

> '[W]e interact a lot. In the sense that, when someone writes to us we immediately respond. They write to us for what? Or [they] ask for information, they also write to us in the form of a comment, or to comment. There may also be some criticism and we reply.'

The grassroots association in which Salvatore works as a communication manager is not very big, meaning that the amount of information they have to process is certainly significant, but not to the point of stressing his daily work at an unsustainable rate. This is, instead, the case of another Italian grassroots association involved in the fight against corruption to which Daniela belongs. She, for instance, explained how difficult yet important it is to identify a positive and sustainable way to handle all the comments that her association receives on different social media profiles. In this non-stop action of interacting with what people write on their social media walls, they achieve three main aims. They develop the skill of separating important information from "noise", deciding when and how to react to a specific category of comments. They eliminate part of this "noise", in particular when it takes the form of uncivil reactions. They accumulate this knowledge for a better reaction when the publication of certain content could result in a significant boost of responses from people in a short time frame. When this happens, Daniela gives one of her social media managers the task of moderating the comments they receive on their social media profiles, as emerges from the last part of the following interview extract.

> '[I]n fact, because of the internal organization of work, we know that if on Wednesday of that week one of our lobbying videos comes out, that afternoon, we have to give the social media manager 3 hours to reply. He must not be disturbed and must do that because it is very important and time-consuming.'

When this practice is performed in public, it cannot be left to chance; a wider audience than the actors involved in the interaction itself could see how the movement organization interacts with its sympathizers and bystanders. Moreover, other people can judge how a movement organization takes care of these interactions. The responses to a comment can give further information about the activities of one's movement organization. The style that activists use to give these responses unquestionably contributes to building the public image of the movement organization. Many of the activists we interviewed showed great awareness of this aspect, even if not all movement organizations under examination wanted to sustain connections or managed to create them in the same way.

Seen from this perspective, funded and structured movement organizations seem more capable of coping with the data stream, especially when the volume and velocity of the data sequences increase abruptly. Moreover, the more a movement organization improves its ability to activate attention within and outside digital environments, the more this will generate a larger amount of data to process, develop, sustain, and nurture interactions with people outside the movement organization. When this happens, activists recognize that it is essential for them to act: bystanders may not welcome a complete or significant lack of responsiveness. However, the bigger a movement organization becomes, the more resources it can rely on, even if this direct relationship between relevance and economic availability does not concern all organizations. In the likely case of having to generate more resources, this ability is not a sufficient condition for them to decide to manage this copious flow of digital data efficiently. Indeed, movement organizations also need to pursue the explicit goal of dealing with the pressing and incessant flow of digital data. Moreover, they need to acquire heterogeneous and multifaceted professional skills to do it at best. This last point is not insignificant: different digital platforms require different forms of expertise, such as the ability to answer an email rather than a Facebook comment and vice versa. Indeed, professional management of the practice of sustaining connections when dealing with bystanders within popular digital environments cannot be improvised. It demands diverse and skilled professional figures who are not easy to identify and instruct, and who are – most of all – indispensable. Very often, activists either have the money to hire these professional figures or simply limit themselves to highly inefficient handling of digital data when these come in the form of a massive flow.

Writing on smartphones to keep connections alive

Although focusing on different kinds of actors, the previous sections have described how activists need to master the ability to meet someone in person and exchange messages in those digital environments where personal and physical presence is not required. Regarding the latter type of communicative exchange, our investigation reveals a very complex scenario in all three countries under examination. A primary, unexpected trend nonetheless seems to emerge: the centrality of writing through smartphones in the attempt to keep connections alive. Activists continuously type on their smartphones and in their everyday routine, they mainly exchange information through written forms of communication. They do this regardless of the fact that the devices they use can easily support phone calls, voice messages, and other oral forms of communication. Nevertheless, when sustaining this specific practice, smartphones are not the only device that activists carry in their pockets or keep on their tables. Activists also extensively rely on other technological devices – such as laptops – to keep strategic connections alive. Alternating these different devices, they mainly perform their political activities through their personal email while exchanging messages through individual chats on WhatsApp and, sometimes, making phone calls. Although the latter is still a relevant way of staying in touch with people, activists put media technologies that support written exchanges at the centre of the practice of sustaining connections. The activities of checking and replying to messages received from a variety of people – be they fellow activists or the movement organizations' supporters – seem to occupy most of the time that activists devote to the practice of sustaining connections. As we will see in what follows, reading and writing skills are highly relevant in the framework of this practice, since most of the time activists deal with written messages instead of phone calls or audio messages.

Emails play a central role in the three countries. Although research on this specific form of written communication suggests that it is 'less valuable for building and sustaining close social relationships than face-to-face contact and telephone conversations' (Cummings et al, 2002: 103), the activists we interviewed greatly value email messages, putting them at the centre of the practice of sustaining connections.

As to the countries' peculiarities, consistently with what we have already seen in previous chapters, we found that activists in Italy make a stronger association between WhatsApp and the practice of sustaining connections. Compared to emails, WhatsApp tends to give a conversation an intimate tone, for example when people use emojis or a colloquial style (Dodds, 2019). At times, activists need to adopt a warmer and more intimate style of communication to trigger that trustful relationship that is so fundamental for nurturing a specific, long-term connection with another social or political actor. This applies to both everyday non-political relations (Baxter, 2018) and more political ones, such as the interactions among social movements' participants (della Porta and Diani, 2020).

Instant messaging apps like WhatsApp also characterize the practice of sustaining connections in Spain and Greece, albeit on a less significant scale. Talking precisely about WhatsApp, Adrian, a Spanish activist, made an interesting consideration. During his interview, the activist focused on the relationship between different modalities of mediated communication, such as writing text messages versus talking on the phone. He meticulously explained how his massive daily use of WhatsApp has resulted in his relationships with other social, political, or media actors now being based on text messages only. He got rid of vocal conversations almost entirely; chats have replaced phone calls.

> 'Phone calls are … rarer every time. People don't call you anymore, which is good. They write messages … So I think there was a time in which we called each other a lot more, and I think through WhatsApp and all these tools we don't call so much anymore, so I think calling someone gets serious. It's like, "ok, I need to call this person". And I mean, I don't write a message or an email or something.'

Many of the activists we interviewed spoke about a similar experience in terms of the overall dismissal of phone calls because of the widespread use of text messages, as we also pointed out in Chapter 5, devoted to the practice of political organizing. Consistently, Lenhart (2012) pointed out that a general trend in favour of written forms of communication had already begun in the second decade of the twenty-first century, limiting phone calls mainly to the extraordinary moments of one's life. For activists, this switch implies different consequences and challenges, which we will discuss in the remainder of this section.

As in the case of other practices, the use of a specific digital media device often affects the time of grassroots politics. In this case, the extensive employment of instant messaging services like WhatsApp shapes the timing of communication. Writing, instead of calling someone over the phone, does not require synchronism. This frees the recipient of the message from the imperative to immediately respond to the sender, as would be the case with a phone call. As a result, WhatsApp and similar services have pushed phone calls to the sideline. According to many of the activists we interviewed, a communicative exchange among two actors that is pivoted on the use of an instant messaging app implies a sense of protection of, and even respect for, their counterpart in the interaction, as studies on the use of various communication services have also demonstrated (Rettie, 2007). Simona underlines this aspect in the following extract:

> 'If someone calls me and it's something interesting, I'll even talk to them on the phone. [But] me having to phone someone, no. I hate that stuff: I feel like I'm disturbing them. I never know if they're doing something … Before I call, if they're not a friend of mine, I send a WhatsApp: "Can I call you?" … I find [the phone call] an aggressive way to communicate: you force the person you call to talk to you.'

If phone calls are considered too invasive, or even aggressive, as Simona claims, it is natural that activists consider messages written via instant messaging services a more discreet – and somehow gentle – way to develop their connections.

Finally, writing rather than calling also affects the pleasure, habit, and emotional involvement that a particular form of communication can elicit. For instance, Simona said that she hates "talking to people on the phone. I avoid the phone if I can. Maybe because I also write a lot for my work, and so I prefer writing". Some activists may therefore consider it much more enjoyable to pivot their relationship with another activist, journalist, policy maker, or supporter on written rather than oral communication, or the other way around. This is not a secondary aspect. The practice of sustaining connections demands an investment of time to accomplish it at best; to do so through a form of communication that puts activists at ease helps them to live their activism with far more enthusiasm.

Conclusion

In this chapter, we have cast light on the extent to which various types of digital media are interlaced with the activists' practice of sustaining connections with other actors both within and outside the social movement milieu. We have shown that activists mostly rely on three types of connections: those with fellow activists who belong to other movement organizations and other political actors who can support them as allies in the arena of institutional politics; those with people who actively support movement organizations although they are not necessarily part of them in any formal way; and, those with the even more dispersed ensemble of bystanders (that is potential sympathizers or just curious people) who randomly interact with the activists' movement organizations. We have shown that, through its main activities, the practice of sustaining connections also changes depending on the actors that activists involve in it and, consequently, the type of digital and non-digital media that activists employ to perform them.

We have argued that when activists need to exchange information with relevant political and social actors, or with fellow members of their grassroots organization, they still see no better option than face-to-face communication. For them, there is no alternative than to meet in person, perhaps on a regular base and in a welcoming office. Activists value the possibility of looking an interlocutor in the eyes and sharing the same physical space because it increases their chances of turning the first contact with relevant actors into a fruitful relationship. From this viewpoint, the general understanding of physical spaces and the face-to-face encounters that happen in them is strongly related to the creation of trust between activists and those with whom they work more closely, being positioned outside the social movement milieu along with other fellow activists and potential allies.

By contrast, in its production of digital data sequences, the data stream takes on greater importance when activists seek to build and maintain relationships with their supporters, who are often dispersed throughout the territory and linked to the activists' organizations in varying ways. Again, we have nevertheless seen that some movement organizations favour face-to-face relationships at the expense of those mediated through digital media. Yet, most of the organizations we examined use at least a couple of digital media, which they see as an effective way to nurture the relationship with their supporters. Indeed, our interviewees often revealed a tendency precisely toward a practical combination of digital and face-to-face interactions, depending on the situation and the need of the moment. Once again, it is a matter of using the heterogeneous aspect of the data stream to one's advantage, carefully choosing among the different possibilities for interaction to get to know one's supporters better, connect with them, and strengthen the supporters' ties with the movement organization.

Additionally, we have discussed how activists also take care of daily engagements with that dispersed array of bystanders who enter into contact with activists' political fights for various reasons and, in some cases, even coincidentally. What characterizes the day-to-day management of the connections with this second type of actor is the fact that these connections could occur through somewhat private interactions – thanks to one-to-one messages – but also public exchanges that, instead, rely on a many-to-many flow of communication. In this case, the heterogeneity of the data stream is also reflected in the coexistence of data sequences that are virtually accessible to anyone and others that are available only outside public scrutiny. Activists relate to their supporters, sympathizers, and curious – or disturbing – citizens via email, in social media chats, or even on WhatsApp, but they also respond to public comments on digital platforms such as Facebook and Twitter, to mention only those they employ the most. Knowing how to alternatively and professionally manage the data sequences that are private and those that are, instead, public is therefore an essential skill for activists who want to sustain the practice of sustaining connections at best. Although we have highlighted the important role of face-to-face encounters in this process, we have also argued that digital writing skills must not be underestimated, in particular when there is no relevant political or social actor on the other side of the activists' screen. Indeed, when the latter engage in the practice of sustaining connections, they mainly do so by using a smartphone and typing on its keyboard. In other words, they connect with people through content that is communicated through writing.

Overall, the most important point that we have raised is the fact that movement organizations do not curate these interactions in a seemingly automatic manner. Activists need to devote attention to this practice and perform it through ad-hoc activities that recur systematically: reading messages, filtering them, and deciding how to reply to them are not random and episodic activities: they are interlinked; activists need to be aware of their consequences; and they require continuous attention and time. As with other practices that we have discussed in previous chapters, activists again rely on a general understanding of the digital media they employ and, additionally, the data sequences they generate. For instance, they know that adapting to the fast pace of social media platforms like Facebook when connecting with their supporters may not be good for their internal decision-making processes, which they want to preserve in all their slowness. In other cases, activists strive to consistently and continuously process the data sequences that they deal with to keep existing connections alive and develop new ones from scratch. The main goal for activists is, therefore, to curate interactions that prefer speed to other features of the movement organizations they belong to.

When this happens, movement organizations may also need to rely on professional help, for example that of social media managers. In turn, this means that they need both economic and human resources to face the requests for interaction that they receive online through digital media services. Activists need to craft different ways of interacting online with the various types of actors they could enter into contact with, ranging from fellow activists who are part of movement coalitions to those bystanders who have casual encounters with the activists' organizations. Some of these actors could be reached more easily through a strategic reply on Twitter or a quick message via Facebook Messenger, email, or SMS, not to mention oral forms of communication either mediated by technology (for example phone calls) or free from any technological interference (for example physical encounters). What matters here is the fact that different ways of communicating need distinctive skills that a single activist, whether they are paid for this activity or not, is usually not able to fulfil alone. Hence, the resources that movement organizations may invest in the practice of sustaining connections are relevant, especially when they are embedded in various types of digital media, some of which have the effect of quickly multiplying the activists' interactions with sympathizers, bystanders, and even curious people who casually enter into contact with the activists' organizations.

To conclude, in this chapter we have shown how the practice of sustaining connections with other actors can take on different meanings depending on the types of digital – or non-digital – media that activists use. However, when talking about media, we have left out one of the most important connections for activists: that with journalists working for legacy media, who are therefore particularly crucial in giving (or not) visibility to the activities of the movement organizations in which the activists we interviewed are embedded. The next chapter addresses this very issue, focusing on the practice of sustaining connections from the perspective of the not always easy relationship between activists and journalists.

7

The Fragile Interactions Between Activists and Journalists

Anna is an Italian freelance journalist who works in Rome. The national newspaper she works for pays her per piece. This means that if she does not write anything, she receives no money. What is worse, she may write something and still not get paid; if her piece is not published, it has been a waste of time and, more importantly, a decrease in her monthly income, which is never stable or certain. To face such uncertainty, she needs to juggle multiple jobs. Until a few years ago, she collaborated with a notorious Italian magazine, curating a blog on its website. Initially, the magazine paid her €400 per month, but this amount steadily declined; toward the end of her collaboration, she had to curate the blog for free. The magazine's rationale behind this decision was that Anna had gained visibility thanks to the blog and that this should be enough of a payment for her. One day, she diplomatically criticized a cover page of that same magazine on her Facebook profile. A few days later, "I do not know how, but that Facebook post I published arrived on the desk of the magazine's director, who did not like it at all and decided to close my blog." Although Anna lost her unpaid collaboration with the magazine owing to a post on Facebook, she says she cannot do without the social media platform:

> 'I often use Facebook to do an investigative report. For example, I had to do one on graduates who have converted to more practical activities: the journalist who started as a pizza maker, the philosopher as a pastry chef. So I go to my personal profile on Facebook and I ask my Facebook friends: "Does anyone know any graduates who have converted to something different?" In my work, finding and building the news, I launch pleas [and] requests for help. All journalists do it.'

For Anna, Facebook is not only a place to get information, but also an occasion to promote herself and the news pieces she publishes elsewhere.

However, the promotion phase does not end with Facebook: "When I have finished writing all my articles, the second step is to always promote them using different types of communicative environments." Anna does so through her own website and a Twitter profile. As a freelancer, this second step is crucial for her. Not having a fixed contract, hence no regular income, she needs to disseminate her pieces and build her journalistic brand to increase the chances of being hired by other media companies and having her pieces published – in other words, getting paid. However, gaining visibility through a personal website, Facebook, or Twitter requires having the time to manage all these different media channels, and time is both a precious and scarce resource for a freelance journalist:

> 'I take very little care of my personal website, because I don't have much time to do it. And there is another thing that I should do better: to also publish my pieces on Facebook or Twitter. To be honest, I publish on Facebook and Twitter whatever I write on my blogs. But I don't do this with the necessary perseverance. I do it randomly, when I have the time to do it, when I have the energy.'

Even when journalists would prefer not to engage in such promotional activities, they still have a strong incentive to engage in personal strategies to increase their visibility when they work freelance, without a fixed contract. The degree, heterogeneity, and magnitude of these strategies may vary depending on personal choices. What remains fairly stable is the precariousness of journalists, which is closely linked to another factor: new forms of newsroom routines and the different working relationships and lifestyles of freelance journalists compared to those on permanent contracts.

Again, Anna's case is emblematic. Since she is a freelance journalist, she almost always works outside a newsroom, something that she dislikes because it increases the distance between her and those who, instead, work inside newsrooms and in more stable positions. With newsrooms increasingly relying on freelance journalists, this distinct dichotomy between an in-group and an out-group of journalists is common in the print press as well as other news-making outlets. In this regard, literature focusing on journalists and their working conditions considers the growth of unregulated and precarious freelance journalists among the journalistic workforce as one of the main factors that determine a sharp decline in the quality of journalistic output. Despite some notable exceptions, journalism today is less about hard news and the in-depth investigation that goes with it, and more about soft, lifestyle news, with entertainment content, style and logic increasingly blending with those of journalistic information (Reinemann et al, 2012; Otto et al, 2017).

In short, Anna's precarious working conditions and her irregular interactions with colleagues who work in the newsrooms of the national newspapers she freelances for put her in a difficult professional position. However, there is at least one aspect of her work that Anna values to a great extent: the relatively high level of freedom that she enjoys when writing her news pieces. She can cover any issue she wants to, with the angle she favours. This is not a common feature among journalists in Greece, Italy, and Spain, where the journalistic profession traditionally has strong connections with the realm of institutional politics (Hallin and Mancini, 2004). As Anna told us, the national newspaper she works for:

> 'is the only newspaper where you do not receive any kind of pressure from your superiors and you can write whatever you want. You can conduct all the investigative reports you want, on anything you want. The absurd thing is that every newspaper has frightening conflicts of interest. My newspaper has no conflicts of interest. You can write investigative reports that you can hardly ever write elsewhere and this gives you absolute freedom. This is very remarkable ... I feel totally free, I can really write what I want and have to say.'

However, the experience Anna shared with us is not very common in Southern Europe, where not even the flourishing of new online-only news media outlets – or the more general advent of the Internet and digital media – has managed to undermine the strong links between the political and journalistic realms, as our interviews with experts in Greece, Italy, and Spain also suggest.

Drawing on these premises, this chapter examines how activists engage in the practice of sustaining connections with journalists in the quiet times of politics, that is, when they struggle more to attract the attention of news media outlets because they are not engaged in any form of public protest. Activists deal with the data stream from at least two viewpoints when it comes to their relationship with journalists. On the one hand, they need to gather data on journalists: how they work and what features characterize the news-making routines of the news organizations they work for. As Charlotte Ryan (1991) illustrated when writing about activists' television coverage in the United States, their knowledge of how journalists write news stories, when they do it, and through which format is vital to increase the likelihood of getting media coverage from mainstream media. Gathering data on how the news-making process works is even more important today, as journalists also interact with a large number of digital media services and devices to make their work visible, connect with others, and collect data for their news pieces. On the other hand, activists aim at becoming stable data sources for journalists, and this is particularly relevant when they are not in the streets. When public protest fails to gain the attention of journalists because there isn't any massive public disruption that they see as newsworthy in itself, activists seek to produce data about the contentious issue they care about, transforming them in ways that can be attractive to news organizations and feeding them to journalists. In a sense, then, activists and their movement organizations seek to credit themselves as reliable data sources to whom journalists will automatically refer when writing about this or that social problem.

Activists, though, face important challenges when it comes to establishing and nurturing stable connections with journalists, as we will see later in this chapter. In the next section, we will look more closely at the political parallelism between media and political systems in countries such as Greece, Italy, and Spain (Hallin and Mancini, 2004). We argue that activists have to take into serious consideration certain values that are deeply rooted in the journalistic profession as it developed in Southern European countries from its inception, with journalists frequently defending partisan viewpoints when reporting on events. In countries like Greece, Italy, and Spain, journalists frequently fight alongside specific political actors, who may even own the media organizations they work for. They thus advocate a partial view of the world or system of values, up to the point of being associated and identified with a specific political party. In countries with a high level of political parallelism, journalists do not traditionally behave as watchdogs of power who are detached from any form of political affiliation. Rather, they are like soldiers in a clear political line-up. This contextual feature of the three countries examined in this book poses a threat to activists. At the same time, however, this chapter will also show how activists try to take advantage of political parallelism without succumbing to it.

Then, we will consider the increasing precariousness that affects the journalistic profession. Today, a significant portion of journalists work freelance – hence without any stable or fixed contracts – in a media company, whether it is a newspaper, a radio, a television channel, or an online-only news website. These journalists usually do their job without ever entering the buildings where their companies' newsrooms are located; they work from home, instead. Or they work from the tables of bars and cafeterias, equipped with no more than a laptop, a smartphone, and an Internet connection. They are often forced to work non-stop, including at weekends and overnight, to secure a decent and satisfactory salary at the end of each month. This ongoing transformation within journalism has important consequences for activists; most of the time, activists relate to this type of (precarious) journalist and this is why activists have to be fully aware of precarious journalists' practices and routines. Activists need to know that a specific freelancer may work every night from 10 pm onwards at the table of a posh bar located close to the buildings of power in their country's capital – just the right time and place for activists to build a fruitful relationship of mutual trust with this new type of journalist, who is becoming ever more common in the field of journalism.

Finally, we will discuss an important issue in the practice of establishing connections in the data stream: the security of data exchanges when journalists and activists interact. Although journalists have the deontological mandate to protect their sources of information, the exchange that happens through digital media can jeopardize the activists' information. Digital data sequences are, indeed, incredibly fragile in this regard, mainly when activists operate on a sensitive issue like corruption: activists seem to know that the practice of sustaining connections needs to be performed carefully in the age of widespread digital surveillance. However, in this section, we will illustrate how both activists and journalists have a different awareness of this issue depending on the country in which they live. Overall, the issue of data security is still largely unexplored when it comes to activists engaging with journalists. For instance, we still have scarce knowledge on the way activists face digital security when, on the other side of the screen, there is not a political actor, another grassroots activist, or a lay citizen, but a journalist. We have not yet built systematic scientific knowledge of the strategies that activists imagine and then perform to secure digital communication when they relate to journalists. Moreover, if – as we have already observed in previous chapters – the Italian activists are those who care less about digital security, it is highly important to understand what happens when Italian activists relate to journalists online, in particular in comparison with their Greek and Spanish counterparts.

Activists and the political ties of journalists

As we have also illustrated in Chapter 3, political parallelism remains a relevant feature in activists' general understanding of how journalists are linked to the realm of institutional politics. Activists, indeed, can identify the political leaning of journalists, usually at first sight. Indeed, Southern European journalists are usually well aware of their partisanship. They do not believe journalism means providing neutral and – as much as possible – objective information to citizens. It instead entails taking a side: fighting for that political component of society they support. It is no coincidence that Simone, one of the Italian journalists we interviewed, stressed his political belonging to and partisan role in society, owing to his belief that "partisanship is an ambivalent concept. It can be used both in negative-derogatory terms and in terms of being and belonging to a part, and taking the side of a specific part is the first way to be political in life, as it is in journalism". Such a specific understanding of what partisanship and journalism are leads Simone to think and assume that, as a journalist, he is doing and *has to do* a partisan job. For him, strong partisanship is a natural consequence and inner characteristic of his professional identity as a journalist.

Following this mindset, Simone has a privileged and direct, daily connection with certain political actors, while others fall completely out of his network. Furthermore, working for a well-known printed newspaper, he is a reliable and influential point of reference for many grassroots organizations sharing his political views, attitudes, and values. More than a simple gatekeeper of information and a news provider, Simone is perceived as a political actor, one able to strongly affect the political elaboration of the politically closest activists he interacts with. As he revealed to us,

> 'No one tells me what to say. I was the one who contributed to and formulated a course of action for a social movement ... The possibility that a newspaper like mine gives you is to stay inside the social movements, to discuss things with them, to give back to social movements as much as possible ... to guide them. To make them understand the news and what happens in their community. But writing for my newspaper also allows me to affect the keywords and frames that social movements adopt, and even their general political purposes.'

As his words denote, Simone does not act as the mere megaphone of certain grassroots organizations; he is also part of them. He has daily, intense contact with activists, up to the point of being one of their most prominent figures with strong material as well as symbolic power within different grassroots organizations. This is particularly true in the case of those legacy media that openly follow a specific political line, and that at times develop a strong relationship with those movement organizations that share a similar political alignment, hence becoming 'sympathetic media' for activists (Mattoni, 2012, 2017a).

This very deep-rooted interconnection between journalists and political actors also emerged during our interviews with Greek and Spanish activists. Even in these Southern European countries, activists know very well what the rules of the game are and how the entrenched bond between media and politics works and is materially and symbolically structured. They know how helpful it is to have a 'very close friend' in a journalistic newsroom, regardless of whether they work in older media companies or new online-only media outlets. This friendship can have different forms, causes, and levels of intensity. There are journalists with whom activists share a specific view of the world (Ceron and Splendore, 2018) and others with whom they nurture a historical relationship of friendship because they have known them since their school days or met them in those informal events so important for networking tasks – relaxing moments that end with a beer in a pub talking about anything but politics until three in the morning. In this second case, a geographical factor enters into action. These types of connections can be built only when political and media actors share the same geography of power, that is, the same physical places of power (usually a country's capital city). Activists perceive and know this aspect rather well, in particular when they live outside the so-called bubbles (that is Rome, Madrid, or Athens) and feel excluded by them. Ruben, a Spanish activist who lives in Barcelona and, therefore, outside the "Madrid bubble", explains what not living in Madrid means for his movement organization:

> 'There is something called the M-30, which is the Madrid ring road. The M-30 should not be studied at the urban level, nor should it be studied geographically. It must be studied at the psychiatric level. It's an M-30 syndrome. So, we really shouldn't use an expression like "national level" or "state level". We should rather use an expression like the "Madrid Level". And the people that appear on TV and that we have to watch in the whole of Spain are all people from Madrid. And they only talk to each other, too. Such people only talk to newspaper editors, … a specific newspaper editor only talks to parliamentary leaders, while the rest of the country is getting the country going. These kinds of relations would be understandable in a country like France, because Paris is very big, but Madrid is not that big. Spain is not Madrid.'

At the same time, Miranda, an activist who *is* based in Madrid, made the following suggestion:

> 'I suppose that if you are outside Madrid then you feel some isolation because we are in the center … The way I get information and spread information is what I have been doing all these years, so I know people and people know me. If I go to Barcelona, for example, I know people, but not so many people, that's true.'

She is well aware of the importance of staying very close to the centres of power, even in the era of ubiquitous communication and the progressive digitalization of society. Indeed, if being out of this bubble equals exclusion, being in it means a higher chance for a grassroots organization to establish fruitful connections with media actors and (hopefully) reach positive media coverage. In line with Ruben's and Miranda's words, the case of the following Greek activist also attests to the importance of living, operating, and campaigning in the capital city of his country. As Ivan told us,

> 'there are people that we know, because they work with media that are closer to our political views. So we know them, we find

them everywhere; they might even contact us if they want to create something. Some of them are also part of our political organization, I mean, the general political organization, ... others may be closer, you know. So this is ... I think it's obvious.'

These last three interview extracts raise a relevant consideration: the blend between media and politics in Southern European countries is well structured also at the grassroots level, hence not only at an institutional one. It implies that the interconnections between political parties and the main national news media outlets, both in their older and newer digital formats, do not embrace the whole phenomenon of political parallelism in a certain country alone. Indeed, activists are conscious of how their respective national media system works, so they know that they live in countries in which political parallelism is one of the main structural forces shaping the relationships between political and media actors; they act accordingly, although this becomes difficult when, for example, they operate far from the centres of power in which those close relationships take place. Therefore, they may try to exploit the structural dynamics of journalism to gain the media coverage they harshly strive for as well as to become data sources that are stabler and considered reliable also because of the connections they have managed to establish with a given journalist.

However, political parallelism very often works as a constraining structure that does not favour social movements. If seen from a broader perspective, high levels of political parallelism imply that other kinds of political actors, such as elected officials or professional lobbyists, also exert an influence over journalists, regularly surpassing activists thanks to the greater symbolic and political resources they can rely on. More than benefiting from the potential of political parallelism to influence how and how often different media outlets cover their political stances, grassroots organizations are more frequently silenced by it (Prentoulis and Kyriakidou, 2019). Although political parallelism remains a debated subject of scientific inquiry (van der Pas et al, 2017; Nechushtai, 2018), the ongoing processes of digitalization and datafication in our societies do not appear to have weakened the closely interconnected relationship between media and politics. While scholarly literature is still investigating the extent to which digital media currently influence the role and characteristics of political parallelism (Mattoni and Ceccobelli, 2018), our interviews strongly indicate that, rather than diminishing political parallelism, digital media are actually reinforcing the entrenched links between media and politics in Greece, Italy, and Spain. According to Flavio, an Italian digital entrepreneur and expert in the field of political communication in Italy, digital media:

'Revealed [political parallelism]. This specific type of parallelism was quite evident to political and media insiders. It was not evident to the general public. The Internet has unveiled it; it has unveiled it to the general public. It has unveiled the fact that there is a mixture between these two worlds, [these] somehow also unhealthy [worlds], which leads publishers to develop an interest in politics, publishers to develop an interest in some fields of the economy, and journalists to basically lend themselves to this type of media coverage and support of interests.'

Adrian, an activist based in Spain, also asserted that: "we don't make any difference between printed newspapers and digital newspapers, but we make a difference between 'friends-media', which are normally the more radical projects, and mainstream media".

The main difference in the interconnections between media and politics is not to be located at the level of digital versus paper, or mainstream versus new online-only news media. Rather, it is *still* at the level of "friend vs non-friend" news media, to use Adrian's words. There are media outlets in which it makes sense to invest time and energy if one wants to build a relationship of trust. In other cases, this would imply nothing more than a waste of time. The reason lies in the fact that, when there is a high level of political parallelism, newsworthiness is not the only criterion shaping news-making processes. Instead, it is the source that produces potential news, like someone with whom journalists share a specific political view of the world. As Agata, an Italian activist working on corruption, told us during her interview, "depending on what the position and the tendency of a given media outlet are, their interest in our issues is consequently different. We try to communicate to the whole range of media, but we have realized that some newspapers are more receptive to what we communicate and who we are, others far less".

What activists say is not newsworthy per se. At times, it is newsworthy only for specific media outlets, but again, this does not appear to be a novelty for Southern European social movements. Greek, Italian, and Spanish activists are conscious of the fact that specific information they produce may be transformed into a news item, hence in visibility, only by a specific portion of a national press sector: the news portals that are ideologically close to their world views. Still, this is only the first challenge they have to face when approaching journalists; the second one is the increasing precariousness of the profession of journalism in the present day. A topic we discuss in the next section.

Activists and the increasing precariousness within journalism

As we have already suggested earlier, activists need to face another serious challenge when trying to establish a fruitful and long-standing relationship of mutual trust with journalists: the increasing level of precariousness affecting the field of journalism. This is not a minor challenge, since it requires a complete and substantial reconsideration and adaptation of their strategies aimed at establishing and then maintaining meaningful and relevant connections with journalists. The high level of precariousness that journalists experience within their job has, in fact, deep and significant effects on their daily professional as well as private life, including how they relate to technological innovations such as digital media: for example, the much more intense use of social media by freelancers for purposes of personal branding (Hedman and Djerf-Pierre, 2013). The history of journalism is deeply tied to precariousness (Örnebring, 2020), and journalism in non-Western countries suffers from a widespread precariousness in the overall work context of journalism (Matthews and Onyemaobi, 2020). However, according to recent studies on journalism in Western countries, newsrooms that in the past decade revolved around a permanent journalistic workforce today increasingly count on the work of temporary journalists, who often work as external freelancers or on short-term contracts for newspapers and other news media outlets (Deuze, 2007). Such working conditions have an impact on the content that journalists are willing and able to produce; thus, they may avoid writing pieces that could have legal consequences or focus on quickly produced stories rather than on investigative journalism (Hayes and Silke, 2019). Furthermore, recent research conducted in Italy (Casula, 2021) and Spain (Marín-Sanchiz et al, 2021) suggests that this situation has led to increased uncertainty among the journalistic workforce. There is a progressive increase in the number of freelance journalists who make up the entire workforce of contemporary media outlets. Owing to different, mostly systemic factors (Paulussen, 2012; Ekdale et al, 2014), nowadays the majority of media companies – both online and offline – employ freelancers who cover a significant part, if not the entirety, of the whole newsroom (Gollmitzer, 2014; Örnebring and Conill, 2016).

The journalists who participated in our study frequently reflected on the various difficulties they face in their lives: in particular, the daily struggle to do their job at their best, especially when working in a condition of precarity. Some of the journalists we talked with explained to us that their condition of precariousness has a direct, negative effect on how they practice their profession on a daily basis. We are referring to their perennial search for pieces allowing them to collect that minimum amount of money they need to make ends meet. At times, they argued, this translates into their conscious choice to lower the level of professionalism of their work, an effect of the precariousness of journalism that has already been identified in existing research on this topic (Standing, 2011; Lee-Wright, 2012, Cohen et al, 2019), even though this does not appear to be recurrent and common behaviour among the group of journalists we engaged with. Indeed, during our interviews with journalists, we were told that it can happen that journalists translate and paraphrase newspaper articles from international outlets, only half-heartedly mentioning their source of information.

At the same time, journalists' perpetual and inescapable state of precariousness means that they offer a 24/7 availability to any potential source, which puts them in the position to then propose their piece to different, sometimes multiple, media outlets. Most of the time, this occurs thanks to a specific technological device: their smartphone. It is therefore the norm that precarious journalists do not have a clear-cut division between their private and professional identities, owing also to the lack of a physical distinction between the two. Most of the time, the home is the office of precarious journalists. Mario, another Italian precarious journalist, confirmed this substantial overlap between his professional and private life in his work as a freelance journalist: "I mostly work from home. I call people from home, I write my pieces from home, I propose my pieces from home."

Given that journalism is taking a turn in this direction and a significant amount of journalists are embodying this type of daily routine, the increasing precariousness affecting journalism is becoming more than a challenge for activists, who are well aware of the changes occurring in the field of journalism. For instance, the following words of Federico, an Italian unionist mainly operating in a small Italian city, reveal full awareness of the state of journalism in his country, a perception that also emerged from our interviews with activists in Greece and Spain:

> 'Today there are a lot of young people who want to do this job, who are exploited in a crazy way, who live in a condition of absolute precariousness without having any certainty for the future. So what do they do? They try to collect news and pieces of information as much as possible, even poorly in terms of the quality of information. They write to get those €25 per piece, which is what some newspapers pay them for their work. These young journalists very often write incorrect things in their pieces, just to make a scoop. This is when things go wrong.'

In their effort to build and then maintain trustful and long-lasting connections with journalists, activists need to enter into contact with this specific routine of precarious journalists. As the extracts from the interviews with Anna and Mario indicate, theirs is a daily routine that foresees total availability, which is often guaranteed by the continuous and constant recourse to the smartphone as a crucial work tool – one that some journalists even prefer to face-to-face forms of communication. Overloaded by an incessant and voracious hunt for new pieces, precarious journalists usually consider physical encounters a simple waste of time that can be easily replaced by a phone call, an email, a message on WhatsApp, and so forth.

To conclude, other than political parallelism, activists also have to deal with a second challenge: the increasing precariousness that is transforming the daily life of a significant portion of journalists. This challenge forces activists to adapt to the messy and chaotic routine suffered by precarious journalists and develop a strategy to obtain what they need: media visibility. Before looking into the concrete strategies that activists employ so as to tackle these two challenges, let us first zoom in on a third and final challenge that activists encounter when trying to establish fruitful and meaningful connections with journalists: data security.

The hidden threats of digital media: data security

In our investigation, we have identified a third challenge that strongly shapes the daily interactions between journalists and activists: the level of attention that both devote to securing their communication, in particular when it is mediated by a particular device or digital platform. In fact, when engaging with each other, activists and journalists may feel the need to take precautions. At times, third parties are keen to get access to the information they exchange, and some technological devices and/or media-related services that they decide to employ do not give them the desired level of security. However, activists and journalists should *both* know how to avoid third parties jumping secretly into their conversations. When digital security is at stake, they work as a unique chain in which no single link can function as a weak point. If, while engaging digitally with journalists, activists take precautions to make this communication secure but their counterparts do not, then all their efforts may be in vain. A third party that wishes to spy on activists' communication could simply exploit the weak link in their digital communication – in this hypothetical case, journalists who do not care about digital security – without leaving any traces. This entails that when a communicative exchange between activists and journalists occurs it is not enough to consider how the former face and master the issue of digital security. It is also fundamental to take into due consideration whether and eventually how the other link in this chain, namely journalists, behave in order to avoid unwelcome guests secretly accessing the content of this communication.

In Chapter 5 devoted to the practice of political organizing, we have already paid special attention to the notions of security and surveillance as perceived and experienced by activists when sustaining other practices. We have pointed out that Italian, Spanish, and Greek activists do not approach those topics in the same way, as the following extracts from interviews with Nestor and

Photios from Greece, and Marcos from Spain – all journalists – mirror the positions of Greek and Spanish activists that we have already identified:

> '[The level of security] depends on the level of the query that I have to do. If it's an ordinary query … I call: "hey, how was that case closed? Was it filed?" Well, you can [then] do it. If it is more sensitive, [I send] an audio [message] by Signal. A self-destruct audio and they answer you. And if it is something very delicate: "We meet at 5 pm in the neighbourhood".'

> 'I do not use WhatsApp. Instead, Signal is a heavily cryptographic instant messaging application. It is the only one that Snowden himself recommends. It is best practice for someone being in journalism to deploy best practice, always. The point is that even Snowden uses Signal in order to communicate. I do not really use it, because nowadays I do not have the actual need to communicate with someone in such a heavily crypto way, because I do not do a lot of investigative reporting nowadays. But there is this tool that I do have, on my phone and computer, just in case I need to securely communicate with someone.'

> 'When I want a lot of privacy, I don't use any device. I remove the battery, and I prefer contacts like that, without mobiles. Sometimes I do stuff that could be dangerous. You should take precautions, but without exaggerating.'

By contrast, Italian journalists never mentioned instant-messaging apps like Signal in their interviews. Furthermore, when asked about privacy and surveillance, they answered saying things like "we will make something up", highlighting the lack of a structured and well-established behavioural routine when dealing with sensitive sources and information that was therefore replaced by improvisation. The following interview extract is a perfect example of how, according to our interviewees, Italian journalists approach issues of surveillance and digital security. When asked how he would handle a cryptographic message received from an anonymous source, Mario gave this reply: "I have a good friend who is an engineer. I call him and I use him to decipher anything. We can do it. We leave nothing behind: nothing is left aside. If things are interesting, we get them. We find the way."

Regardless of the will to solve a problem that is very complex for a journalist with no familiarity at all with cryptographic language, Mario makes unpredictable circumstances guiding him. He does not follow a set of well-rooted and established norms, rules, and routine practices, and his training as a journalist did not involve any updates on the issue of digital security, as the fact that he deals with sensitive sources would require. Displaying the same attitudes that we found among activists, the Italian journalists we interviewed also hardly care about surveillance, approaching it differently compared to their Spanish and Greek counterparts.

What, then, does this imply for the practice of sustaining connections related to the daily exchanges of information between activists and journalists? How does the fear of being spied on by an external actor affect the concrete daily choices of both journalists and activists when they need to enter into contact with each other and maintain a technology-mediated relationship of trust? Although these seem to be relevant concerns, the activists and journalists who participated in our study did not seem to engage too much with them. Even in the case of activists and journalists working on sensitive issues such as corruption, for whom we expected that the fear of surveillance would have been a constant and pressing concern, we rarely encountered cases of people defending themselves in any way against potential leaks within their technology-mediated conversations. As we have already made clear in previous chapters, differences across countries do occur, with Greece and Spain being much more advanced than Italy when it comes to data security. However, as a general trend, there is a lack of attention.

In some cases, this lack of attention seems to lead down dangerous roads. For instance, as we learn from our interviews, when high-risk subjects (for example *pentiti di mafia*, that is former members of the Italian mafia who collaborate with police authorities) contact journalists via Facebook Messenger and then give them very sensitive information that could put them, their beloved ones, and the police forces watching over their safety in serious personal danger. As Carla, a freelance journalist working on Italian mafia and corruption revealed to us,

'I was contacted by some *pentiti di mafia* on Facebook. They contacted me autonomously. I couldn't believe it. One with an anonymous identity, under a protection program: nobody has to know where they are! And he wanted to do an interview, with his name and all. It seemed crazy to me.'

As we have already mentioned, exceptions occur, but only among Greek and Spanish journalists. Even in those cases, the exceptions are not caused by systemic and structural choices and factors, such as established norms and rules within journalism or within the single journalistic organization in which journalists are employed (McGregor and Watkins, 2016); it is more the result of a single and, therefore, episodic personal approach. Thanks to a bottom-up demand for digital security, for example by different grassroots movement organizations that journalists regularly relate to, those technology-mediated conversations could escape surveillance also in Greece, Italy, and Spain. Activists may be those who sensitize journalists to issues of data security, refusing to communicate with them if not in very secure and safe digital environments. However, journalists may respond by no longer caring about the topics that the activists want them to cover, which leads to a lack of visibility for activists. Pressured to communicate via instant messaging apps such as Signal or through email systems with higher level of encryption, journalists could react with a sort of 'How boring!' or 'This is too complicated!' attitude, consequently deciding to devote their (limited) time and attention to different political actors.

In sum, along with enduring political parallelism and the increasing precariousness of journalism, the issue of digital security also poses a significant and pressing challenge for activists when they are working hard to activate and then keep alive relevant and meaningful connections with journalists. The next section discusses some of the concrete strategies that activists have employed in Greece, Italy, and Spain to face these challenges in an attempt to develop stable connections with journalists in the three countries.

Activists' concrete strategies for establishing connections with journalists

Before discussing how activists deal with political parallelism and the pervasive precariousness of the journalistic profession, it is worth remembering that activists have never been an influential or eminent source for journalists (Gitlin, 1980; Gamson and Wolfsfeld, 1993). An official declaration of a grassroots organization is rarely covered by mainstream media, even in the case of those media outlets closer to its political views. Activists have never had the same level of newsworthiness as a political party, a party leader, or even a simple parliamentarian. To merely play the game of political parallelism has never been enough for them, nor is it in the present. Furthermore, if it is true that precarious journalists – rather than traditional ones – may be much more predisposed to deal with activists in an attempt to collect interesting and newsworthy stories to then transform them into paid pieces, this is valid also for other social, economic, and political actors with more resources and a better organization, which may easily attract the attention of precarious journalists.

However, it is precisely the combination of these two challenges that makes activists look for the most effective activities for maintaining links with journalists. As our interviewees point out, these activities – when taken together – usually represent an intense, non-stop, and professional public relations ensemble of interactions, which are sometimes performed regardless of political parallelism. A good example comes from the interview with Miranda, the Spanish activist with whom we opened the previous chapter. Miranda knows very well that journalists nowadays have a routine characterized by a shortage of time and work overload owing to the pressing demand to produce a higher amount of news on a daily basis. Again, this appears to be particularly true for precarious journalists, who are rarely willing to leave their work desk to grasp that piece of information they could collect more easily, cheaply, and enjoyably in front of their computer screen. As Miranda said,

> 'When you say "I want to do a press conference", some of them say "really?" So what we do is to say "a breakfast conference". We invite them to have breakfast with us and then they feel like, "ok". Because [if] they do not want to come, they say something like "send me your press release, send me your audio, if you want, send me an email, a video, and that's it. I don't need to go".'

It goes without saying that political parallelism is no more than a starting point (in this case, Miranda and the journalists sharing a similar political view of the world), after which something more has to occur: giving the journalists "ready-made news", thus making them work a minimum amount of time. In other words, activists must make the necessary efforts so that journalists do not waste time, thus supporting their will not to leave their work desk.

These skills are detached from the relational and political dynamics that result from operating in a country with a high level of political parallelism. They are, instead, more related to news management and inside lobbying activities, as we have already pointed out in the previous chapter. What activists have to do is to (also) lobby their journalists. Yet, having friends in journalistic newsrooms is not enough for them to gain media coverage, especially a positive one. Activists also have to cuddle them, so to speak, as they try to do with their supporters and sympathizers. Jorge explicitly mentioned doing this during our chat:

> 'Sometimes we have these kinds of meetings when we find out that some journalist is coming, and he or she starts to say: "I really like what you guys do", and so on. So we start building a personal relationship with that person. And then sometimes I call in an informal way to take a coffee or something, in order to talk about us or what we are doing, and so on. But this is an informal level, rather than a very strategic and planned thing.'

Nevertheless, even though activists like Miranda or Jorge engage in activities that, in principle, may sustain the creation and management of meaningful connections with journalists, they sometimes fail to obtain the desired result. For instance, they end up wasting all the time they invested in constructing and cultivating those relations with journalists, failing to transform these into better, continuous, and likely positive media coverage in the media outlets that activists want to be aired on. Occasionally, all their efforts result in nothing more than a huge failure.

In other cases, though, the practice of sustaining connections takes another direction, as the case of Papios demonstrates. Papios is a leading member of a Greek grassroots association defending the rights of journalists. For this reason, he knows and has very close contact with hundreds of journalists. More than just former colleagues, these journalists are personal friends to him. Talking about his current role as an activist with a professional background in journalism, Papios highlighted the importance of having relations that transcend work-related practices and that are ingrained in the sphere of friendship. There are, in fact, some cases in which media coverage of his grassroots organization is highly necessary. What happens is that Papios just takes his phone and directly calls one of his *journalist friends*, asking for a personal favour: "It's personal. These are colleagues who worked together for 20, 30, 40 years. We know each other."

However, the depth, frequency, and strategic power of these relations of friendship with journalists are not the norm for the activists we interviewed in Greece, Italy, and Spain. Other than Papios, only very few activists admitted that they can play the card of friendship when engaging in the practice of sustaining connections with journalists. Conversely, the opposite happens if we look at our interviews with institutional actors; for them, to have more than one close friend in journalism seems to be very normal. Two good examples are those of Mauricio, a regional Spanish parliamentarian, and Dimitria, a member of a Greek government agency, who described their relationship with certain journalists in these terms:

> 'Sometimes I exchange messages with journalists who are closest at times; sometimes we have a more friendly relationship. They are friends rather than journalists.'

> '[B]ecause my previous job was at the Ministry of Economy, I have a group of people that I know very well, so I contacted them. They are my friends now. So I asked them to come to the presentation.'

What these extracts tell us, albeit indirectly, is that friendships between political institutional actors and journalists seldom blossom and flourish in front of a digital screen. It is more a matter of connections that individuals usually obtain at a young age – for example by going to the same high school – or by attending those very informal and sometimes even exclusive groups and events that require physical presence. Activists often lack or cannot rely on this kind of personal background or daily routine.

That said, even though activists cannot exploit their personal friendship with journalists, sometimes they nonetheless succeed in getting what they need from this relationship. They do so through a *do ut des* mechanism: they exchange favours with journalists. This is the case of Adrian, who described how he builds a connection with the press in the following way:

> '[W]e know that if we really want our videos to go viral, it is better to put them on two specific news media outlets at the national level. In other cases, they come to us and they ask us for help in researching something, because they know that we are closely connected to different people. So it always goes in both directions. We therefore go to them and ask them for favours, in terms of disseminating our stuff, or they come to us and ask for something. It's a two-sided relationship.'

This interview extract allows us to highlight a final feature that describes how activists create, handle, and nurture their connections with journalists. Adrian does not mention any journalist or personal contact in a specific newsroom; he just refers to a whole media organization. This suggests that he does not exchange favours with specific journalists, but with an entire press company. We consider this point relevant because, based on all the interviews we collected and thinking of the Italian freelance journalists with which we opened this chapter, we believe that what Adrian described in his interview is more an exception than the norm. Activists tend to relate to single journalists, not to whole newsrooms. When they rely on *do ut des* mechanisms, there is almost always a specific journalist involved. As Ruben, another Spanish activist, explicitly reported during his interview, "to be honest, we try to have contacts with journalists rather than with entire media organizations". Journalists work ever more as lone wolves. Hence, it is much easier for activists to relate to a single individual that they trust and can engage with every day, rather than to entire newsrooms. Their relationship is therefore a personal one, with all the pros and cons that come along with it. On the one side, building on one-to-one interactions, such personal relationships nurture a connection based on mutual trust. On the other side, though, depending too much on personal relationships seems to be a strong limit, especially if we consider the uncertain working conditions of precarious journalists: if the latter ceased to be employed in the news media organization through which activists aim to get media coverage, their movement organizations would no longer be able to maintain their role as valuable data sources within that news media organization.

Considered under different aspects, the challenges resulting from, on the one hand, the enduring high level of political parallelism that still affects Greece, Italy, and Spain and, on the other hand, the increasing precariousness within journalism combine in determining what strategies activists employ to win these challenges. The third challenge that we have reflected upon is related to how activists and journalists engage with each other when it comes to securing one's digital communication. These actors seem to be surrounded by a specific and unique socio-technological context, mainly linked to the country they live in, that somehow influences their daily choices on whether and how to interact with each other. However, overall, journalists rarely seem to guide activists toward digital security. There are, of course, exceptions, such as Italian journalists intervening to protect their sources when the latter – be they activists or not – use digital media in a very naïve and, most of all, insecure manner (as in the aforementioned case of Carla, who has to deal with *pentiti di mafia* on Facebook Messenger). However, as a general trend, it seems that the practice of creating and nurturing fruitful connections with journalists does not add anything new when it comes to understanding how activists deal with digital security, compared to what we have highlighted in previous chapters: Southern European activists generally underestimate how digital security works, and those activists who do pay attention to it usually come either from Spain or Greece. It is the contextual background in which activists operate that seems to advise them to take digital security seriously. Other factors, such as that relating to specific media actors like journalists, do not seem to play a role in this regard.

Unlike the former two challenges that activists face when engaging with journalists to create and then nurture meaningful connections with them, activists seem to behave much more passively when it comes to digital security. Our interviewees appear unable to even only grasp the potential threats behind exchanging sensitive information via digital media, and this is true for both the activists and other actors they interact with, such as journalists. In fact, only one exception emerged from our interviews: a movement organization that represents a national point of reference when it comes to digital security. In the words of Marcos, a Spanish journalist who regularly relates to this grassroots organization so as to protect his communication from potential third-party intrusions:

> 'We are very close to people who come from the world of hackers, and who periodically update us on security and privacy on the Internet. And, in fact, when a new person enters our newsroom, we give them the dossier on how to secure their communications. And we also do updates. Sometimes, those people alert us and say: "Hey, there's a problem here, be careful with it".'

Although this is an exceptional case, the strategy that these activists employ is to create a personal, but also general and diffused, media environment in which each link in the chain – journalists included – will at least be aware of the potential threats of communicating through digital media. This strategy is aimed at spreading good practices that not only widen the awareness of how digital media work but also successfully deal with the related challenge of digital security. The fact that this specific Spanish movement organization is openly and directly involved in digital security matters further supports the finding that, as a general trend, the Southern European activists we interviewed tend to relate to the digital as if no threats whatsoever are implied in it. Compared to the challenges of political parallelism and journalists' precariousness, that of digital security still seems to be largely underestimated. As a direct consequence, activists fail to transform the challenge of digital security into a potential opportunity. This happens not because they are unable to do so, but simply because they have not yet recognized the issue of securing their digital communication as a challenge. In other words, they lack a strategy because they lack awareness, which therefore makes this challenge a potential and serious threat to them, but one that they neither see nor acknowledge as such.

Conclusion

This chapter has focused on the daily interactions between activists and journalists. The latter are vital media actors for the former since they allow them to perform the practice of gaining visibility much more efficiently. That is why activists need to establish deep, meaningful, and long-lasting connections with journalists. However, in Southern Europe, this nowadays happens in a context in which journalism is still firmly anchored in one of its historical roots, namely political parallelism. Furthermore, journalists experience an increasing level of precariousness that usually translates into a profound transformation of the concrete actions and daily routine that journalists perform in order to collect, elaborate, and then produce the news. Finally, the widespread availability of digital media for journalists and activists alike brings along potential threats, such as a data security breach in the digitally mediated interactions between activists and journalists.

With regard to the challenges resulting from the pervasive presence of political parallelism in Greece, Italy, and Spain, combined with the progressive precariousness of journalism in these three Southern European countries, activists face several difficulties in finding the right strategies to perform at best the practice of establishing connections with journalists. It is no coincidence, then, that the practice of sustaining connections with journalists demands very heterogeneous strategic moves: for instance, trying to meet journalists face to face also in informal contexts and in episodic, extemporaneous situations, that is, outside institutional settings. This usually happens only if activists visit the places journalists haunt, like the buildings of power located in a country's capital city. Indeed, the geographical factor also helps to explain why some activists do not succeed in performing the practice of sustaining connections with journalists: Greek activists who do not live and operate in Athens, Spanish activists based outside Madrid, or Italian activists living far from Rome are more limited in their ability to create and maintain solid and fruitful connections with the media actors of their respective countries. However, our interviews with activists living and operating in Rome, Madrid, and Athens revealed that movement organizations do not always succeed in getting what they want from their daily efforts to engage in different ways with journalists. According to our interviewees, the main reason for this lies in the lack of relational capital, which they need to get the most from their connections with journalists. Conversely, institutional political actors almost automatically own this relational capital, which can lead party leaders, parliamentarians, or even government agents to call journalists friends, bypassing the standard and 'colder', professional relationship with journalists that activists must resort to. Hence, a *do ut des* mechanism is sometimes the only strategy that activists can activate to obtain what they want from their connections with journalists in a context shaped by a high level of political parallelism and increased precariousness in the field of journalism. Despite these difficulties, activists there seem to be tackling the two combined challenges by proactively developing heterogeneous and multifaceted strategies to successfully engage with journalists.

The same cannot be said for the third challenge, data security, where activists seem to be much less proactive, especially in Italy. Our interviews demonstrated that technology-mediated communications between activists and journalists are handy in that they accelerate and facilitate the creation and maintenance of strong linkages of trust between them. However, they also have a weak spot: they are vulnerable. Third-party actors can easily enter into these communications without being noticed, putting at risk the safety of activists, journalists, and other people linked to them. Confirming what we have claimed in previous chapters, Greek and Spanish activists and journalists perceive this potential threat and then try to behave accordingly to protect their communication. Vice versa, Italian activists act as if there never was a pre- and post-Snowden era, as opposed to activists in other (Western) countries (Ermoshina and Musiani, 2017). In fact, every Italian activist we engaged with relates to other social, political, and media actors with a quasi-total indifference to issues of surveillance and data security.

Regardless of the specificity of the Italian media and political scenario, making communication via digital devices secure does not result in a systematic and established practice in the whole of Southern Europe. Rather, it stands out as an irregular and intermittent factor related to agency, not the result of any codified and stratified norms and habits that are rooted in journalism as a profession as well as in the daily life of activists. Even in the practice of sustaining connections, most activists enter into contact with the digital data sequences of the general data stream they face every day without a deep awareness of the threats and potentially harmful consequences of this activity, no matter if there is a fellow activist, a policy maker, or indeed a journalist on the other side of the screen.

8

Activists' Practices and Agency in the Data Stream

In this book, we have explained how activists in three Southern European countries deal with digital media and the related data in the quiet times of grassroots politics. We have analysed the qualitative data of our empirical investigation through the lens of practice theories, according to which the material, symbolic, and social dimensions co-constitute each other and the practices of which they are part. Thanks to the analysis of these three interlinked dimensions, the concept that emerged most forcefully from our investigation was that of the data stream, which proves to be a powerful heuristic to describe and explain how activists cope with digitalization and datafication in the ordinary, routine activities that sustain the grassroots political work of their movement organizations. The data stream, as we have observed in the introduction, is an essential aspect of activists' and movement organizations' practices: in the previous chapters, we have shown that activists are constantly immersed in the data stream, even when they seek to abandon it. In those moments, the only thing that they can do is to act on it to change its rhythm, making it slower, more manageable, and less pressing.

The main result of our investigation, therefore, has been that of casting a light on the agency that activists exert – or seek to exert – not so much over digital media as such, but over the whole data stream, more specifically. In this regard, we have furthermore illustrated that such an agency can come in many shapes, bringing along and answering to a variety of challenges depending on who the activists are, what their movement organizations do, and where they are located. Despite these differences, though, there is one common aspect: no matter where activists are situated, their agency over the data stream is particularly important for them and their movement organizations to perform the practices related to their grassroots political engagement. In this conclusive chapter, we hence discuss such agency further from three different angles.

As a first step, we will consider agency discussing how the four practices are connected to each other and we will argue that the practice of information gathering has a prominent role in anchoring the other three practices that emerged as important for activists. In short, the activists' agency over the data stream passes to a great extent through the construction, arrangement, and employment of data; as a result, the data become information that is able to sustain other practices. In our opinion, this is an important finding since social movement scholars seldom pay attention to the practice of information gathering when seeking to understand how movement organizations work and with what outcomes, both during the peak of mobilizations and in the quiet times of politics.

Then, we will examine agency over the data stream, outlining some of the skills that activists in Greece, Italy, and Spain developed to wield control over the heterogeneous, ubiquitous, and perpetual stream of data that they have to manage on a daily basis. More specifically, we will consider the challenges that activists have to face, and how they face them, discussing each of the three main features of the data stream. In terms of its heterogeneity, we claim that it is not sufficient to simply point at the hybridity that activists experience when engaging in grassroots politics; while hybridity is nowadays almost a fact, what is relevant is to understand that it comes in different configurations and that these matter for activists. By considering the data stream ubiquitous, we argue that we need to pay more attention to those spaces where activists construct data beyond and outside digital media, recognizing the still important role of face-to-face interactions for activists and their movement organizations when coping with the data stream. When focusing on the perpetual unfolding of the data stream, we highlight the interplay between different temporalities that activists engage with in a purposeful manner to manage the data stream, its never-ending development, and its frequent moments of acceleration.

Finally, we will argue that how activists and their movement organizations exert their agency over the data stream is also very indicative of the extent to which they relate to digitalization and datafication in different contexts. Hence, we will discuss the situated nature of digitalization and datafication. Far from being homogeneous waves of mediatization in societies, their specificities will be considered in each of the three countries and in connection to the movement organizations contexts that we investigated. Even in relatively similar countries, like those at the centre of our research, we could indeed detect differences in the way activists and their movement organizations deal with digital media and the related data. More specifically, we will focus on some of the factors that seem to be relevant to understand such dissimilarities and, additionally, on the way digitalization and datafication manifest themselves differently according to the practice at stake.

Overall, we consider this book as the beginning of a new line of inquiry that seeks to explore the interactions of movement organizations with the data stream from the perspective of activists, looking at how they interact with digital media and data to foster their activities beyond the realm of data activism and, in many cases, even beyond big data as such. This chapter therefore ends with a discussion of the questions that have arisen at the end of our research journey. We indeed hope that our qualitative, explorative research may serve as the basis for further investigations to capture, describe, and explain how activists in other parts of the world – that is, beyond the three Southern European countries that we have examined here – integrate media at large into their activities and exercise their agency over the data stream, also in times of massive mobilization.

The interconnection of practices in the daily life of grassroots politics

Throughout this book, we have treated the four practices as distinct from one another for analytical reasons. However, in the daily unfolding of activists' grassroots political engagement, the four practices have more than one point of connection. More specifically, we found that they are connected in at least three different ways: first of all, temporally, in the sense that the performance of a practice in the present is often able to facilitate the performance of another practice in the future. This is easily understandable if we think of the practice of sustaining meaningful connections, which is closely tied to the practice of gaining visibility: nurturing a connection with a journalist who works for legacy media, for instance, can put activists in a better position to obtain mainstream media coverage for their movement organization in a future moment. Viewed from this perspective, one practice leads to another, through a chain of activities that follow each other over time.

Furthermore, different practices connect with each other through the activities that characterize the practice, because the same activity can play a role in different practices at the same time. In this regard, the activity of meeting someone for an informal chat can be inserted in the practice of information gathering, in the practice of political organizing, and in the practice of sustaining connections. Thus, an activist can meet a fellow activist to better understand the internal political debate in their movement organization, to coordinate their efforts toward the organization of a press conference, and to further nurture their relationship of mutual trust. Indeed, there are moments in which activists perform more than one practice at the same time, hence overlapping them in the same space.

Finally, practices connect with each other in a similar way as we have just described, but through the use of the same digital media service in the framework of different activities. While this is not always the case and activists do use different digital media services to support different activities, as we have shown in the book, some digital media services do seem to work as connectors of different practices. A good example in this regard is the use of instant messaging services, especially in Italy and Spain; they have emerged as one of the most crucial digital media services that activists employ in all four practices that we have discussed in the book. For instance, activists employ WhatsApp to keep in touch with journalists and other relevant actors who could become their supporters in case of mobilizations. At the same time, they use the same instant messaging platform to feed journalists news pieces about their activities in the hope of increasing the chance of getting news media coverage. They also employ WhatsApp to participate in the decision-making activities of their movement organization, exchanging messages with their fellow activists, sharing information with them, and partaking their political analyses. The distinction between one practice and another therefore becomes particularly blurred. Furthermore, activists use WhatsApp to sustain their interactions with friends, family members, and other groups of people with whom they interact beyond their grassroots political engagement. Hence, as we have already discussed in Chapter 5 on the practice of political organization, the fuzziness of the boundaries between practices that pertain to different domains of activists' lives can also bring about a collapse of different contexts. The pervasive presence of certain digital media devices and services certainly contributes to creating such a challenging experience.

There is, then, yet another relevant way practices are interconnected one with the other. When thinking about how different practices stand in relation to one another, we know from practice theories that some practices may become more important than others in certain domains of social life, and these practices have an anchoring function, in the sense that they become essential to support other practices (Swidler, 2001). Conceptualizing media as practices, Nick Couldry (2004) already argued that they can have an ordering function regarding other practices that do not involve media. In our research, where we looked at digital and non-digital media in the framework of four practices, we found a similar anchoring (or ordering) process, in that one practice stood out as particularly relevant: the practice of information gathering.

Activists constantly gather information that is relevant for the daily political work of their organizations and related to the contentious issues they focus on, including pieces of legislation, statistics, and other types of data, stories, and testimonies. They also try to learn what others say about the contentious issues they care about; they are interested in knowing the viewpoints of activists who work for other organizations, but also those of institutional political actors, potential opponents, and other types of stakeholders. This type of information is vital for activists, as they are then able to map the contentious field in which they operate and see how it changes, sometimes even overnight. More broadly speaking, we argue that activists need to have access to information on what is happening at the broader political level: what are the most relevant issues in the institutional political agenda, and what are people speaking about in a given moment? This information is crucial to position the activists' organizations in the broader political realm that they are part of – albeit usually from a marginal position. It is exactly to avoid being pushed to the margins of the political realm that activists need to know when the moment has come to be more visible in the public debate, to nurture specific connections, or to change their organizational routines.

In short, the practice of information gathering seems to be particularly relevant for activists, for their other practices, and for the related activities. As such, it has the ability to anchor (Swidler, 2001) the other three practices that emerged from our research: political organizing, gaining visibility, and sustaining connections. The presence of a heterogeneous, yet ubiquitous and perpetual, data stream strictly linked to the dynamics of digitalization and datafication throws activists into data sequences that, to acquire relevance and become useful, must be forcefully processed and then assembled into meaningful information for activists and their movement organizations. Gathering, assembling, collecting, storing, and making sense of all the different data that activists harvest and construct in the data stream are all vital activities that sustain the practice of information gathering. The latter is hence a practice that is not just important in itself but also for the other three practices. Consequently, the agency that activists exert towards the practice of information gathering is particularly relevant. Indeed, based on our findings, we can make the assumption that to understand activists' engagement with digital media, and with all kinds of media more in general, a key starting point is to understand the practice of information gathering. In other words, it is not possible to grasp how activists organize, become visible, and establish connections with other social actors without first considering how they seek and produce information. This finding has profound implications for our understanding of grassroots politics in the data stream, also in times of mobilization.

Rethinking activists' agency in the data stream

Activists' agency in the data stream entails much more than the necessary skills to understand how algorithms work. In fact, more than just focusing on how a specific type of digital media might constitute a powerful leverage in their hands, activists develop both a general and practical understanding of how to combine different types of data sequences taken from the data stream so that they may successfully integrate them into their practices of grassroots political engagement. In other words, they develop an epistemic knowledge – based mostly on their daily experience and hence on previous practices they have performed in the past – of how various technological devices can sustain them and their movement organizations. It has become clear from the previous chapters that such knowledge is neither solely dependent on the material qualities of those digital and non-digital media that activists interact with nor exclusively reliant on the values, beliefs, and ideas that activists have with regard to the same digital and non-digital media. It is, rather, a variable interplay between these two dimensions – the material and the symbolic ones – that, in turn, are linked to the social conditions of activists and their movement organizations. It is at the intersection of the material, symbolic, and social dimensions of their practices, that activists exert their agency in the data stream. To understand more deeply what this agency is made of, and what it means exactly, in what follows we discuss it according to the three features that characterize the data stream and that we introduced earlier in this book.

First, the data stream is heterogeneous in that it not only includes those data that can be defined as big data, strictly speaking, but all kinds of data that activists produce, harvest, aggregate, and spread in the course of their grassroots political engagement. We know from the extant literature that when movement organizations and activists engage in public protests, they do so by employing and combining a variety of digital and non-digital media, to the point that some scholars consider hybridity as one of the most characteristic qualities of mobilizations and social movements today (Treré, 2018). In the previous chapters, we have shown that such a hybridity is also a relevant feature when considering the quiet times of politics, that is, when movement organizations go back to their ordinary activities of grassroots political engagement. We have also illustrated how this hybridity becomes even more layered in the data stream, in that it entails not just the combination of different types of media technologies but also the – often challenging – combination of different data sequences in an attempt to produce meaningful information that activists can use to their advantage in the practices that characterize their grassroots political work. It is no coincidence that the practice of information gathering is central for activists.

In short, hybridity in the data stream goes beyond the combination of various types of digital and non-digital media, as it also implies the combination of different types of data sequences and, even more importantly, the creation of hybrid assemblages of data and media, where these two entities nurture each other, albeit not always in a straightforward and unproblematic manner. As we have shown in the previous chapters, for instance, activists gather data about the contentious issues they care about through the online websites of research institutions, aggregate and discuss such data after face-to-face meetings with their fellow activists, and then arrange the same data so as to spread them via their social media profiles. In this case, various digital media services and non-digital media technologies are at stake: online websites, face-to-face discussions, social media platforms. Through each of them, activists develop specific activities around data, which thus become relevant for at least two different practices: information gathering and gaining visibility. Seen from this perspective, the activists' agency over the data stream is strictly related to their ability to embed various type of data – digital and non-digital, big and small – in their broader repertoire of communication, hence working at the frontiers of media-related and data-related practices even when they cannot be considered data activists in the strict sense. In sum, the activists' agency in the data stream is twofold, simultaneously directed at the opportunities and challenges of digitalization and datafication.

The data stream is also ubiquitous because data are simply everywhere and related to all kinds of technological devices and services: from the algorithms that directly work with data, ordering and clustering them in new data assemblages, to the activists' face-to-face conversations with political allies, among others. In the previous chapters, we have shown that activists decide to go beyond the digital data sequences, instead referring to the data that they can gather through face-to-face encounters with their fellow activists, political allies, and potential supporters. In each of the four practices that we have presented in this book, the materiality of the physical meeting, where the bodies become the ultimate technology through which activists perform their activities, acquire a role that is not possible to underestimate. When having face-to-face meetings, activists are unable to escape the data stream in its entirety, but they can counterbalance the data sequences that are most pervasive and tied to the incessant employment of digital media services: emails, instant messages, and posts in social media platforms. Even when such meetings are not physical but, say, one-to-one conversations over the phone, the data sequences that activists come into contact with are certainly more rarefied, but equally relevant. More specifically, we have shown that, in the practice of information gathering, activists' interactions with their personal, trusted contacts are relevant to filter the otherwise abundant – and sometimes even messy – amount of data that comes from legacy media and social media alike. Furthermore, although the practice of political organizing nowadays deeply revolves around the use of digital media and the related data, activists greatly value the possibility of meeting in person to speak about both the political strategies and the logistic details of their movement organizations. The same goes for the practice of establishing connections with other actors, both in the realm of politics and in that of media. Having lunch together or meeting for a beer after work are two informal moments in which activists nurture their precious links with other fellow activists, supporters of their movement organizations, policy makers, and even journalists. The physical space of face-to-face interactions thus becomes part of the data stream because it is during these meetings that activists harvest relevant data, process those that they have gathered elsewhere, and combine them, creating effective assemblages to sustain other activities within the practices they perform. In societies that are digitally saturated and increasingly datafied, the data stream is everywhere. However, when the activists' activities in grassroots politics involve interactions that are mainly mediated through their bodies alone, spaces emerge in which activists can develop critical reflections on digital data, and their importance also in relation to other data; at the same time, such spaces become relevant not so much to escape the data stream, but to perform activities through which some data sequences in the data stream become more manageable.

Finally, the data stream is perpetual because it neither has an end, in time, nor an ending: as we have seen in the previous chapters, activists do not seem to find a way out of the data stream and are in constant contact with it. On the one hand, there are all those data – some of which are big data, strictly speaking, while others are not – that are related to the combined use of many types of digital media services and the algorithms that sustain their functioning. On the other hand, there are other data that come in less pervasive and more scattered data sequences, which are equally important for activists: a public declaration by a political opponent in the national television news; a blog comment by a potential supporter published on an alternative informational website; a precious piece of information given in confidence by a fellow activist during an informal chat over a cup of coffee. In the case of data sequences that originate from and propagate through digital media, a common feature in all the four practices that we have discussed in this book is that the data stream is not only perpetual, but also in a constant state of acceleration that risks overwhelming activists. This is especially true when considering the practices of information gathering, gaining visibility, and political organizing: in all three cases, we have shown, in the respective chapters, how the activists' constant connection with digital media devices and their services ties them to data sequences that give them not only a sense of immediacy with regard to the activities they perform, but also a sustained sense of urgency, even in those moments that are usually characterized by a slower pace, because mobilizations are not ongoing. These data sequences also bring along a sense of perpetual presence, in which immediate actions and reactions seem to shape grassroots politics more than longer reflections and articulated discussions. Yet, it would be deceptive to say that, in the present day, activists and movement organizations are at the mercy of the accelerated times of grassroots politics. On the contrary, the activists' agency over the data stream also implies the ability to combine different temporalities so as to return, albeit not permanently, to a slower pace in grassroots politics, carving out moments of political discussion through the combination of different types of digital media and the related data sequences; in doing so, they also give back an important role to other, unmediated forms of communication, as in the case of face-to-face interactions. The alternation between the acceleration and deceleration of the data stream, through which activists seek to exert some control over the rhythm of its perpetual unfolding, is a significant aspect of their agency.

In this section, we have offered an overview of the ways in which activists and their movement organizations deal with the data stream, paying particular attention to its challenges and how activists face them. Next, we will broaden our sight to discuss how activists experience digitalization and datafication in different practices and contexts.

Different shades of digitalization and datafication

In the previous chapters, we have presented and discussed how activists deal with digital and non-digital media during the quiet times of politics in the framework of the four activists' practices that emerged from the analysis of the data gathered in Greece, Italy, and Spain. We discussed the four practices separately because we wanted to highlight the differences between them. Indeed, one important finding of our research is the relevance of digital media and the related data for activists not so much in general terms, but in the framework of four specific practices. For instance, the daily grassroots political activities in which WhatsApp is used are different and hence come with a diverse range of challenges, whether it is the practice of political organizing – in which WhatsApp and similar instant messaging services are pervasive – or that of establishing connections with other political actors or journalists, in which WhatsApp and similar devices are less prevalent. It is not just a matter of how often activists employ certain digital media across the four practices, but also in what way they use them. To stick to the example of WhatsApp, in the previous chapters, we have shown that activists employ it as an additional communicative backbone of their movement organizations, turning it into a sort of permanent activist assembly, so that the practice of political organizing is not only constantly unfolding in the activists' smartphones but also doing so at a fast pace. Instead, when we look at the practice of sustaining connections with journalists, activists employ WhatsApp as a direct one-to-one communication channel in the attempt to become valuable, and stable, data sources for journalists who work for legacy media. In short, in our discussion of the four practices, we have valued the different levels of digitalization and datafication in each of them; instead of assuming that the two waves of mediatization equally affect all activists' activities in the quiet times of politics, we have argued that they interplay differently depending on what part of their grassroots political engagement we are focusing on. The analysis that we have presented in the previous chapters in fact reveals the multifaceted nature of mediatization, which we will summarize in three points.

First, throughout the book, we have argued that mediatization is situational and, as such, also activists' agency concerning the broader digitalization and datafication processes is. As is known, different waves of mediatization have followed one another in the past centuries (Couldry and Hepp, 2016). The notion of mediatization, and more specifically that of digitalization and datafication, conveys some important trends related to the role that media, at large, have played and continue to play in society. However, seeking to grasp the meaning of digitalization and datafication for the people who experience them – in this case activists – has led us to develop a more fine-grained understanding of such waves of mediatization. In other words, we have argued that activists and their movement organizations do not experience digitalization and datafication in the same manner everywhere and at all times: the country in which grassroots political engagement happens, the contentious issues activists care about, and the type of movement organization they are inserted in are all factors that seem to intertwine with the activists' experience of digitalization and datafication. For instance, in Chapter 5, devoted to the practice of political organizing, we have shown that only those activists belonging to the most resourceful movement organizations have the luxury of meeting face to face during national meetings; this allowed them to balance the otherwise pervasive online meetings with activists scattered across the country in question, who sustained the coordination of the national movement organizations. Additionally, in the same chapter, we have shown that the contentious issue at stake was also relevant to explain the use of face-to-face meetings; those movement organizations tackling corruption employed face-to-face interactions more than those devoted to labor issues. We have linked such a difference to the type of information that activists deal with, with corruption being potentially a much more sensitive issue than labor when it comes to leaked information.

In a similar way, while discussing the practice of gaining visibility in Chapter 3, we have argued that Greek activists also include non-digital forms of alternative media in their activities in the capital city, Athens, where they make a broad use of printed flyers, leaflets, and posters to make their presence visible in the streets. We put this habit in relation to the distribution of political and economic power in the country, which tends to be much more concentrated in the capital city on which movement organizations focus large part of their efforts, also in terms of visibility. Similarly, the Greek activists we interviewed were more reluctant to establish and nurture connections with the supporters of their movement organizations through digital media, hence greatly preferring the use of face-to-face interactions, as we have demonstrated in Chapter 6, which reflects on the practice of sustaining connections. In short, both the general and practical understanding of the four practices is tied to the specific situations in which activists interact with the varied ensemble of digital media.

Second, and in connection with the previous point, we have claimed that digitalization is an inherently non-homogeneous process, since individual activists and their movement organizations interlace with digital media at different paces and with different results. While digitalization affects all four practices under investigation, it is clear that it encounters them according to different configurations. For instance, in Chapter 2, on the practice of information gathering, we have shown that news media websites are relevant when gathering data on political elites, but when our interviewees described what they did on an ordinary day of grassroots political engagement, they also discussed at length the role of other news media like the print press, television, and radio. More importantly, social media platforms have a specific role in the practice of information gathering: activists employ them to understand what other movement organizations, potential allies, and scattered supporters think about the political issue of the day. However, face-to-face interactions are important to validate the information activists acquire through digital and non-digital media. In short, while digitalization is certainly and widely present in the lives of activists, we always need to put it into a broader perspective. At times, activists employ digital media because they are the most immediate way to perform a practice, but this does not mean that they are the activists' preferred choice or the solution that they consider most effective. For this reason, during their grassroots political engagement, there are moments in which they put digital media aside and rather engage with other forms of communication. This is why we cannot consider digital media and technologies as something that can homogeneously sustain the activists' grassroots political work on a daily basis: recognizing the uneven employment of digital media allows us to understand that, while our societies are deeply digitalized, activists and their movement organizations may not always decide to be so.

Third, looking at datafication from the viewpoint of activists who were not protesting at the time of the empirical research, we developed a more fine-grained understanding of what datafication means for grassroots politics beyond stages of mobilization and in Southern Europe. We illustrated that there are, of course, some movement organizations that put (big) data at the centre of their collective actions, among those that we investigated. Activists who belong to organizations that gather and elaborate data to increase the transparency of parliamentary activities, for instance, base much of their daily political engagement on activities that involve data. They develop digital media platforms that allow them and the general public to find information about what the elected MPs do when they are in Parliament, assembling existing data about parliamentary activities and making them easily searchable for the broader public. At the same time, they gain visibility for the contentious issue they care about by releasing reports that elaborate on the collected data, once again transforming the raw data into relevant information that is easy to understand even for the least specialist audiences. While these types of movement organizations may not deal with big data in the strict sense, they certainly ensure that their collective actions overlap with the use of data for their political engagement. These organizations engage in data activism and therefore also deal – to some extent – with datafication. And, they do so from an empowering political stance according to which activists do not submit to data: they actively engage in their creation, combination, and visualization through various forms of storytelling.

That said, most of the movement organizations we took into consideration, and the activists in them, developed another take on data. For instance, when activists deal with the algorithms that characterize a commercial social media platform like Facebook, they also engage in data but from a less empowering position. While they certainly seek to understand how algorithms manage the data they create and try to circulate online, they often do not have the ability or the resources to engage in them efficiently and effectively. As such, activists experience datafication and exert agency towards it in a twofold manner. On the one hand, activists and their movement organizations cannot escape datafication and its logic, which is present in the data stream as well. The moment in which they include social media platforms in their daily activities, they implicitly decide to at least be in touch with it. On the other hand, they avoid adhering to its logic in the strictest sense: their general understanding of datafication relies on the assumption that its dynamics and consequences are difficult to know; this translates into avoidance, according to which activists engage in other data sequences within the data stream than those that are more solidly related to algorithms and big data. In so doing, they seek to escape datafication in the full sense of the word.

Final claims and new lines of research

In this book, we have presented the outcomes of an explorative qualitative research project on how activists and their movement organizations employ digital media, in combination also with non-digital media, to perform their grassroots political engagement when they do not occupy themselves with public protests. As we have claimed in Chapter 1, while we know a lot about digital media in times of mobilization, our knowledge of activism in the quiet times of politics is more limited, especially when it comes to media at large. By filling this gap in the literature, we have considered how the material, symbolic, and social dimensions of activists' practices entangle when it comes to the place and role of various types of media in the activists' ordinary engagement with grassroots politics. Starting from this perspective, we have made three major advancements that pave the way for further lines of research.

First, we have identified the four activists' practices that seem most relevant for movement organizations during the quiet times of politics: information gathering, gaining visibility, political organizing, and sustaining connections. Next, we have argued that the former has the ability to anchor the three other practices; we should therefore devote special attention to how activists harvest, combine, and present various types of information to better understand how they become visible, organize, and connect with other actors who are near to them, including supporters, allies, and opponents. Furthermore, we have contended that visibility is particularly relevant even when activists are not trying to be seen by others through their public protests. As such, we might put into question the traditional distinction between latency and visibility stages, since activists and their movement organizations nowadays seek for visibility also during latency stages, mainly due to the widespread presence of digital media, including social media platforms. Due to the latter, activists have to deal with a pervasive algorithmic visibility that they find difficult to manage and which activists try to cope with through attentive care towards their reputation among different audiences. Building a reputation, in fact, assumes a central role in order to emerge, get noticed, and in some way go beyond a visibility otherwise only dictated by the algorithmic logics governing social media platforms. In this regard, further research is however needed on how and why activists curate their visibility during stages of latency and with what consequences for their movement organizations. Another point we have made is related to the time of political organizing, which seems to suffer from a strong acceleration and a perpetual presence that activists manage in various ways. While the movement organizations' meetings and assemblies were once face-to-face events, where to take stock of their experiences and plan their present and future activities, the extensive use of instant messaging platforms has expanded and extended the moments and spaces for collective decision-making moving fluidly from a face-to-face meeting to a mailing list to an instant messaging chat group. Novel assemblages emerge, where we find different times of grassroots political engagement as well as different individual and collective commitments, and which deserve further investigation to understand what happens to the various forms of decision-making that traditionally characterize grassroots politics, including deliberative and participatory ones. Finally, we have illustrated how the daily grassroots political engagement of activists highly revolves around the establishment and nurturing of connections between them and multiple types of actors. In this regard, we have furthermore shown that the practice of establishing connections seems to rely more on writing and less on other forms of communication: activists write messages in instant messaging services, read replies to comments in social media platforms, and compose emails on their laptops. The widespread use of digital media seems to give back a centrality to written forms of communication when activists connect with others. This raises questions about how writing through digital media is shaping the way in which activists interact with different types of audiences and with what consequences for the quality of such relationships.

Second, we have concretely illustrated the situated nature of activists' practices and the role that digital media play in them. We did this by engaging in a comparison at three different levels, because we were looking at activists operating in three different countries, who engage in two different contentious issues, and who are involved in two different types of movement organizations. In several parts of the book, we have focused on the similarities that we found when activists integrate digital media into the daily activities that constitute their grassroots political engagement. From this perspective, we underlined what activists working in different settings have in common despite their differences. For instance, the importance of face-to-face interactions regardless of the widespread use of digital media is a common trait that we have underlined for all three countries. At the same time, a particularly relevant part of the practice of political organizing is the acceleration of time, which is also a shared trait of Greek, Italian, and Spanish activists and brings with it certain features that permeate other practices as well, like the tendency toward immediacy that we have discussed in connection to algorithmic visibility. Such commonalities are probably due to the fact that activists incorporate similar types of media into their practices, no matter where they are located and to which movement organizations they are affiliated. This is not surprising, since we are dealing with global digital media services and devices, which have similar features across countries. Likewise, all three countries have a media system that is comparable in terms of the configuration of its legacy media and the traits that characterize the journalistic profession.

Nevertheless, we also found some significant differences. Let us mention only a couple of them, beyond those that we have already outlined earlier in this chapter: Italian activists seem to be less concerned about the data security in the data stream than those living in Greece and Spain; activists who are located in Spain consider a social media platform like Facebook irrelevant to their political activities, while Italian and Greek activists greatly value it. We have explained such differences with broader, general, and practical understandings that activists have about their country, intended as both a political framework and a media environment with specific features that activists perceive as relevant. While there are structural differences, in this book, we have shown that activists assign different meanings to them; consequently, the symbolic dimension in practices becomes particularly relevant not just to describe, but also to explain how activists interact with media. That said, we acknowledge the fact that further comparative research in this direction will be able to cast light on certain aspects that we have evoked in this book but without discussing them in depth.

Finally, our analysis of how digital media intertwine with the four practices led us to theorize the data stream, a heuristic that we employed throughout the book in association with our findings, and to adopt a broadened understanding of data that goes beyond the now common understanding of data as big data. Considering activists' engagement in grassroots politics through the lenses of the data stream allowed us to go beyond the distinction between digitalization and datafication and capture them by looking at their points of contact. At the same time, the emphasis on the data stream enabled us to appreciate the activists' interactions with data also when they do not engage with forms of activism that are explicitly and largely tied to big data in the first place, as in the case of data activism. This is important because even those activists and movement organizations that do not put big data at the centre of their efforts nowadays have to deal with big data and data analytics. Still more importantly, we have shown that activists engage in all kinds of data because the data stream is, in fact, heterogeneous and comes in a variety of data sequences, each specifically linked to one type of digital media. From this perspective, we argue that, to appreciate activists' agency in contemporary societies, we need to understand it in relation to the data stream as a whole, with the activists' ability to exploit the heterogeneity of its data sequences in creative ways, at times also to oppose its ubiquitous and perpetual presence in the activists' routine activities. This book is a first step in the direction of a line of research that we find particularly promising, and we hope that other investigations in the near future will unpack how activists experience and engage in the data stream in other countries beyond Southern Europe, considering also what happens to the data stream in moments of mobilization and how it intersects with contentious issues other than corruption and precariousness. Moreover, we believe that the data stream may be a promising heuristic even beyond the realm of activism. As we have also noted throughout this book, activists and their movement organizations are not the only ones who participate in and experience the data stream. Other actors associated with the realm of politics are doing the same, including lay citizens, journalists, politicians, lobbyists, and others. All of these actors deal with its main qualities and intersect with its multiple data sequences in different ways: as such, each of them develops specific types of agencies towards the data stream that are worth investigating, also comparatively, in order to better understand how political participation unfolds in times of digitalization and datafication.

Methodological Appendix

In this Appendix, we will discuss our research design and methods, explaining the crucial choices that we made concerning the sampling, gathering, and analysis of the data on which this book is based. We will briefly clarify from which viewpoint we tell the story of how activists deal with the data stream, namely from a micro-level angle, and why we decided to adopt this particular perspective. Related to this, we will also discuss our choices regarding the countries on which our empirical investigation focuses, as well as the types of activists and movement organizations that are discussed in our book.

Without necessarily looking for causal explanations, the purpose of the research project was to explore how the process of mediatization is interlaced with the daily life of grassroots politics during stages of latency, understanding their similarities and differences from a qualitative standpoint. To do this, we decided to investigate how digital media as well as non-digital media, including face-to-face interactions, are interlaced with the daily practices of grassroots politics. We focused on more than one country and more than one type of movement organization, and we relied on a comparative cross-country research design that investigates the daily life of grassroots politics in three countries in Southern Europe: Greece, Italy, and Spain. While we did not compare the countries as such, but rather instances of grassroots politics in each of them, it is important to stress that we selected the three countries because they provide similar contexts in which activists interact with digital and non-digital media. Indeed, Greece, Italy, and Spain share the same type of media system (Hallin and Mancini, 2004) in which activists conduct their daily grassroots political work. As such, they have many features in common concerning the historical development of the journalistic profession and the relationship between legacy media and institutional political actors, among others. Furthermore, the three countries had similar scores in the 2016 Network Readiness Index of the World Economic Forum, which assesses 'country preparedness to reap the benefits of emerging technologies and capitalize on the opportunities presented by the digital transformation and beyond' (Baller et al, 2016: 3), including measures related to the diffusion of digital media and other digital technologies at the individual level. In designing our research, we also kept another aspect unchanged: in all three countries, we selected activists who were embedded in movement organizations working on two contentious issues that – albeit different – were not linked to public protest at the time of conducting the empirical research. These were corruption and transparency, on the one side, and temporary work and labor rights, on the other. Hence, another relevant similarity that all movement organizations we entered into contact with during the project shared was the following: they were in a stage of latency and, therefore, not involved in any kind of mobilization. However, other aspects did change. First, the fact that movement organizations in the three countries were inserted in different movement cultures that varied according to not only the country at stake but also the political leaning of the movement organization. While some presented themselves as being somehow politically neutral, which was especially the case of anti-corruption movement organizations, others openly situated themselves in specific activist traditions, like anarchism, post-autonomy, or the hacker culture. Second, some movement organizations had a structured hierarchy and could count on a good wealth of material resources, while others were highly unstructured, lacking any formal hierarchy, and relying on limited material resources. These two endogenous aspects help to understand the constitutive entanglements of the symbolic, material, and social dimensions at the level of the activists' practices and related activities. Indeed, their relevance has emerged from our data analysis, as we have also stressed in several parts of this book.

As we have already explained in the introduction, the cross-country comparative research design was complemented with a specific theoretical framework: that of practice theories. We started from the assumption that to understand how, why, and with what consequences movement organizations engage with digital and non-digital media, we must look at their practices: what they do on an ordinary day of grassroots political work and how they employ digital and non-digital media to do what they do.

We were looking for a method of data gathering that would allow us to do cross-country comparative fieldwork within the research project's constraints. Hence, while participant observation is probably the most common method of data gathering when investigating practices, we decided not to employ it because it would have required intensive fieldwork on a small sample of movement organizations in the three countries. Instead, we decided to broaden the number of movement organizations by relying on semi-structured interviews with activists. We are aware that the employment of semi-structured interviews has its limits when studying practices: instead of observing practices as they unfold before us, through semi-structured interviews, we gather accounts of practices as activists recall them. In this regard, Davide Nicolini (2010) is straightforward in stating that it is not possible to study practice-building through methods such as surveys and interviews alone. However, our investigation was not about practices as they unfolded, but rather focused on the role that digital and non-digital media play in the daily practices of grassroots politics. Other scholars already employed in-depth interviews with research participants to gather data on specific types of practices. Indeed, when researchers cannot experience the performance of practices firsthand, it is always possible to find research participants who have performed those practices and ask them to talk about what they did and how (Pouliot, 2013). In this regard, Reijo Savolainen's investigations on activists' information practices makes large use of in-depth interviews, which are his primary source of data; he employs them to understand the role of various sources of information for activists (and a group of unemployed people) and the strategies they develop to employ and share the information they gather. In-depth interviewing as a method to gather data about practices certainly suffers from the limit of not allowing researchers to see practices unfold as research participants perform them. At the same time, it has the invaluable feature of allowing researchers to access the practical knowledge of practices through someone – namely the research participant – who engages in those practices on a daily basis (Bueger and Gadinger, 2018) and who is asked to provide information about what they do in the framework of their everyday activities (Pouliot, 2013). Such practical knowledge is accessible through interviews because practices always include an element of self-reflection and, hence, people can articulate what they do and what they say in reference to a particular situation. Of course, through in-depth interviews we only get a narrative of those doings and sayings, but what was relevant for our investigation was exactly the reflections and interpretations that accompany the narrative. At the same time, it was important for us to have some comparable information about the material side of practices, that is, how activists embedded digital and non-digital media in their daily activities. Hence, in such narratives we certainly welcomed – and looked for – the activists' understandings of the practices they performed in connection to grassroots politics, but we also wanted to get an idea of the digital technologies that they usually interacted with while performing these practices.

For this reason, we developed a specific method of data gathering that revolves around the creation of a map able to depict the interviewees' daily engagement with digital and non-digital media in the framework of their grassroots political work. Participant-led maps are a promising visual tool for data gathering in qualitative methods, to facilitate the interactions between the interviewer and the interviewees and cross-case comparisons (Bravington and King, 2019). The use of maps created by and with participants is no novelty, neither in media studies (Hepp et al, 2016) nor in social movement studies (Wood, 2003; Benski, 2010), although their use in the latter is uncommon. Furthermore, Reijo Savolainen (2008) employed maps to investigate information practices, asking research participants to position themselves in their daily information horizon, hence visualizing those sources of information that were nearer to the interviewees and those that were more distant to them. Drawing on these studies, we envisioned the creation of a map that put research participants and their ordinary grassroots political work at the centre, without focusing on any specific practice, as we will explain more in detail later. Furthermore, we decided to employ the resulting map as a starting point for semi-structured interviews with participants to grasp the role that digital and non-digital media have in the various activities that activists perform on a daily basis to sustain their grassroots political work. The focus on activities, and not on whole practices, was not random; we considered activities as the entry point to understand and reconstruct practices in the stage of data analysis.

In short, we developed a specific interview protocol that we named *media in practices interview maps*, through which we collaborated with research participants to obtain a map related to what activists did with digital and non-digital media in the framework of several daily activities related to their grassroots political engagement. This protocol revolved around two stages within the same interview session, involving one research participant at a time. In the first stage, the interviewer drew a map based on the research participant's answer to one initial open question:

> 'If you think about an ordinary day, what is the first thing you do when you wake up that is connected with your political work, and what are the other things that you would normally do throughout the day, until you go to bed? Could you specify if you use any digital media to do this? Or do you also use other types of media?'

Additionally, to contextualize the use of media, we deliberately asked research participants to include in their accounts those moments in which they employed face-to-face interactions.

The opening question triggered a narrative in which the research participant would tell us about a typical day of political engagement, and the role that media had in their politically oriented activities. When drawing the map in the presence of the research participants, the interviewer wrote down the different actions mentioned during the interview, the type of device with which these were performed (for example a smartphone or a laptop), and the type of services used in connection with each device (for example an instant messaging platform or a cloud storage space). As it is clear from Figure A.1, the resulting map therefore included a configuration of three different elements: (1) an action, connected to (2) a service, connected to (3) a device. We obtained such a configuration from summarizing what activists told us during the interview. For instance, when an activist explained to us

Figure A.1: An example of a media in practices map

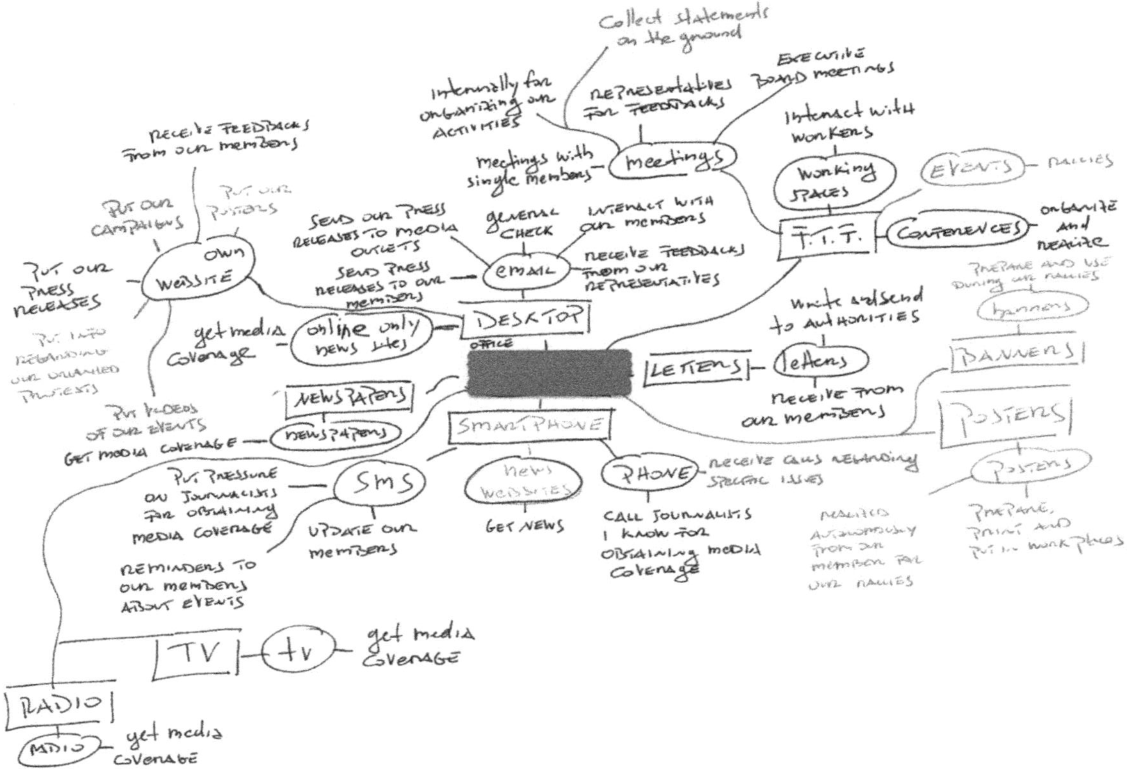

that the first thing she did in the morning was to read the main news on the homepage of a national newspaper website on her smartphone, we drew the following configuration: read the news, newspaper website, smartphone.

Beyond this, all maps also included three main different times of grassroots politics, each represented by a different color. Black stands for the ordinary unfolding of activists' grassroots political engagement, the main topic of this part of the interview. Green is related to those activities that activists perform from time to time and, in any case, not on a regular basis during latency stages. Red, instead, refers to what activists would do in moments of increased visibility for the interviewee's organization and/or when this organization entered a stage of mobilization. We added this additional temporal layer to put activists' practices and the role of media in these practices in a broader temporal context, after having drawn the first two layers that referred to the stage of latency. We did this by asking activists to tell us what they would add to the resulting map with regard to any actions that they would perform beyond the ordinary and routine activities of times of latency. All the activists we interviewed enriched the map with further actions and the related services and devices.

Once the map was completed, the second stage of the interview consisted of a set of open questions that started from a broad reflection on the map and continued with other questions about actual and potential situations related to the use of media in the interviewee's daily political work. Commenting on both the map and questions related to fictional scenarios was relevant to elicit the research participant's thoughts on the tacit knowledge and imaginaries related to the practices they performed in connection to their daily grassroots political work (Pouliot, 2013). In this regard, Davide Nicolini (2009) developed a specific interview protocol that he named 'interview with the double', asking research participants to give instructions on how to do their job (and related tasks) to an imaginary double that would need to substitute them. Through this interview technique, it is possible to acquire data about the normative and moral elements that characterize practices (Nicolini, 2009). While we did not ask the research participants to think about an imaginary double, their reflections on the map and questions about fictitious situations aimed at gathering further data on activists' practices: not so much on their normative and moral elements, but certainly on the symbolic dimension of imaginaries, beliefs, and values concerning the daily life of grassroots politics and the role of digital and non-digital media in it. In line with the spirit of semi-structured interviews, we used a similar interview guide for all the interviews as reported in Figure A.2, making some inevitable changes during the interview when activists raised unexpected or interesting topics.

We interviewed a total of 45 activists in three countries (N = 18 in Italy, 16 in Spain, 11 in Greece). Activists were selected following a purposive

Figure A.2: The interview guidelines

- What kind of reflections does your map suggest about the way you engage with politics?

- Looking at the map, I notice that you did not include X (devices, services/platforms/outlets and/or activity). Can you explain what the reason for this is? Is this because of the specific issue you are working on (temporary work vs. anti-corruption)?

- While drawing the map you said that you use X to perform activity Y. Can you explain exactly how and why? Is this because of the specific issue you are working on (temporary work vs. anti-corruption)?

- Looking at the map, I notice that you perform the same activity using different devices (or services/platforms/outlets). Can you explain why? Is this because of the specific issue you are working on (temporary work vs. anti-corruption)?

I would now like you to think about the activities related to your political work that we have summarized in this map.

- Imagine what you would do if, for one day, you didn't have any Internet connection. What would you do differently? How would your map change?

- Still imagining scenarios different from the one represented by the map, if you had a 'magic button' that could make it easier for you to carry out communication activities related to your political work, what would it do? What would this 'magic button' do?

Finally, I would like to understand what importance you give to the various elements included in the map.

- Of all the activities indicated in this map, which do you consider indispensable, and are there any that you could do without? If so, for what reason?

- If instead we talk about the services you use (for example, here you have included WhatsApp, Facebook...), which do you consider truly indispensable and which could you do without? For what reason?

- Finally, if we reason in terms of devices (for example, you mentioned smartphones, TV, newspapers), which are truly indispensable and which could you do without? For what reason?

sampling technique that allowed us to include activists involved in the most relevant movement organizations, engaged either in the struggle against corruption and the lack of accountability or in the fight against precariousness and for workers' rights.

To select the initial sample of participants, we drew on our knowledge of the field in each of the three countries, which we had gained from previous research projects on the same contentious issues (Mattoni and Vogiatzoglou, 2014; Mattoni, 2017a; Treré et al, 2017). We complemented our expertise through desk research, consultation of secondary sources, and with the support of a country expert in the case of Greece. After a preliminary round of interviews, we employed a snowball sampling technique to reach out to other potential research participants, which we selected on the basis of our initial criteria. The resulting sample is a combination of activists who work in various types of movement organizations, ranging from informal and grassroots activists' groups – mainly dependent on their members' voluntary work to survive – to more structured movement organizations, which pay activists to achieve their objectives. Our sample is therefore internally diverse, although all the movement organizations that we included in it coordinate their efforts with other movement organizations when engaging in mobilizations around the two contentious issues, sustaining various types of collective actions that range from the more contentious ones (for instance, the organization of general strikes) to the least contentious ones (for instance, the organization of an online petition). It makes no difference if we are dealing with a trade union, a political collective, or a third-sector association: all the movement organizations that we selected have been engaged in some form of collective action in the past and they indeed become active nodes of social movements when they engage in waves of mobilization.

Regarding the specific identities and political-professional roles of the research participants interviewed, two main categories were identified. These categories include individuals holding high-level communicative and/or organizational roles within their respective social movement organizations. In some cases, to capture both communicative and organizational aspects, two different members from the same social movement organization were interviewed – one with specific organizational roles and the other with communicative roles. Furthermore, concerning the gender and age of the research participants, the interviews involved 11 women and 34 men, ranging in age from the late twenties to the early sixties. Finally, all the interviews were conducted in person, within the 'headquarters' of the social movement organizations whenever they had one. As for the social movement organizations they belong to, they are both well-established ones and much newer organizations. This means that the research participants belong to social movement organizations characterizing the social movement milieu of the three countries even well before the beginning of the current century, but also to other movement organizations, with a stronger anchoring to the digitalization and datafication of our society. These latter groups were born as a result of and owe their existence to the impact of these two latest waves of mediatization.

The interviews produced two integrated data sets: first, 45 maps, which included chains of devices, services, and actions related to the daily political work of the interviewees; second, the corresponding semi-structured interviews, which included information on the meanings that the interviewees attach to their use of media. Interviewing activists allowed us to access two types of relevant information on practices and the role of media technologies in them. On the one hand, we gathered data from the micro-perspective of activists' experiences and imaginaries about what they can do with digital media to sustain their grassroots political work on a daily basis. On the other hand, we also gathered data on the movement organizations to which the interviewees belong; this means that we were able to reconstruct the role of digital media at the meso level, focusing not just on individual actors but also on collective ones. For the coding of such materials, we employed the software MAXQDA.

We coded the maps following an inductive strategy to obtain configurations of devices, services, and actions starting from what the interviewees told us about their ordinary and routine engagement with mediated and non-mediated actions. This means that we did not start our coding from an existing list of devices, services, and actions; rather, that list emerged recursively as the analysis developed. As for the actions, we obtained a list of 136 actions that we further analysed. Next, we started from the actions of the most recurring configurations and engaged in a second round of coding to group the configurations within broader practices. This means, once again, that we did not start from a preconceived list of activists' practices; rather, we inductively reconstructed them through two rounds of analysis of the maps. The emergence of the four practices is, therefore, the first relevant finding that we obtained through our analysis. In short, as a result of this second round of inductive analysis we grouped the actions into four practices that emerged as the more central for activists' everyday political engagement during latency stages: political organizing (17 actions), sustaining connections (20 actions), information gathering (31 actions), and gaining visibility (48 actions). The remaining 20 actions were heterogeneous, and we put them into a fifth group, which we decided not to take into consideration in the subsequent analysis. Next, we employed the complex configuration function in MAXQDA to understand what the most common configurations of actions-services-devices were per each type of practice. The following tables show the 20 most common configurations per practice in each country, that is, those that activists mentioned most frequently during the first stage of the map-in-practices interviews. While not significant at the representative level, these tables have allowed us to look at the map dataset from a comparative perspective and keep a bird's-eye view on what activists told us about their daily employment of digital and non-digital media in connection with their grassroots political activism (Tables A.1–A.4).

In each of the 45 semi-structured interviews, we employed a deductive coding strategy that started from the four main practices we had identified in a previous stage of our analysis. Other than coding for interview extracts that relate to specific types of practices, we also coded for the meanings that activists assigned to the digital and non-digital media they employed in the framework of the four different practices, this time in an inductive way. Overall, we obtained a coding scheme that included both codes on the activists' representation of the actions in the four practices and codes on the activists' evaluation of the digital and non-digital media that they employed. In this case, too, we moved the analysis ahead by comparing the coded materials across countries and activists' movement organizations.

In an attempt to shed light also on the concrete effects of digital media on the daily life of journalists, a crucial component for understanding activists' practices, we complemented our data set with 14 media in practices interview maps with journalists who work in television, printed press, and online-only media outlets. All cover either corruption or work-related issues. As a further measure of comparison, we conducted seven media in practices interview maps with institutional actors to provide additional contextual data for our cross-national analysis. This final subset of interviewees is composed of three national parliamentarians, two governmental agents, one regional council member, and one media consultant working for a prominent national politician. All these institutional actors – three from Greece, two from Italy, and two from Spain – are actively engaged with the two issues we selected for the composition of our data set. We analysed both the maps and the subsequent interviews with journalists and institutional political actors, following the same procedure as in the case of interviews with activists. We used the results of this analysis to support the writing of Chapters 6 and 7, both revolving around the practice of sustaining meaningful connections.

All the interviews we collected in Italy were in Italian, those collected in Spain were in Spanish and those collected in Greece were in English. We then transcribed the interviews in the language in which they were collected and analysed them as such. We only translated into English those interview extracts that we decided to include in the book and that were originally in Italian or Spanish. In the case of interviews conducted in English, the interview extracts were in some cases revised to eliminate grammatical errors without changing the meaning of the interview extract.

Finally, this book also relies on 19 expert interviews with seven different categories of digital media experts working at the crossroads of media and politics. Unlike our media practices interview maps, these 19 expert interviews follow a more traditional, semi-structured interview format. To collect information that will allow for a better contextualization of the content of our book, we interviewed tech lawyers, digital entrepreneurs, governmental agents, free culture promoters, traditional and citizen journalists, and a digital corporation manager. Among these 19 experts, seven are from Italy, six from Greece, and six from Spain. With this second set of interviews, we aimed to collect the main historical and contextual factors that could help explain the similarities and differences between Italy,

Spain, and Greece at the level of digital media adoption, adaptation, and evolution, and at the intersection of the four practices. While we did not directly quote these interviews in the book, the information we gathered through expert interviews was important to reconstruct the overall context in which activists perform their practices as well as to interpret some of our results.

In addition to these 85 interviews (see Table A.5 for details), we complemented our data in two directions. First, we conducted archival research on the civil society actors' organizations as well as on the journalists' media outlets, to gather basic information about their history, recent development, and main features. We did this mainly by using the Internet as an archive of information and focusing on the official websites of civil society actors' organizations and journalists' media outlets. Second, we gathered macro data on the media consumption patterns and different media penetration in Greece, Italy, and Spain. The data come from various sources, including the International Telecommunication Union, the Digital News Report of the Reuters Institute for the Study of Journalism, and national data sources such as CENSIS in the case of Italy.

METHODOLOGICAL APPENDIX

Table A.1: The 20 most common configurations of actions-services-devices in each country (practice of political organizing)

Activities in the practice of political organizing	Devices	Services	Greece	Italy	Spain
a_organize workflow own organization	d_face-to-face	s_meeting with co-workers/collaborators	3	11	12
a_organize workflow own organization	d_smartphone	s_phonecall	4	8	7
a_organize workflow own organization	d_smartphone	s_chat app WhatsApp group	2	8	8
a_organize workflow own organization	d_smartphone	s_chat app WhatsApp individual chat	0	8	6
a_participate in meeting own organization/coalition	d_face-to-face	s_meeting with co-workers/collaborators	0	6	4
a_organize workflow own organization	d_laptop	s_software VoIP	1	5	2
a_organize workflow own organization	d_smartphone	s_text messages	2	6	0
a_organize workflow own organization	d_laptop	s_email personal	3	2	3
a_organize workflow own organization	d_smartphone	s_chat app Telegram	0	2	5
a_organize workflow own organization	d_face-to-face	s_assembly of own organization/movement	3	1	1
a_participate in meeting own organization/coalition	d_face-to-face	s_assembly of own organization/movement	0	4	1
a_organize workflow own organization	d_smartphone	s_email personal	1	4	0
a_share documents with other colleagues/activists	d_smartphone	s_email personal	1	2	1
a_share documents with other colleagues/activists	d_laptop	s_email personal	0	1	3
a_organize face-to-face meetings	d_smartphone	s_phonecall	1	1	2
a_organize workflow own organization	d_laptop	s_chat app WhatsApp individual chat	0	1	3
a_participate in meeting own organization/coalition	d_laptop	s_software VoIP	1	3	0
a_organize workflow own organization	d_laptop	s_platform for teamwork	0	3	0
a_participate in meeting own organization/coalition	d_personal computer	s_software VoIP	0	3	0
a_organize public events	d_face-to-face	s_public debates and conferences	0	1	2

193

Table A.2: The 20 most common configurations of actions–services–devices in each country (practice of sustaining connection)

Activities in the practice of sustaining connection	Devices	Services	Greece	Italy	Spain
a_check received messages	d_smartphone	s_email personal	4	6	6
a_speak with (trusted) journalists	d_smartphone	s_phonecall	4	4	4
a_speak with activists and political actors	d_face-to-face	s_meeting with activists and political actors	2	3	6
a_check received messages	d_laptop	s_email personal	4	3	3
a_reply to received messages	d_laptop	s_email personal	2	0	8
a_speak with (trusted) journalists	d_face-to-face	s_meeting with journalist	1	5	3
a_reply to received messages	d_smartphone	s_email personal	1	1	5
a_reply to received messages	d_laptop	s_Facebook page own organization	2	2	2
a_speak with (trusted) journalists	d_smartphone	s_chat app WhatsApp individual chat	0	5	1
a_speak with other actors	d_face-to-face	s_meeting with other actors	1	1	3
a_check received messages	d_smartphone	s_chat app WhatsApp individual chat	0	2	3
a_check received messages	d_personal computer	s_email personal	1	4	0
a_speak with activists and political actors	d_smartphone	s_phonecall	1	3	0
a_speak with (trusted) journalists	d_laptop	s_email personal	0	1	3
a_listen to citizens' needs and problems	d_face-to-face	s_meeting with citizens	2	2	0
a_reply to received messages	d_smartphone	s_Facebook messenger	1	2	1
a_check received messages	d_smartphone	s_email own organization	2	1	1
a_reply to received messages	d_laptop	s_Facebook messenger	1	3	0
a_speak with (trusted) journalists	d_smartphone	s_text messages	1	3	0
a_reply to received messages	d_smartphone	s_Facebook page own organization	1	1	2

Table A.3: The 20 most common configurations of actions-services-devices in each country (practice of information gathering)

Activities in the practice of gathering information	Devices	Services	Greece	Italy	Spain
a_gather relevant information for own work/own organization	d_television	s_television newscasts and talk shows	7	9	3
a_gather relevant information for own work/own organization	d_radio	s_radio programme on current affairs	5	5	3
a_check media coverage on own organization	d_television	s_television newscasts and talk shows	2	3	8
a_check media coverage on own organization	d_print press	s_newspapers national	2	2	8
a_gather relevant information for own work/own organization	d_laptop	s_website informational	8	1	2
a_gather relevant information for own work/own organization	d_print press	s_newspapers national	6	4	1
a_gather relevant information for own work/own organization	d_smartphone	s_website informational	6	0	3
a_read (listen/watch) news	d_print press	s_newspapers national	1	7	0
a_check media coverage on own organization	d_radio	s_radio programme on current affairs	2	2	4
a_monitor own organization (news) media outlet	d_laptop	s_website own organization	2	0	5
a_monitor what is going on	d_smartphone	s_Facebook page own organization	2	2	2
a_monitor own social media data and audience interactions	d_laptop	s_Facebook page own organization	2	2	2
a_monitor what is going on	d_laptop	s_Facebook page own organization	2	2	1
a_gather relevant information for own work/own organization	d_print press	s_newsweek national	1	4	0
a_read (listen/watch) news	d_smartphone	s_newspapers national	2	1	1
a_gather relevant information for own work/own organization	d_smartphone	s_Facebook own profile/page	1	3	0
a_read (listen/watch) news	d_laptop	s_newspapers national	3	0	1
a_gather relevant information for own work/own organization	d_laptop	s_Facebook own profile/page	2	2	0
a_gather relevant information for own work/own organization	d_laptop	s_newspapers national	2	1	1
a_monitor what is going on	d_laptop	s_Twitter personal profile	1	0	3

Table A.4: The 20 most common configurations of actions-services-devices in each country (practice of gaining visibility)

Activities in the practice of gaining visibility	Devices	Services	Greece	Italy	Spain
a_publish own written/audio/video (news) media content	d_laptop	s_website own organization	8	5	6
a_release interviews	d_radio	s_radio programme on current affairs	4	7	5
a_release interviews	d_television	s_television newscasts and talk shows	2	8	3
a_participate in public event	d_face-to-face	s_public debates and conferences	3	4	4
a_share own opinion in public discussions/debates	d_face-to-face	s_public debates and conferences	1	5	3
a_organize public event	d_face-to-face	s_public debates and conferences	2	4	3
a_record video/take pictures of events	d_photo/videocamera	s_software digital audio/photo/video recording	1	6	1
a_publish info on own organization activities/events	d_laptop	s_website own organization	3	0	5
a_publish own written/audio/video (news) media content	d_smartphone	s_Facebook page own organization	0	3	4
a_record video/take pictures of events	d_smartphone	s_software digital audio/photo/video recording	3	3	1
a_publish own written/audio/video (news) media content	d_laptop	s_Facebook page own organization	2	2	3
a_publish info on own organization activities/events	d_laptop	s_Facebook page own organization	1	2	4
a_release interviews	d_print press	s_newspapers national	3	2	2
a_publish own written/audio/video (news) media content	d_personal computer	s_website own organization	0	7	0
a_produce/co-prod declarations/calls/documents own organization	d_laptop	s_Google drive	0	3	3
a_send press release own organization to media	d_laptop	s_email personal	4	0	2
a_repost own org content from other platforms/websites	d_smartphone	s_Facebook own profile/page	1	1	4
a_repost own org content from other platforms/websites	d_laptop	s_Facebook own profile/page	2	3	1
a_repost own org content from other platforms/websites	d_laptop	s_Facebook page own organization	1	3	2
a_publish own written/audio/video (news) media content	d_personal computer	s_Facebook page own organization	0	5	1

Table A.5: List of research participants interviews (names are fictional)

Number	Name	Role	Main contentious issue	Place of interview	Date of interview
Italy					
1	Marta	activist	temporary work and labor rights	Bologna	13/03/17
2	Stefano	activist	temporary work and labor rights	Rome	06/07/17
3	Francesco	institutional actor	temporary work and labor rights	Rome	17/07/17
4	Franco	institutional actor	temporary work and labor rights	Rome	05/07/17
5	Martino	activist	temporary work and labor rights	Florence	15/06/17
6	Mauro	activist	temporary work and labor rights	Turin	03/07/17
7	Gianluca	activist	temporary work and labor rights	Florence	13/03/17
8	Federico	activist	temporary work and labor rights	Terni	18/03/17
9	Simone	journalist	temporary work and labor rights	Rome	28/04/17
10	Anna	journalist	temporary work and labor rights	Rome	15/05/17
11	Alessandro	activist	temporary work and labor rights	Rome	28/04/17
12	Fabio	activist	temporary work and labor rights	Rome	15/05/17
13	Simona	activist	temporary work and labor rights	Milan	12/09/17
14	Mario	journalist	corruption and transparency	Rome	02/08/17
15	Carla	journalist	corruption and transparency	Turin	12/06/17
16	Domenico	activist	corruption and transparency	Verona	04/07/17
17	Emilia	activist	corruption and transparency	Rome	05/07/17
18	Riccardo	activist	corruption and transparency	Turin	12/06/17
19	Davide	activist	corruption and transparency	Turin	03/07/17

(continued)

Table A.5: List of research participants interviews (names are fictional) (continued)

Number	Name	Role	Main contentious issue	Place of interview	Date of interview
20	Luca	activist	corruption and transparency	Milan	15/06/17
21	Salvatore	activist	corruption and transparency	Rome	02/08/17
22	Giovanni	activist	corruption and transparency	Rome	11/09/17
23	Daniela	activist	corruption and transparency	Rome	15/09/17
24	Agata	activist	corruption and transparency	Milan	25/08/17
25	Flavio	expert	media, digitalization, and datafication	Milan	06/07/16
26	Marcello	expert	media, digitalization, and datafication	Rome	11/07/16
27	Beatrice	expert	media, digitalization, and datafication	online interview	22/08/16
28	Paolo	expert	media, digitalization, and datafication	Rome	13/06/16
29	Oreste	expert	media, digitalization, and datafication	Turin	02/08/16
30	Valeria	expert	media, digitalization, and datafication	online interview	14/07/16
31	Gabriele	expert	media, digitalization, and datafication	Rome	20/09/16
Spain					
32	David	activist	temporary work and labor rights	Madrid	08/05/17
33	Armando	activist	temporary work and labor rights	Madrid	08/05/17
34	Marisol	journalist	temporary work and labor rights	Madrid	10/05/17
35	Alvaro	activist	temporary work and labor rights	Madrid	10/05/17
36	Julia	activist	temporary work and labor rights	Madrid	10/05/17
37	Bruno	activist	temporary work and labor rights	Madrid	15/06/17
38	Enrique	activist	temporary work and labor rights	Barcelona	20/11/18
39	Jorge	activist	temporary work and labor rights	Barcelona	23/11/18

Table A.5: List of research participants interviews (names are fictional) (continued)

Number	Name	Role	Main contentious issue	Place of interview	Date of interview
40	Miguel	activist	temporary work and labor rights	Barcelona	28/11/18
41	Mauricio	institutional actor	temporary work and labor rights	Vitoria-Gasteiz	03/12/18
42	Diego	activist	temporary work and labor rights	Barcelona	10/12/18
43	Abril	activist	corruption and transparency	Valencia	06/05/17
44	Santiago	institutional actor	corruption and transparency	Madrid	12/06/17
45	Carlos	activist	corruption and transparency	Madrid	13/06/17
46	Tobias	activist	corruption and transparency	Madrid	09/05/17
47	Rodrigo	activist	corruption and transparency	Madrid	15/06/17
48	Marcos	journalist	corruption and transparency	Barcelona	22/11/18
49	Hilario	journalist	corruption and transparency	Valencia	21/11/18
50	Ruben	activist	corruption and transparency	Barcelona	29/11/18
51	Adrian	activist	corruption and transparency	Barcelona	30/11/18
52	Miranda	activist	corruption and transparency	Madrid	04/12/18
53	Letizia	expert	media, digitalization, and datafication	online interview	29/06/16
54	Leo	expert	media, digitalization, and datafication	online interview	18/07/16
55	Alonso	expert	media, digitalization, and datafication	online interview	05/07/16
56	Bernardo	expert	media, digitalization, and datafication	online interview	18/07/16
57	Maria	expert	media, digitalization, and datafication	online interview	17/06/16
58	Francisco	expert	media, digitalization, and datafication	online interview	12/07/16
59	Cristobal	expert	media, digitalization, and datafication	online interview	22/08/16

(continued)

Table A.5: List of research participants interviews (names are fictional) (continued)

Number	Name	Role	Main contentious issue	Place of interview	Date of interview
Greece					
60	Timotheos	journalist	temporary work and labor rights	Rome	05/04/17
61	Petro	activist	temporary work and labor rights	Athens	19/09/17
62	Eusebios	journalist	temporary work and labor rights	Athens	01/11/17
63	Kosmas	activist	temporary work and labor rights	Athens	08/12/17
64	Eustratios	activist	temporary work and labor rights	Athens	06/12/17
65	Hektor	activist	temporary work and labor rights	Athens	24/10/18
66	Papios	activist	temporary work and labor rights	Athens	09/11/18
67	Kosta	activist	temporary work and labor rights	Athens	08/11/18
68	Sebastian	activist	temporary work and labor rights	Athens	08/11/18
69	Ivan	activist	temporary work and labor rights	Athens	23/10/18
70	Philippos	activist	corruption and transparency	Athens	19/09/17
71	Eulalia	activist	corruption and transparency	Athens	30/10/17
72	Nestor	journalist	corruption and transparency	Athens	05/12/17
73	Kyprianos	journalist	corruption and transparency	Athens	28/11/17
74	Iris	institutional actor	corruption and transparency	Athens	10/10/18
75	Dimitra	institutional actor	corruption and transparency	Athens	25/10/18
76	Helene	institutional actor	various	Athens	30/10/17
77	Photios	journalist	various	Athens	02/11/17
78	Orestes	journalist	various	Athens	05/12/17

METHODOLOGICAL APPENDIX

Table A.5: List of research participants interviews (names are fictional) (continued)

Number	Name	Role	Main contentious issue	Place of interview	Date of interview
79	Dionysius	journalist	various	Athens	09/10/18
80	Delphina	activist	various	Athens	06/11/18
81	Niketa	expert	media, digitalization, and datafication	Athens	20/07/16
82	Anatolios	expert	media, digitalization, and datafication	Athens	19/07/16
83	Constantine	expert	media, digitalization, and datafication	Athens	21/07/16
84	Zenas	expert	media, digitalization, and datafication	Athens	19/07/16
85	Marcurios	expert	media, digitalization, and datafication	Athens	18/07/16

Notes

Chapter 1

1. Although Twitter had already changed its name to X by the time of the book's publication, we decided not to use this name. Instead, we opted to stick with the name 'Twitter' as it was known during the empirical research that underlies this book.

Chapter 3

1. RAI1 is the flagship channel of RAI, the Italian public broadcaster.
2. According to European Commission, Directorate-General for Communication (2018), Greek, Italian, and Spanish citizens who listen to the radio *almost every day* make up 39 per cent, 35 per cent, and 33 per cent of the entire population respectively, while the same data are more than double regarding television: 86 per cent in Greece, 90 per cent in Italy, and 88 per cent in Spain.

Chapter 4

1. *Citizens United v. Federal Election Commission*, 558 U.S. 310 (2010).

References

Ahva, L. (2017) "Practice theory for journalism studies", *Journalism Studies*, 18(12): 1523–41.
Andrejevic, M. (2013) *Infoglut: How Too Much Information is Changing The Way We Think and Know*, New York: Routledge.
Atton, C. (2002) *Alternative Media*, London: Sage Publications.
Atton, C. (ed) (2015) *The Routledge Companion to Alternative and Community Media*, London: Routledge.
Bakardjieva, M. (2009) "Subactivism: lifeworld and politics in the age of the internet", *The Information Society*, 25(2): 91–104.
Baldassar, L. (2015) "Guilty feelings and the guilt trip: emotions and motivation in migration and transnational caregiving", *Emotion, Space and Society*, 16: 81–9.
Baller, S., Dutta, S., and Lanvin, B. (2016) *The Global Information Technology Report 2016: Innovating in The Digital Economy*, Geneva: World Economic Forum.
Barad, K. (2007) *Meeting the Universe Halfway: Quantum Physics and the Entanglement of Matter and Meaning*, Durham: Duke University Press.
Barassi, V. (2015a) *Activism on the Web: Everyday Struggles against Digital Capitalism*, London: Routledge.
Barassi, V. (2015b) "Social media, immediacy and the time for democracy: critical reflections on social media as 'temporalizing practices'", in D. Lina and O. Leistert (eds) *Critical Perspectives on Social Media and Protest: Between Control and Emancipation*, New York: Rowman and Littlefield International, pp 73–90.
Barassi, V. and Fenton, N. (2011) "Alternative media and social networking sites: the politics of individuation and political participation", *The Communication Review*, 14(3): 179–96.
Bauman, Z. (2012) *Liquid Modernity*, Cambridge, MA: Polity Press.
Baxter, J. (2018) "'Keep strong, remember everything you have learnt': constructing support and solidarity through online interaction within a UK cancer support group", *Discourse & Society*, 29(4): 363–79.
Baym, N. (2015) *Personal Connections in the Digital Age*, Hoboken, NJ: John Wiley & Sons.

Belair-Gagnon, A. and Frisch, N. (2017) "Mobile sourcing: a case study of journalistic norms and usage of chat apps", *Mobile Media & Communication*, 6(1): 53–70.

Bennett, W.L. (2005) "Social movements beyond borders: understanding two eras of transnational activism", in A. della Porta and S. Tarrow (eds) *Transnational Protest and Global Activism*, Lanham, MD: Rowman & Littlefield, pp 271–94.

Bennett, W.L. and Segerberg, A. (2013) *The Logic of Connective Action: Digital Media and the Personalization of Contentious Politics*, Cambridge: Cambridge University Press.

Benney, J. (2011) "Twitter and legal activism in China", *Communication, Politics & Culture*, 44(1): 5–20.

Benski, T. (2010) "Emotion maps of participation in protest: the case of women in black against the occupation in Israel", *Research in Social Movements, Conflicts and Change*, 31: 3–34.

Bifet, A., Gavaldà, R., Holmes, G., and Pfahringer, B. (2018) *Machine Learning for Data Streams: With Practical Examples in MOA*, Cambridge, MA: MIT Press.

Bimber, B. (2003) *Information and American Democracy: Technology in the Evolution of Political Power*, Cambridge: Cambridge University Press.

Bishop, S. (2019) "Managing visibility on YouTube through algorithmic gossip", *New Media & Society*, 21(11–12): 2589–606.

Blee, K.M. (2012) *Democracy in the Making: How Activist Groups Form*, New York: Oxford University Press.

Borgman, C.L. (2016) *Big Data, Little Data, No Data. Scholarship in the Networked World*, Boston, MA: MIT Press.

Bosi, L. and Zamponi, L. (2015) "Direct social actions and economic crises: the relationship between forms of action and socio-economic context in Italy", *Partecipazione e Conflitto*, 8(2): 367–91.

Bourdieu, P. (1977) *Outline of a Theory of Practice*, Cambridge: Cambridge University Press.

Bourdieu, P. (1990) *The Logic of Practice*, Cambridge, MA: Polity Press.

Bracciale, R. and Martella, A. (2017) "Define the populist political communication style: the case of Italian political leaders on Twitter", *Information, Communication & Society*, 20(9): 1310–29.

Brants, K. and Voltmer, K. (eds) (2011) *Political Communication in Postmodern Democracy: Challenging The Primacy of Politics*, New York: Springer.

Bräuchler, B. and Postill, J. (2010) *Theorising Media and Practice*, New York: Berghahn Books.

Bravington, A. and King, N. (2019) "Putting graphic elicitation into practice: tools and typologies for the use of participant-led diagrams in qualitative research interviews", *Qualitative Research*, 19(5): 506–23.

Briffault, R. (2012) "Super PACs", *Minnesota Law Review*, 96: 1644.

Bucher, T. (2012) "Want to be on the top? Algorithmic power and the threat of invisibility on Facebook", *New Media & Society*, 14: 1164–80.

Bucher, T. (2017) "The algorithmic imaginary: exploring the ordinary affects of Facebook algorithms", *Information, Communication & Society*, 20(1): 30–44.

Bucher, T. (2018) *If… Then: Algorithmic Power and Politics*, New York: Oxford University Press.

Bueger, C. and Gadinger, F. (2014) "Die formalisierung der informalität: praxistheoretische überlegungen", *Informelle Politik*, Springer VS: Wiesbade, pp 81–98.

Bueger, C. and Gadinger, F. (2018) *International Practice Theory: New Perspectives*, Houndmills: Palgrave Macmillan

Casero-Ripollés, A. and Izquierdo-Castillo, J. (2013) "Between decline and a new online business model: the case of the Spanish newspaper industry", *Journal of Media Business Studies*, 10(1): 63–78.

Castells, M. (2009) *Communication Power*, New York: Oxford University Press.

Castells, M. (2015) *Networks of Outrage and Hope: Social Movements in the Internet Age* (2nd edn), Cambridge, MA: Polity Press.

Casula, C. (2021) "Local broadcast journalists and the trap of professional heterogeneity", *Professions and Professionalism*, 11(1): e3912.

Ceccobelli, D. and Di Gregorio, L. (2022) "The triangle of leadership: authenticity, competence and ordinariness in political marketing", *Journal of Political Marketing*, 2: 113–25.

Ceccobelli, D., Quaranta, M., and Valeriani, A. (2020) "Citizens' engagement with popularization and with populist actors on Facebook: a study on 52 leaders in 18 Western democracies", *European Journal of Communication*, 35(5): 435–52.

Ceron, A. and Splendore, S. (2018) "Social TV, pluralism and journalistic authority", *Problemi dell'Informazione*, 2: 181–206.

Chadwick, A. (2007) "Digital network repertoires and organizational hybridity", *Political Communication*, 24(3): 283–301.

Chadwick, A. (2013) *The Hybrid Media System: Politics and Power*, New York: Oxford University Press.

Chadwick, A. and Dennis, J. (2017) "Social media, professional media and mobilisation in contemporary Britain: explaining the strengths and weaknesses of the citizens' movement 38 Degrees", *Political Studies*, 65(1): 42–60.

Chadwick, G. (2013) *A Systems View of Planning: Towards a Theory of The Urban and Regional Planning Process*, Amsterdam: Elsevier.

Chen, H.T. (2018) "Spiral of silence on social media and the moderating role of disagreement and publicness in the network: analyzing expressive and withdrawal behaviors", *New Media & Society*, 20(10): 3917–36.

Chenou, J.M. and Cepeda-Másmela, C. (2019) "#NiUnaMenos: data activism from the Global South", *Television & New Media*, 20(4): 369–411.

Cohen, I.J. (1996) "Theories of action and praxis", in B.S. Turner (ed) *The Blackwell Companion to Social Theory*, Oxford, UK: Wiley-Blackwell, pp 73–111.

Cohen, N., Hunter, A., and O'Donnell, P. (2019) "Bearing the burden of corporate restructuring: job loss and precarious employment in Canadian journalism", *Journalism Practice*, 13(7): 817–33.

Cook, K.S., Hardin, R., and Levi, M. (2005) *Cooperation Without Trust?*, New York: Russell Sage Foundation.

Costanza-Chock, S. (2003) "Mapping the repertoire of electronic contention", in A. Opel and D. Pompper (eds) *Representing Resistance: Media, Civil Disobedience and the Global Justice Movement*, Greenwood, NJ: Praeger, pp 173–91.

Couldry, N. (2000) *The Place of Media Power: Pilgrims and Witnesses of The Media Age*, London: Routledge.

Couldry, N. (2004) "Theorising media as practice", *Social Semiotics*, 14(2): 115–32.

Couldry, N. (2012) *Media, Society, World: Social Theory and Digital Media Practice*, Cambridge, MA: Polity Press.

Couldry, N. and Hepp, A. (2016) *The Mediated Construction of Reality*, Cambridge, MA: Polity Press.

Couldry, N. and Mejias, U.A. (2019) *The Costs of Connection: How Data Is Colonizing Human Life and Appropriating It for Capitalism*, Redwood: Stanford University Press.

Cress, D.M. and Snow, D.A. (2000) "The outcomes of homeless mobilization: the influence of organization, disruption, political mediation, and framing", *American Journal of Sociology*, 105(4): 1063–104.

Crete-Nishihata, M., Oliver, J., Parsons, C., Walker, D., Tsui, L., and Deibert, R. (2020) "The information security cultures of journalism", *Digital Journalism*, 8(8): 1068–91.

Cretu, A.E. and Brodie, R.J. (2007) "The influence of brand image and company reputation where manufacturers market to small firms: a customer value perspective", *Industrial Marketing Management*, 36(2): 230–40.

Cummings, J.N., Butler, B., and Kraut, R. (2002) "The quality of online social relationships", *Communications of the ACM*, 45(7): 103–8.

Davis, G.F., McAdam, D., Richard, W., Mayer, S., and Zald, N. (eds) (2005) *Social Movements and Organization Theory*, Cambridge: Cambridge University Press.

Deibert, R. and Rohozinski, R. (2011) "Contesting cyberspace and the coming crisis of authority", in R. Deibert, J. Palfrey, R. Rohozinski, and J. Zittrain (eds) *Security, Identity, and Resistance in Asian Cyberspace*, Cambridge, MA: MIT Press, pp 21–41.

della Porta, D. and Diani, M. (2020) *Social Movements: An Introduction*, Hoboken, NJ: John Wiley & Sons.

Dencik, L. and Wilkin, P. (2018) "Digital activism and the future of worker resistance", in G. Meike (ed) *The Routledge Companion to Media and Activism*, London: Routledge, pp 125–33.

Deuze, M. (2007) *Media Work*, Cambridge, MA: Polity Press.

Diani, M. (2015) *The Cement of Civil Society: Studying Networks in Localities*, Cambridge: Cambridge University Press.

Diani, M. and Mische, A. (2015) "Network approaches and social movements", in D. della Porta and M. Diani (eds) *The Oxford Handbook of Social Movements*, Oxford, UK: Oxford University Press, pp 306–25.

Dodds, T. (2019) "Reporting with WhatsApp: mobile chat applications' impact on journalistic practices", *Digital Journalism*, 7(6): 725–45.

Downing, J. (2001) *Radical Media: Rebellious Communication and Social Movements*, Thousand Oaks, CA: Sage Publications.

Driessens, O., Raeymaeckers, K., Verstraeten, H., and Vandenbussche, S. (2010) "Personalization according to politicians: a practice theoretical analysis of mediatization", *Communications*, 35(3): 309–26.

Dubois, E. and Blank, G. (2018) "The echo chamber is overstated: the moderating effect of political interest and diverse media", *Information, Communication & Society*, 21(5): 729–45.

Dumitrica, D. and Felt, M. (2020) "Mediated grassroots collective action: negotiating barriers of digital activism", *Information, Communication & Society*, 23(13): 1821–37.

Earl, J. and Kimport, K. (2011) *Digitally Enabled Social Change: Activism in the Internet Age*, Boston, MA: MIT Press.

Ekdale, B., Tully, M., Harmsen, S., and Singer, J. (2014) "Newswork within a culture of job insecurity", *Journalism Practice*, 9(3): 383–98.

Elmer, G., Langlois, G., and McKelvey, F. (2014) "The permanent campaign online: platforms, actors, and issue-objects", in K. Kozolanka (ed) *Publicity and the Canadian State: Critical Communications Perspectives*, Toronto: University of Toronto Press, pp 240–61.

Engesser, S., Ernst, N. Esser, F., and Büchel, F. (2017) "Populism and social media: how politicians spread a fragmented ideology", *Information, Communication & Society*, 20(8): 1109–26.

Enli, G. (2015) "'Trust me, I am authentic!': authenticity illusions in social media politics", in A. Burns, G. Enli, E. Skogerbø, A.O. Larsson, and C. Christense (eds) *The Routledge Companion to Social Media and Politics*, London: Routledge, pp 121–36.

Ermoshina, K. and Musiani, F. (2017) "Migrating servers, elusive users: reconfigurations of the Russian Internet in the post-Snowden era", *Media and Communication*, 5(1): 42–53.

Etter, M. and Albu, O.B. (2021) "Activists in the dark: social media algorithms and collective action in two social movement organizations", *Organization*, 28(1): 68–91.

Etter, M., Ravasi, D., and Colleoni E. (2019) "Social media and the formation of organizational reputation", *Academy of Management Review*, 44(1): 28–52.

European Commission, Directorate-General for Communication (2018) *Media Use in the European Union – Standard Eurobarometer 88, Autumn 2017 – Report*, European Commission, Available from: https://data.europa.eu/doi/10.2775/116707.

Evans, E.M. (2016) "Bearing witness: How controversial organizations get the media coverage they want", *Social Movement Studies*, 15(1): 41–59.

Fenton N. and Barassi, V. (2001) "Alternative media and social networking sites: the politics of individuation and political participation", *Communication Review*, 14(3): 179–96.

Fiebert, T. and Warren, C.R. (2013) "It's your birthday! Greetings as a function of gender and relationship status on Facebook", *International Review of Social Sciences and Humanities*, 4(2): 206–8.

Fominaya, C.F. (2020) *Democracy Reloaded: Inside Spain's Political Laboratory from 15-M to Podemos*, New York: Oxford University Press.

Gabrys, J., Pritchard, H., and Barratt, B. (2016) "Just good enough data: figuring data citizenships through air pollution sensing and data stories", *Big Data & Society*, 3(2). DOI: 10.1177/2053951716679677

Gad, C. and Jensen, C.B. (2014) "The promises of practice", *The Sociological Review*, 62(4): 698–718.

Galbraith, J.K. (1986) "Power and organization", in S. Lukes (ed) *Power: Reading in Social and Political Theory*, New York: New York University Press, pp 211–28.

Galis, V. and Neumayer, C. (2016) "Laying claim to social media by activists: a cyber-material detournement", *Social media + Society*, 2(3). DOI: 10.1177/2056305116664360.

Gamson, W.A. (1975) *The Strategy of Social Protest*, Homewood: Irwin-Dorsey.

Gamson, W.A. and Wolfsfeld, G. (1993) "Movements and media as interacting systems", *Annals of the American Academy of Political and Social Science*, 528(1): 114–25.

Gazzola, P., Amelio, S., Papagiannis, F., and Michaelides, Z. (2019) "Sustainability reporting practices and their social impact to NGO funding in Italy", *Critical Perspectives on Accounting*, 79. DOI: 10.1016/j.cpa.2019.04.006

Gerbaudo, P. (2012) *Tweets and the Streets: Social Media and Contemporary Activism*, London: Pluto Press.

Gherardi, S. (2009) "Practice? It's a matter of taste!", *Management Learning*, 40(5): 535–50.

Giddens, A. (1979) *Central Problems in Social Theory*, London: Macmillan Education UK.

Gitelman, L. and Jackson, V. (2013) "Introduction", in L. Gitelman (ed) *Raw Data is an Oxymoron*, Cambridge MA: The MIT Press, pp 1–15.

Gitlin, T. (1980) *The Whole World Is Watching. Mass Media in the Making and Unmaking of the New Left*, Berkeley, CA: University of California Press.

Goffman, E. (1959) "The moral career of the mental patient", *Psychiatry*, 22(2): 123–42.

Gollmitzer, M. (2014) "Precariously employed watchdogs? Perceptions of working conditions among freelancers and interns", *Journalism Practice*, 8(6): 826–41.

Goodwin, J. and Jasper, J.M. (2004) "Caught in a winding, snarling vine: the structural bias of political process theory", in J. Goodwin and J.M. Jasper (eds) *Rethinking Social Movements: Structure, Meaning, and Emotion*, Lanham MD: Rowman & Littlefield, pp 3–30.

Gran, A.B., Booth, P., and Bucher, T. (2020) "To be or not to be algorithm aware: a question of a new digital divide?", *Information, Communication & Society*, 24(12): 1779–96.

Gutierrez, M. (2019) "Maputopias: cartographies of communication, coordination and action – the cases of Ushahidi and InfoAmazonia", *GeoJournal*, 84(1): 101–20.

Gutierrez, M. (2018) *Data Activism and Social Change*, New York: Springer.

Haddon, L. (2011) "Domestication analysis, objects of study, and the centrality of technologies in everyday life", *Canadian Journal of Communication*, 36(2): 311–23.

Halkier, B., Katz-Gerro, T., and Martens, L. (2011) "Applying practice theory to the study of consumption: theoretical and methodological considerations", *Journal of Consumer Culture*, 11(1): 3–13.

Hallin, D.C. and Mancini, P. (2004) *Comparing Media Systems: Three Models of Media and Politics*, Cambridge: Cambridge University Press.

Hardin, R. (2002) *Trust and Trustworthiness*, New York: Russell Sage Foundation.

Harlow, S. and Johnson, T.J. (2011) "The Arab spring: overthrowing the protest paradigm? How the New York Times, global voices and twitter covered the Egyptian revolution", *International Journal of Communication*, 5(16): 1359–74.

Hayes, K. and Silke, H. (2019) "Narrowing the discourse? Growing precarity in freelance journalism and its effect on the construction of news discourse", *Critical Discourse Studies*, 16(3): 363–79.

Häyhtiö, T. and Rinne, J. (2008) *Net Working/Networking: Citizen Initiated Internet Politics*, Tampere: Tampere University Press.

Hedman, U. and Djerf-Pierre, M. (2013) "The social journalist: embracing the social media life or creating a new digital divide?", *Digital Journalism*, 1(3): 368–85.

Hepp, A. (2013) *Cultures of Mediatization*, Hoboken, NJ: John Wiley & Sons.

Hepp, A., Roitsch, C., and Berg, M. (2016) "Investigating communication networks contextually: qualitative network analysis as cross-media research", *MedieKultur: Journal of Media and Communication Research*, 32(60): 87–106.

Hoffmann, C.P. and Suphan, A. (2017) "Stuck with 'electronic brochures'? How boundary management strategies shape politicians' social media use", *Information, Communication & Society*, 20(4): 551–69.

Howard, P.N. and Hussain, M.M. (2013) *Democracy's Fourth Wave? Digital Media and the Arab Spring*, New York: Oxford University Press.

Hunt, S. (2005) *The Life Course: A Sociological Introduction*, New York: Palgrave Macmillan.

Hutchinson, J. (2021) "Micro-platformization for digital activism on social media", *Information, Communication & Society*, 24(1): 35–51.

Inglehart, R. (1997) *Modernization and Postmodernization: Cultural, Economic and Political Change in 41 Societies*, Princeton, NJ: Princeton University Press.

Jasper, J.M. (2010) "Social movement theory today: toward a theory of action?", *Sociology Compass*, 4(11): 965–76.

Jasper, J.M. and Duyvendak J.W. (2015) *Players and Arenas: The Interactive Dynamics of Protest*, Amsterdam: Amsterdam University Press.

Jenkins, H. (2006) *Convergence Culture: Where Old and New Media Collide*, New York: New York University Press.

Jeppesen, S., Kruzynski, A., Lakoff, A., and Sarrasin, R. (2014) "Grassroots autonomous media practices: a diversity of tactics", *Journal of Media Practice*, 15(1): 21–38.

Joathan, Í. and Lilleker, D.G. (2020) "Permanent campaigning: a meta-analysis and framework for measurement", *Journal of Political Marketing*, 22(1): 67–85.

Johnson, T.J. and Kaye, B.K. (2010) "Still cruising and believing? An analysis of online credibility across three presidential campaigns", *American Behavioral Scientist*, 54(1): 57–77.

Juris, J.S. (2005) "The new digital media and activist networking within anti-corporate globalization movements", *The ANNALS of the American Academy of Political and Social Science*, 597(1): 189–208.

Juris, J. (2008) *Networking Futures: The Movements against Corporate Futures*, Cambridge, MA: MIT Press.

Karapanos, T. and Gouveia, R. (2016) "Need fulfillment and experiences on social media: a case on Facebook and WhatsApp", *Computers in Human Behavior*, 55: 888–97.

Karpf, D. (2017) *Analytic Activism: Digital Listening and the New Political Strategy*, New York: Oxford University Press.

Katsikas, S.K. and Gritzalis, S. (2017) "Digitalization in Greece: state of play, barriers, challenges, solutions", in A.A. Paulin, L.G. Anthopoulos, and C.G. Reddick (eds) *Beyond Bureaucracy*, New York NY: Springer, pp 355–75.

REFERENCES

Kaun, A. (2016) *Crisis and Critique: A Brief History of Media Participation in Times of Crisis*, London: Zed Books.

Kavada, A. (2013) "Internet cultures and protest movements: the cultural links between strategy, organizing and online communication", in B. Cammaerts, A. Mattoni, and P. McCurdy (eds) *Mediation and Protest Movements*, Bristol: Intellect, pp 75–94.

Kavada, A. and Treré, E. (2020) "Live democracy and its tensions: making sense of livestreaming in the 15M and occupy", *Information, Communication and Society*, 23(12): 1787–804.

Kazansky, B. (2021) "'It depends on your threat model': the anticipatory dimensions of resistance to data-driven surveillance", *Big Data & Society*, 8(1). DOI: 10.1177/2053951720985557.

Kennedy, H. (2018) "Living with data: aligning data studies and data activism through a focus on everyday experiences of datafication", *Krisis: Journal for Contemporary Philosophy*, 1: 18–30.

Kepplinger, H.M. (2002) "Mediatization of politics: theory and data", *Journal of Communication*, 52(4): 972–86.

Kidd, D. (2003) "Indymedia.org: a new communications commons", in M. McCaughey and M.D. Ayers (eds) *Cyberactivism: Critical Theories and Practices of On-Line Activism*, New York: Routledge, pp 47–69.

Kitchin, R. (2017) "Thinking critically about and researching algorithms", *Information, Communication & Society*, 20(1): 14–29.

Klandermans, B. (1992) "The social construction of protest and multiorganizational fields", in A.D. Morris and C. McClurg Mueller (eds) *Frontiers in Social Movement Theory*, New Haven, CT: Yale University Press, pp 77–103.

Klawitter, E. and Hargittai, E. (2018) "'It's like learning a whole other language': the role of algorithmic skills in the curation of creative goods", *International Journal of Communication*, 12: 3490–510.

Klinger, U. and Svensson, J. (2018) "The end of media logics? On algorithms and agency", *New Media & Society*, 20(12): 4653–70.

Kreiss, D. and McGregor, S.C. (2018) "Technology firms shape political communication: the work of Microsoft, Facebook, Twitter, and Google with campaigns during the 2016 US presidential cycle", *Political Communication*, 35(2): 155–77.

Kriesi, H., Tresch, A., and Jochum, M. (2007) "Going public in the European Union: action repertoires of Western European collective political actors", *Comparative Political Studies*, 40(1): 48–73.

Krinsky, J. and Crossley, N. (2014) "Social movements and social networks: introduction", *Social Movement Studies*, 13(1): 1–21.

Krombholz, K., Merkl, D., and Weippl, E. (2012) "Fake identities in social media: a case study on the sustainability of the Facebook business model", *Journal of Service Science Research*, 4(2): 175–212.

Kubitschko, S. (2018) "Acting on media technologies and infrastructures: expanding the media as practice approach", *Media, Culture & Society*, 40(4): 629–35.

Langer, A.I. and Gruber, J.B. (2021) "Political agenda setting in the hybrid media system: why legacy media still matter a great deal", *The International Journal of Press/Politics*, 26(2): 313–40.

Lazarsfeld, P.F., Berelson, B., and Gaudet, H. (1944) *The People's Choice: How the Voter Makes up his Mind in a Presidential Campaign*, New York: Columbia University Press.

Leach, D.K. and Haunss, S. (2009) "Scenes and social movements", in H. Johnston (ed) *Culture, Social Movements and Protest*, Farnham, UK: Ashgate Publishing, pp 255–76.

Lee, A.Y.L and Ting, K.W. (2015) "Media and information praxis of young activists in the Umbrella Movement", *Chinese Journal of Communication*, 8(4): 376–92.

Lee, F.L.F. and Chan, J.M. (2018) *Media and Protest Logics in the Digital Era: The Umbrella Movement in Hong Kong*, New York: Oxford University Press.Lee-Wright, P. (2012) "The return of Hephaestus: journalists' work recrafted", in P. Lee-Wright, A. Phillips, and T. Witschge (eds) *Changing Journalism*, London and New York: Routledge, pp 21–41.

Leizerov, S. (2000) "Privacy advocacy groups versus Intel: a case study of how social movements are tactically using the Internet to fight corporations", *Social Science Computer Review*, 18(4): 461–83.

Lenhart, A. (2012) "Teens, smartphones, & texting: texting volume is up while the frequency of voice calling is down. About one in four teens say they own smartphones", Pew Research Centre [online] 19 March, Available from: https://www.pewresearch.org/internet/2012/03/19/teens-smartphones-texting/ [Accessed 25 September 2023].

Leonelli, S. (2016) *Data-Centric Biology: A Philosophical Study*, Chicago, IL: University of Chicago Press.

Lievrouw, L. (2011) *Alternative and Activist New Media*, Cambridge, MA: Polity Press.

Lilley, S., Grodzinsky, F.S., and Gumbus, A. (2012) "Revealing the commercialized and compliant Facebook user", *Journal of Information, Communication and Ethics in Society*, 10(2): 82–92.

Lovejoy, K. and Saxton, G.D. (2012) "Information, community, and action: how nonprofit organizations use social media", *Journal of Computer-Mediated Communication*, 17(3): 337–53.

Lupien, P. (2020) "Indigenous movements, collective action, and social media: new opportunities or new barriers?", *Social Media + Society*, 6(2). DOI: 10.1177/2056305120926487

Lupien, P., Chiriboga, G., and Machaca, S. (2021) "Indigenous movements, ICTs and the state in Latin America", *Journal of Information Technology & Politics*, 18(4): 387–400.

Lupton, D. (2015) *Digital Sociology*, London; New York: Routledge.

Lupton, D. (2018) "How do data come to matter? Living and becoming with personal data", *Big Data & Society*, 5(2). DOI: 10.1177/2053951718786314

Macintyre, A. (2020) "Adaption to data-driven practices in civil society organizations: a case study of Amnesty International", *Journal of Information Technology & Politics*, 17(2): 161–73.

Magalhães, J.C. and Yu, J. (2017) "Algorithmic visibility: elements for a new media visibility regime", European Consortium for Political Research [online], Available from: https://www.researchgate.net/publication/321245421_Algorithmic_visibility_-_Elements_of_new_regime_of_visibility.

Mancini, P. and Swanson, D.L. (1996) "Politics, media, and modern democracy: Introduction", in P. Mancini and D.L. Swanson (eds) *Politics, Media and Modern Democracy: An International Study of Innovations in Electoral Campaigning and Their Consequences*, Westport, CT: Praeger Publishing, pp 1–26.

Manovich, L. (2011) "Trending: the promises and the challenges of big social data", in M. Gold and K. Minneapolis (eds) *Debates in the Digital Humanities*, Minneapolis, MN: The University of Minnesota Press, pp 460–75.

Marchetti, R. and Ceccobelli, D. (2016) "Twitter and television in a hybrid media system: the 2013 Italian election campaign", *Journalism Practice*, 10(5): 626–44.

Marín-Sanchiz, C.R., Carvajal, M., and González-Esteban, J.L. (2021) "Survival strategies in freelance journalism: an empowering toolkit to improve professionals' working conditions", *Journalism Practice*, 17(3): 450–73.

Marwick, A.E. and boyd, d. (2011) "I tweet honestly, I tweet passionately: Twitter users, context collapse, and the imagined audience", *New Media & Society*, 13(1): 114–33.

Marx, L. (1964) *The Machine in the Garden: Technology and the Pastoral Ideal in America*, New York: Oxford University Press.

Matassi, M., Boczkowski, P.J., and Mitchelstein, E. (2019) "Domesticating WhatsApp: family, friends, work, and study in everyday communication", *New Media & Society*, 21(10): 2183–200.

Matthews, J. and Onyemaobi, K. (2020) "Precarious professionalism: journalism and the fragility of professional practice in the Global South", *Journalism Studies*, 21(13): 1836–51.

Mattoni, A. (2012) *Media Practices and Protest Politics: How Precarious Workers Mobilise*, Farnham, UK: Ashgate Publishing.

Mattoni, A. (2013) "Repertoires of communication in social movement processes", in B. Cammaerts, A. Mattoni, and P. McCurdy (eds) *Mediation and Protest Movements*, Bristol: Intellect, pp 39–56.

Mattoni, A. (2016) *Media Practices and Protest Politics: How Precarious Workers Mobilise*, London: Routledge.

Mattoni, A. (2017a) "A situated understanding of digital technologies in social movements: media ecology and media practice approaches", *Social Movement Studies*, 16(4): 494–505.

Mattoni, A. (2017b) "From data extraction to data leaking: data-activism in Italian and Spanish anti-corruption campaigns", *Partecipazione e Conflitto*, 10(3): 723–46.

Mattoni, A. and Ceccobelli, D. (2018) "Comparing hybrid media systems in the digital age: a theoretical framework for analysis", *European Journal of Communication*, 33(5): 540–57.

Mattoni, A. and della Porta, D. (2014) "Adapting theories on diffusion and transnational contention through social movements of the crisis: some concluding remarks", in D. della Porta and A. Mattoni (eds) *Spreading Protests: Social Movements in Times of Crisis*, Colchester: ECPR Press, pp 277–92.

Mattoni, A. and Vogiatzoglou, M. (2014) "Italy and Greece, before and after the crisis: between mobilization and resistance against precarity", *Quaderni*, 84: 57–71.

Mayer, R.C., Davis, J.H., and Schoorman, F.D. (1995) "An integrative model of organizational trust", *Academy of Management Review*, 20(3): 709–34.

Mazzoleni, G. and Schulz, W. (1999) "'Mediatization' of politics: a challenge for democracy?", *Political Communication*, 16(3): 247–61.

McAdam, D. McCarthy, J.D., and Zald, M.N. (1996) *Comparative Perspectives on Social Movements: Political Opportunities, Mobilizing Structures, and Cultural Framings*, Cambridge: Cambridge University Press.

McCarthy, J.D. and Zald, M.N. (1977) *The Trend of Social Movements in America: Professionalization and Resource Mobilization*, Morristown NJ: General Learning Press.

McCurdy, P. (2011) "Theorizing 'lay theories of media': a case study of the Dissent! network at the 2005 Gleneagles G8 Summit", *International Journal of Communication*, 5: 619–38.

McGregor, S.E. and Watkins, E.A. (2016) "Security by obscurity: journalists' mental models of information security", *Journal of the International Symposium of Online Journalism*, 6(1): 33–49.

McKenzie, P.J. (2003) "A model of information practices in accounts of everyday-life information seeking", *Journal of Documentation*, 59: 19–40.

McMillan, K. (2017) *The Constitution of Social Practices*, London: Routledge.

Melucci, A. (1989) *Nomads of the Present: Social Movements and Individual Needs in Contemporary Society*, Philadelphia: Temple University Press.

Mercea, D. and Mosca, L. (2021) "Understanding movement parties through their communication", *Information, Communication and Society*, 24(10): 1327–43.

Milan, S. (2015) "When algorithms shape collective action: social media and the dynamics of cloud protesting", *Social Media+ Society*, 1(2). DOI: 10.1177/2056305115622481.

Milan, S. (2017) "Data activism as the new frontier of media activism", in V. Pickard and G. Yang (eds) *Media Activism in the Digital Age*, London: Routledge, pp 151–63.

Milan, S. (2018) "Political agency, digital traces, and bottom-up data practices", *International Journal of Communication, Special Section 'Digital Traces in Context'*, 12: 507–25.

Milan, S. and Barbosa, S. (2020) "Enter the WhatsApper: reinventing digital activism at the time of chat apps", *First Monday*, 25(1). DOI: 10.5210/fm.v25i12.10414.

Milan, S. and Van der Velten, L. (2016) "The alternative epistemologies of data activism", *Digital Culture & Society*, 2(2): 57–74.

Milne, E. (2012) *Letters, Postcards, Email: Technologies of Presence*, London: Routledge.

Mische, A. (2008) *Partisan Publics: Communication and Contention Across Brazilian Youth Activists Networks*, Princeton NJ: Princeton University Press.

Molaei, H. (2015) "Discursive opportunity structure and the contribution of social media to the success of social movements in Indonesia", *Information, Communication & Society*, 18(1): 94–108.

Molyneux, L. and Mourão, R.R. (2019) "Political journalists' normalization of Twitter", *Journalism Studies*, 20(2): 248–66.

Monterde, M.A. and Postill, J. (2014) "Mobile ensembles: the uses of mobile phones for social protest by Spain's Indignados", in G. Goggin and L. Hjorth (eds) *Routledge Companion to Mobile Media*, London: Routledge, pp 429–38.

Morozov, E. (2011) *The Net Delusion: The Dark Side of Internet Freedom*, New York: Public Affairs.

Myers, D.J. (1994) "Communication technology and social movements: contributions of computer networks to activism", *Social Science Computer Review*, 12(2): 250–60.

Nechushtai, E. (2018) "From liberal to polarized liberal? Contemporary U.S. news in Hallin and Mancini's typology of news systems", *The International Journal of Press/Politics*, 23(2): 183–201.

Newman, N., Fletcher, R., Kalogeropoulos, A., and Nielsen, R.K. (2019) *Reuters Institute Digital News Report 2019*, Reuters Institute for the Study of Journalism, Available from: https://ssrn.com/abstract=3414941.

Newman, N., Fletcher, R., Kalogeropoulos, A., Levy, D.A.L., and Nielsen, R.K. (2018) *Reuters Institute Digital News Report 2018*, Reuters Institute for the Study of Journalism, Available from: https://ssrn.com/abstract=3245355.

Nicolini, D. (2009) "Articulating practice through the interview to the double", *Management Learning*, 40(2): 195–212.

Nicolini, D. (2010) *Practice Theory, Work, and Organization: An Introduction*, Oxford: Oxford University Press.

Norris, P. (2011) *Democratic Deficit: Critical Citizens Revisited*, Cambridge: Cambridge University Press.

Nothhaft, C. (2017) *Moments of Lobbying: An Ethnographic Study of Meetings Between Lobbyists and Politicians* [Doctoral dissertation], Örebro: Örebro högskola.

Odilla, F. and Mattoni, A. (2023) "Unveiling the layers of data activism: the organising of civic innovation to fight corruption in Brazil", *Big Data & Society*, 10(2).

Orlikowski, W.J. (2007) "Sociomaterial practices: exploring technology at work", *Organization Studies*, 28(9): 1435–48.

Örnebring, H. (2020) "A social history of precarity in journalism: penny-a-liners, bohemians and larrikins", *Australian Journalism Review*, 42(2): 191–206.

Örnebring, H. and Conill, R.F. (2016) "Outsourcing newswork", in T. Witschge, C.W. Anderson, D. Domingo, and A. Hermida (eds) *The SAGE Handbook of Digital Journalism*, London: Sage, pp 207–21.

Otto, L., Glogger, I., and Boukes, M. (2017) "The softening of journalistic political communication: a comprehensive framework model of sensationalism, soft news, infotainment, and tabloidization", *Communication Theory*, 27(2): 136–55.

Paulussen, S. (2012) "Technology and the transformation of news work: are labor conditions in (online) journalism changing?", in E. Siapera and A. Veglis (eds) *Handbooks in Communication and Media*, Oxford: Wiley-Blackwell, pp 192–208.

Petre, C., Duffy, B.E., and Hund, E. (2019) "'Gaming the system': platform paternalism and the politics of algorithmic visibility", *Social Media + Society*, 5(4). DOI: 10.1177/2056305119879995.

Picard, R.G. (2014) "Twilight or new dawn of journalism? Evidence from the changing news ecosystem", *Digital Journalism*, 2(3): 273–83.

Pizzimenti, E. (2017) "The evolution of party funding in Italy: a case of inclusive cartelisation?", *Modern Italy*, 22(1): 71–85.

Pleyers, G. (2020) "The pandemic is a battlefield: social movements in the COVID-19 lockdown", *Journal of Civil Society*, 16(4): 295–312.

Poell, T. and Rajagopalan, S. (2015) "Connecting activists and journalists", *Journalism Studies*, 16(5): 719–33.

Poell, T. and van Dijck J. (2015) "Social media and activist communication", in C. Atton (ed) *The Routledge Companion to Alternative and Community Media*, London: Routledge, pp 527–37.

Poovey, M. (1998) *A History of the Modern Fact: Problems of Knowledge in the Sciences of Wealth and Society*, Chicago: University of Chicago Press.

Postill, J. (2009) "Introduction: theorising media and practice", in B. Bräuchler and J. Postill (eds) *Theorising Media and Practice*, New York: Berghahn Books, pp 1–34.

Pouliot, V. (2013) "Methodology", in R. Adler-Nissen (ed) *Bourdieu in International Relations: Rethinking Key Concepts in IR*, London: Routledge, pp 45–58.

Prentoulis, M. and Kyriakidou, M. (2019) "Media and collective action in Greece: from indignation to solidarity", *International Journal of Communication*, 13: 22–40.

Prior, M. (2007) *Post-Broadcast Democracy: How Media Choice Increases Inequality in Political Involvement and Polarizes Elections*, Cambridge: Cambridge University Press.

Quattrociocchi, W., Scala, A., and Sunstein, C.R. (2016) "Echo chambers on Facebook", SSRN, Available from: https://ssrn.com/abstract=2795110.

Reckwitz, A. (2002) "Toward a theory of social practices: a development in culturalist theorizing", *European Journal of Social Theory*, 5(2): 245–65.

Reed, T.V. (2019) *The Art of Protest: Culture and Activism from the Civil Rights Movement to the Present*, Minneapolis: University of Minnesota Press.

Reinemann, C., Stanyer, J., Scherr, S., and Legnante, G. (2012) "Hard and soft news: a review of concepts, operationalizations and key findings", *Journalism*, 13(2): 221–39.

Rettie, R. (2007) "'Texters not talkers: phone call aversion among mobile phone users'", *PsychNology Journal*, 5(1): 33–57.

Roig, A., San Cornelio, G., Ardèvol, E., Alsina, P., and Pagès, R. (2009) "Videogame as media practice: an exploration of the intersections between play and audiovisual culture", *Convergence*, 15(1): 89–103.

Rojo, L.M. (2014) "Occupy: the spatial dynamics of discourse in global protest movements", *Journal of Language and Politics*, 13(4): 583–98.

Romanov, A., Semenov, A., Mazhelis, O., and Veijalainen, J. (2017) "Detection of fake profiles in social media: literature review", *WEBIST 2017 – Proceedings of the 13th International Conference on Web Information Systems and Technologies*, pp 363–9. DOI: 10.5220/0006362103630369.

Røpke, I. (2009) "Theories of practice – new inspiration for ecological economic studies on consumption", *Ecological Economics*, 68(10): 2490–7.

Rosenberg, D. (2013) "Data before the fact", in L. Gitelman (ed) *"Raw Data" is an Oxymoron*, Cambridge, MA: MIT Press, pp 15–40.

Rucht, D. (2004) "The quadruple 'A': media strategies of protest movements since 1960s", in W.B. Van de Donk (ed) *Cyberprotest: New Media, Citizens and Social Movements*, London, New York: Routledge, pp 25–48.

Ryan, C. (1991) *Prime Time Activism: Media Strategies for Grassroots Organizing*, Boston, MA: South End Press.

Ryan, C. and Jeffreys, K. (2019) *Beyond Prime Time Activism: Communication Activism and Social Change*, New York: Routledge.

Savolainen, R. (2008) *Everyday Information Practices: A Social Phenomenological Perspective*, Lanham, MD: The Scarecrow Press.

Schatzki, T.R. (1996) *Social Practices: A Wittgensteinian Approach to Human Activity and the Social*, Cambridge: Cambridge University Press.

Schatzki, T.R. (2002) *The Site of the Social: A Philosophical Account of the Constitution of Social Life and Change*, Pennsylvania: Penn State Press.

Schrock, A.R. (2015) "Communicative affordances of mobile media: portability, availability, locatability, and multimediality", *International Journal of Communication*, 9: 1229–46.

Schudson, M. (1998) *The Good Citizen: A History of American Civic Life*, Cambridge, MA: Harvard University Press.

Scott, S.V. and Orlikowski, W.J. (2014) "Entanglements in practice: performing anonymity through social media", *MIS Quarterly*, 38(3): 873–93.

Shin, D. (2019) "Toward fair, accountable, and transparent algorithms: case studies on algorithm initiatives in Korea and China", *Javnost-The Public*, 26(3): 274–90.

Shove, E., Pantzar, M., and Watson, M. (2012) *The Dynamics of Social Practice: Everyday Life and How It Changes*, London: SAGE.

Siles, I. and Boczkowski, P.J. (2012) "At the intersection of content and materiality: a texto-material perspective on the use of media technologies", *Communication Theory*, 22(3): 227–49.

Silverstone, R., Hirsch, E., and Morley, D. (1992) "Information and communication technologies and the moral economy of the household", in R. Silverstone and E. Hirsch (eds) *Consuming Technologies: Media and Information in Domestic Spaces*, London: Routledge, pp 15–31.

Sloan, R.H. and Warner, R. (2018) "When is an algorithm transparent? Predictive analytics, privacy, and public policy", *IEEE Security & Privacy*, 16(3): 18–25.

Sobieraj, S. (2011) *Soundbitten: The Perils of Media-Centered Political Activism*, New York: NYU Press.

Sotirakopoulos, N. and Sotiropoulos, G. (2013) "'Direct democracy now!': the Greek indignados and the present cycle of struggles", *Current Sociology*, 61(4): 443–56.

Splendore, S. and Curini, L. (2020) "Proximity between citizens and journalists as a determinant of trust in the media: an application to Italy", *Journalism Studies*, 21(9): 1167–85.

Standing G. (2011) *The Precariat: The New Dangerous Class*, London: Bloomsbury Academic.

Stephansen, H.C. (2016) "Understanding citizen media as practice: agents, processes, publics", in M. Baker and B.B. Blaagaard (eds) *Citizen Media and Public Spaces*, London: Routledge, pp 25–41.

Strömbäck, J. (2008) "Four phases of mediatization: An analysis of the mediatization of politics", *International Journal of Press Politics*, 13(3): 228–46.

Stroud, N.J. (2010) "Polarization and partisan selective exposure", *Journal of Communication*, 60(3): 556–76.

Sunstein, C.R. (2017) *#Republic: Divided Democracy in the Age of Social Media*, Princeton, NJ: Princeton University Press.

Swidler, A. (2001) "What anchors cultural practices?", in T.R. Schatzki, K.K. Cetina, and E. von Savigny (eds) *The Practice Turn in Contemporary Theory*, London: Routledge, pp 74–92.

Tatarchevskiy, T. (2011) "The 'popular' culture of internet activism", *New Media & Society*, 13(2): 297–313.

Theodoropoulou, I. (2015) "Politeness on Facebook: the case of Greek birthday wishes", *Pragmatics*, 25(1): 23–45.

Thompson, J.B. (2005) "The new visibility", *Theory, Culture & Society*, 22(6): 31–51.

Tilly, C. (2002) *Stories, Identities and Political Change*, Washington, DC: Rowman & Littlefield.

Tilly, C. (2005) *Identities, Boundaries, and Social Ties*, Boulder, CO: Paradigm Publishers.

Tilly, C. (2006) *Regimes and Repertoires*, Chicago: The University of Chicago Press.

Treré, E. (2018) *Hybrid Media Activism: Ecologies, Imaginaries, Algorithms*, London: Routledge.

Treré, E. and Bonini, T. (2022) "Amplification, evasion, hijacking: algorithms as repertoire for social movements and the struggle for visibility", *Social Movement Studies*. DOI: 10.1080/14742837.2022.2143345

Treré, E., Jeppesen, S., and Mattoni, A. (2017) "Comparing digital protest media imaginaries: anti-austerity movements in Greece, Italy & Spain", *tripleC: Communication, Capitalism & Critique. Open Access Journal for a Global Sustainable Information Society*, 15(2): 404–22.

Tsagarousianou, R. (1999) "Electronic democracy: rhetoric and reality", *Communications*, 24(2): 189–208.

Tsui, L. (2015) "The coming colonization of Hong Kong cyberspace: government responses to the use of new technologies by the umbrella movement", *Chinese Journal of Communication*, 8(4): 1–9.

Tufekci, Z. (2017) *Twitter and Tear Gas: The Power and Fragility of Networked Protest*, New Haven, CT: Yale University Press.

Uldam, J. (2018) "Social media visibility: challenges to activism", *Media, Culture & Society*, 40(1): 41–58.

Vaccari, C. and Valeriani, A. (2021) *Outside the Bubble: Social Media and Political Participation in Western Democracies*, New York: Oxford University Press.

Valenzuela, S., Correa, T., and de Zuniga, H.G. (2018) "Ties, likes, and tweets: using strong and weak ties to explain differences in protest participation across Facebook and Twitter use", *Political Communication*, 35(1): 117–34.

van der Pas, D.J., van der Brug W., and Vliegenthart, R. (2017) "Political parallelism in media and political agenda setting", *Political Communication*, 34(4): 491–510.

Van Dijck, J. and Poell, T. (2013) "Understanding social media logic", *Media and Communication*, 1(1): 2–14.

Velkova, J. and Kaun, A. (2021) "Algorithmic resistance: Media practices and the politics of repair", *Information, Communication & Society*, 24(4): 523–40.

Warde, A. (2005) "Consumption and theories of practice", *Journal of Consumer Culture*, 5(2): 131–53.

Waters, S. (2018) "The effects of mass surveillance on journalists' relations with confidential sources", *Digital Journalism*, 6(10): 1294–313.

Wesch, M. (2009) "YouTube and you: experiences of self-awareness in the context collapse of the recording webcam", *Explorations in Media Ecology*, 8(2): 19–34.

Willson, M. and Kinder-Kurlanda, K. (2021) "Social gamers' everyday (in)visibility tactics: playing within programmed constraints", *Information, Communication & Society*, 24(1): 134–49.

Wood, E.J. (2003) *Insurgent Collective Action and Civil War in El Salvador*, Cambridge: Cambridge University Press.

Zaharopoulos, T. and Paraschos, M.E. (1993) *Mass Media in Greece: Power, Politics and Privatization*, Westport, CT: Prager.

Zhu, Q., Skoric, M., and Shen, F. (2017) "I shield myself from thee: selective avoidance on social media during political protests", *Political Communication*, 34(1): 112–31.

Index

4Chan 45
15-M 118

A

accelerated times 174, 179, 180
accessibility of organizations 136
advertising 84
affective/emotional connections 111
 see also teleoaffective structures
age of users 44, 69
agency over the data stream 77, 101, 165, 167–81
algorithms
 algorithmic literacy 53, 178
 algorithmic visibility 35, 180
 appropriation of 6
 blackbox algorithms 81–2, 97
 conversion of data into information 12
 data analytics 42–3
 datafication 178
 Google 42–3
 perpetuity of the data stream 174
 proprietary algorithms on social media 37
 reconstruction of grassroots political debates via social media and algorithms 38–43
 and reputation 85–90
 reserve engineering 82–3
 temporalities of data 31
allies, potential, connecting with 50, 52, 59, 126, 135
alternative media 58–9, 66, 70–4, 75, 77, 176
always-on visibility 2
analytic activism 79
anchoring practices 21, 170, 171
Android devices 40
anti-austerity 5
anti-corporate globalization movement 5
anti-corruption 33, 55–6, 117, 118, 137, 149, 176, 183
applied practice theories 15–16
Arab Spring protests 104
Athens 73, 151, 165
Atton, C. 17
audience breadth 60
audience engagement 58, 123–44

audience information, gathering 39, 41
audio files 64, 139
authenticity 111
 see also trusted information
authoritative sources 36, 72, 76
autonomous media 58–9, 70–4

B

backstage/front-stage practices 21–2
Bakardjieva, M. 10
Baller, S. 182
banners 70
Barad, K. 19
Barassi, V. 6, 10, 90, 131
Barbosa, S. 105
Bennett, W.L. 5, 98, 103, 104
Benney, J. 89
bias 36–7, 148
Bifet, A. 12
big data 5–9, 12–13, 80, 174, 177, 181
blackbox algorithms 81–2, 97
Blee, K.M. 7
blogs 72, 145, 146
Boczkowski, P.J. 20
Borgman, C.L. 12
Borsi, L. 8
boundaries, dissolution of 92, 109–12, 114, 120–1, 170
Bourdieu, P. 15, 127
Brazil 126
breadth of voices 60
bystanders 5, 59, 133–8, 141

C

capital cities 73, 151, 176
capitalism 10, 37
Castells, M. 94, 103
casual interactions 124, 125, 143
Ceccobelli, D. 36, 82, 152
centres of power 151
Chadwick, A. 4
Chan, J.M. 32
claims-making 125
click bait 85
cloth technologies 73

coalitions of movement organizations 126, 129
Cohen, I.J. 16
collective actors in organizational work 103
collective nature of activism 13
collective organizations versus individuals in social media 90–91
comments 42, 131, 133, 137, 142, 179
community-building activities 131–2
connection building as less-researched practice 2
connections, activist-audience 123–44
constant connectivity 110
  see also perpetuity of the data stream
content providers, social movement organizations seen by legacy media as 65
context collapse 110–11, 170
context for information gathering 44–5
conversion of data into information 12, 47, 178
'cooking' data 57, 63, 64
Couldry, N. 9, 15, 16, 17, 75, 170, 176
COVID-19 8
credibility 86, 89–90, 152
  see also trusted information
cross-media outcomes 88, 98
cross-media strategies 56
cross-platform strategies 56
cross-practice effects 89
cryptographic messages 157
Cummings, J.N. 139
current affairs programming 34
current affairs via Facebook 38

D

daily political work 104–6
danger, personal 158
data, definition of 11
data abundance 46–8, 51, 53–4, 134, 136, 137–8, 174
data activism 5–6, 173
data analytics 40–2, 53, 79, 82–3, 167–81
data coding/data analysis (research) 190–1
data in practice 18
data quality 38, 95–6, 98–9, 113, 132
data security 115–18, 122, 149, 156–9, 162, 165
  see also surveillance and privacy
data sequences
  engaging in private interactions 135–6
  information gathering 30, 46–8
  intensity of data sequences 134
  private social media profiles 92–3
  public versus private 133–4
  sponsored posts 83
  surveillance and privacy 149
  sustaining connection 143
data stream
  agency over the data stream 167–81
  definition of 11–15

heterogeneity of the data stream 43–4, 77, 136, 172, 181
hybridity of the data stream 4, 106, 168, 172–3
immersion in 109–10, 167
information 13
information not synonymous with data 12
interrupting 112–15
public versus private 133–4
perpetuity of the data stream
  27/4 nature 101, 104, 109, 121, 148, 155, 174
  activists' agency 171, 174
  constant connectivity 110
  face-to-face interactions 121
  information gathering 43–4
  journalistic profession 148
  see also data abundance
surveillance and privacy 115–18
ubiquity of the data stream 43–4, 46–8, 96–7, 121, 168, 171, 173
  see also data abundance
as useful heuristic 181
'data-as-stakes' 6
datafication 8–11, 33, 76, 152, 167, 168, 174, 175–8
decision-making processes 102, 170, 179
deferred temporalities 44
della Porta, D. 60, 89, 139
device on which social media is accessed 39–40, 43, 44, 94–7, 99, 114–15, 139
Diani, M. 60, 89, 102, 125, 139
digital capitalism 10
digital media and activism 3–7
digitalization 8–11, 103, 105–6, 130, 152, 167, 168, 175–8
direct action at newspaper offices 65–6
direct news 47–8
direct social actions 7–8
disintermediation 47–8, 51, 57, 66
dispersed/integrative practice 22–3
dissolution of boundaries 92, 109–12, 114, 120–1, 170
do ut des 162, 165

E

Earl, J. 5
echo chambers 87
emails
  gaining visibility 74
  political organizing 100, 105, 113, 116
  sustaining connection 134, 135–6, 139
emblematic characters 65
embodied practices 127, 173–4
emojis 139
encrypted emails 116
Etter, M. 6, 85, 88
expert interviews 191–2
expertise 138
  see also understanding of algorithms

INDEX

F

Facebook
  age of users 44
  for current affairs 38–9
  data analytics 41, 42
  digitalization of society 130
  gaining visibility 66–70
  Greece 2, 67–8, 69–70, 76, 82, 130, 180
  information gathering 38–9
  Italy 2, 38, 67–8, 69–70, 76, 180
  journalistic profession 145–6
  legacy media pages 35
  making personal connections 123–4
  Messenger 123, 124, 129, 135, 136, 143
  presencing 75
  privacy 2, 100
  private interactions, sustaining connections through 135
  reconstruction of grassroots political debates via social media and algorithms 38–9
  sensitive information 100
  social networks 39
  sponsored posts 83–4
  sustaining connection 130–1, 133, 143
  temporalities of data 44, 45
  transparency 37
  unfriending 114
face-to-face interactions
  in the data stream 14
  gaining visibility 89
  importance of 3, 118–20, 121, 173–4, 176
  information gathering 49–51, 52
  journalistic profession 156
  making personal connections 124
  nurturing connections with supporters 129
  political organizing 101, 103
  preference for 176, 180
  surveillance and privacy 117
  sustaining connection 126–9, 132, 141
fake profiles 91
fast data 44–5, 53, 95, 101, 107, 113, 174
favour exchanges 162, 165
fax communication 70, 73–4
feedback, quick 108, 136, 137
filter bubbles 6, 87
filtered information 32, 47, 48–51, 54, 173
fine-grained analysis 41, 42
flyers 59, 70, 73, 176
following other activists on social media 52
framing of messages 32
friend vs non-friend news media 153, 161
funding 83, 119, 138
future research 178–81

G

Gabrys, J. 12
gaining visibility 55–77
  algorithms 79–80, 81–99
  as front-stage practice 22
  future research 179
  individualization of visibility 90–4
  interconnection of practices 169–71
  as key practice 21
  as political practice 23
  reputation management 85–90
  social media 39, 66–70
  through direct action 65–6
Galis, V. 81
Gerbaudo, P. 5
Gherardi, S. 20
Giddens, A. 15
Gitelman, L. 11
global justice movement 70
globalization and technology 4
Google 42–3
Google Hangout 116
Google News 42
Gran, A.B. 81
grassroots politics
  and the data stream 13
  digital media and big data in the quiet moments 7–8
  four practices of grassroots politics in the data stream 20–4
  framing of messages 32
  media-centred approach 17
  organizational structures of protest 5
  practice theories 16
  reconstruction of grassroots political debates via social media and algorithms 38–43
Greece
  acceleration of time 180
  alternative media 70, 72–3, 176
  Athens 73, 151, 165
  data security 163, 180
  dissolution of boundaries 110–11
  emails 135
  Facebook 2, 67–8, 69–70, 76, 82, 130, 180
  face-to-face interactions 130
  information gathering 29, 53
  instant messaging platforms 139–40
  journalistic profession 147, 161, 182
  legacy media 34, 37, 49, 59–60, 61, 62, 65, 76
  media and political systems 147, 148, 150–2, 153, 182
  organizational work 100
  personal networks 49
  smartphones 104, 105–6
  social media 43, 67–8, 69–70, 82
  surveillance and privacy 116, 121–2, 156–9, 163, 165, 180
  sustaining connection 139–40
  text messages 108–9
guerrilla pamphleting 73
Gutierrez, M. 6, 10

223

H

hackers 17, 118, 163
hashtags 51
Haunss, S. 7
headlines 33
Hepp, A. 9, 15, 176
heterogeneity of the data stream 43–4, 77, 136, 172, 181
Hong Kong Umbrella Movement 114
Huffington Post 35
human/non-human arrangements 4
hybrid organization types 103
hybridity of the data stream 4, 106, 168, 172–3

I

immediacy
  algorithmic visibility 81, 94–7, 98–9, 180
  information gathering 38
  political organizing 107, 108, 110, 113, 120
  sustaining connection 131, 137–8
immersion in data stream 109–10, 167
incomplete information 113
independent websites 70–2, 77
in-depth interviews 184
individualization of visibility 90–4, 98, 130
Indymedia 4, 70–2
information, conversion of data into 12, 47, 178
information gathering 29–54
  as anchoring practice 21, 170–1
  as backstage practice 22
  defining the practice of 31–3
  filtering activities 173
  finding solid information 30
  future research 179
  interconnection of practices 169–71
  as key practice 21
  as less-researched practice 2
  as mundane practice 23–4
  non-homogenous digitalization processes 177
information overload 47, 53–4, 134, 136
information professionals 63
inside-lobbying 126
Instagram 93, 133
instant messaging platforms
  algorithmic visibility 95
  future research 179
  gaining visibility 64
  immediacy 108
  interconnection of practices 170
  political organizing 101, 105, 111–12
  slowing down and interrupting the data stream 113
  surveillance and privacy 157
  sustaining connection 132, 139–40
  see also Messenger; Signal; Telegram; WhatsApp
instantaneous data 44
intensity of data sequences 134
interconnection of practices 169–71
International Labour Organization 14
Internet access/connection quality 95–6
interorganizational dynamics 103, 104
interpersonal trust 87
'interview with the double' 187
interviews (media) 55
interviews (research) see in-depth interviews; semi-structured interviews
Italy
  acceleration of time 180
  alternative media 70, 73
  data abundance 46
  data analytics 41, 53
  data security 116, 118, 121–2, 149, 156–9, 165, 180
  device on which social media is accessed 95
  emails 135
  Facebook 2, 38, 67–8, 69–70, 76, 180
  face-to-face interactions 118–19, 127
  fax communication 73–4
  information gathering 33–4
  instant messaging platforms 170
  journalistic profession 147, 154, 155, 162, 182
  legacy media 35, 36, 37, 55, 60, 61, 62, 76, 88–9
  media and political systems 147, 148, 149–50, 152–3, 182
  organizational work 101
  personal networks 49
  smartphones 104, 105–6, 107
  social media 43, 67–8, 69–70, 85–6, 88, 91, 92
  surveillance and privacy 116, 118, 121–2, 149, 156–9, 165, 180
  WhatsApp 139

J

Jackson, V. 11
Jeppesen, S. 18
journalistic profession 145–66
  concrete strategies for connecting with 159–64
  freelancers 27, 63, 74, 145–6, 148, 153–6
  information gathering 47, 49
  nurturing connections with 63, 76, 125, 145–66
  partisanship 149–50
  precarity 153–6, 162, 164
  preference for 'ready-to-use' information 63–4, 160
  radio programmes 60
  reputation management 88
  trusted information 86
Juris, J.S. 5

K

Karpf, D. 79
Kennedy, H. 9, 10
Kimport, K. 5
Kitchin, R. 82
Klandermans, B. 103
Kriesi, H. 126

L

labor rights 43, 100, 183
landlines 115
language of data collection 191
laptops/desktop computers 94–5, 99, 105–6, 115
latency, focus on moments of
  algorithmic visibility and legacy media on social media 84
  alternative media 70–1
  gaining visibility 56–7, 60, 62, 75, 93, 179
  gaps in research 178–9
  information gathering 33
  as key research focus 2–3, 7–8
  laptops/desktop computers 94–5
  reputation management 89
  strategic adaptation to legacy media 63–5
  sustaining connection 126, 129
Lazarsfeldt, P.F. 87
Leach, D.K. 7
leaflets 70, 73, 176
Lee, F.L.F. 32
legacy media
  access based on online reputation 88
  becoming a data source for 62–6
  centrality of 33–8
  gaining visibility 57, 59–62
  hybridization of communication repertoires 4
  information gathering 29–30, 32, 52
  not neutral spaces 62, 63, 76
  as political actors 63
  reputation management 88
  strategic adaptation to 63–5
Lenhart, A. 140
Leonelli, S. 11, 12
likes 41, 89
local dimensions of data 14
local newspapers 61
logic of numbers 60, 89
logos 86, 90
low-tech media 73, 76
  see also face-to-face interactions; paper technologies

M

Madrid 151, 165
Madrid terrorist attach 94
mafia 158
magazines 33–4
mailing lists 113
mainstream media *see* legacy media
Manovich, L. 11
mapping daily engagement (research method) 184–7
mapping of all media 43
Matassi, M. 115
materiality 94–7, 98–9, 172
Mattoni, A. 4, 6, 12, 17, 36, 106, 150, 152
McAdam, D. 102
McKenzie, P.J. 32, 36
McMillan, K. 16, 19
media as practices 17
media in practice 18
media in practices interview maps 184–7
mediatization 8–11, 121, 122, 175, 176
Mejias, U.A. 9
Melucci, A. 7
Menéame 43
Messenger 123, 124, 129, 135, 136, 143
meta-data 53
meta-processes 8–11
meta-skills 81
methods 182–92
Milan, S. 6, 10, 11, 93, 105, 116
Mische, A. 125, 126
misinformation 94
mobile devices 94–7
  see also smartphones
mobilizations 32, 33, 102, 103, 104, 105, 171, 172
moderation of comments 42, 137
'modes of coordination' 102
'money equals speech' 97
monitorial citizens 97
movement parties 5
multimodality of data stream 106
multiple channels, correspondents using 136
  see also hybridity of the data stream
multiple sources of data 113
multiple temporalities of data 43–5, 51

N

national newspapers 61, 147
Network Readiness Index of the World Economic Forum 182
networked social movements 103
networking culture in modern activism 5, 89, 123–44, 150–1
  see also face-to-face interactions; relationship-building practice
Neumayer, C. 81
Newman, N. 70
news monitoring platforms 30
news websites 34, 35
newscasts 60
newspapers
  centrality of 33–8
  direct action at offices 65–6

gaining visibility 59
information gathering 29–30
local newspapers 61
movements' own 61
national newspapers 61, 147
print newspapers 34, 35, 36, 45, 52, 61–2, 150
reputation management 88–9
setting media agenda 30
newsworthiness 153, 159
Nicolini, D. 183, 187
'noise' 36, 48, 51, 68, 123, 135, 137

O

Odilla, F. 6
official social media accounts 82
online access to television programmes 34
online-only news outlets 147
oral versus written communication 139
organizational structures 5, 101
organizational work 100–22
Orlikowski, W.J. 19
overwhelm 46, 47, 53–4, 134, 136, 174
 see also data abundance

P

packaging of information 63
paid services/content 82–4, 87
pamphlets 73
paper technologies 73
 see also print newspapers
participant observation 183
participant-led maps 184–7
performances 58
personal networks 49
personal social media profiles 67, 79, 80, 90–4, 98, 134
petitions 89
phone calls 100, 105, 115, 117, 127, 128, 139, 140–1, 173
Pleyers, G. 8
podcasts 36
political celebrity 9
political organizing
 accelerated times of organizational work 100–22
 as backstage practice 21, 22
 future research 179
 interconnection of practices 169–71
 as key practice 21
 as political practice 23
 practice of political organization 102–4
political parallelism 62, 149, 152–3, 160, 164
political power dispersion 73
political/mundane practices 22–4
Poovey, M. 11
popularity 89
positioning of movements within broader milieu 67–8

posters 59, 70, 73, 176
Postill, J. 15
potential allies 50, 52, 59, 126, 135
power dynamics 73, 120, 151
practice approach 15–20
practice of political organization 102–4
practice theories 15–16, 18, 57, 127, 167, 170
precarity 63, 65, 76, 146, 147, 148, 153–6, 164
presencing 75
press conferences 160
press releases 61, 160
press reviews 35, 36
print newspapers 34, 35, 36, 45, 52, 61–2, 150
privacy 100, 115–18, 121, 149, 156
private interactions, sustaining connections through 135–6
private social media profiles *see* personal social media profiles
proactive releases of data 64
pro-democracy protests 104
producers and consumers of data, activists are both 14
professional services, using 41, 138, 143
professional video recordings 95–6
protests
 journalistic profession 148
 legacy media 59
 organizational structures of protest 5
 organizational work 102
 and technological change 4–5
'proxy' access to information 36
public debates, participation in 67–8
public interactions, sustaining connection through 136–8, 142
public viewpoints, gathering 51
pyramid organizational structures 101

Q

quality of data 38, 95–6, 98–9, 113, 132
quiet moments 7–8
 see also latency, focus on moments of

R

radical media 58–9, 70–4
radio programmes 34, 36, 52, 59, 60, 65–6
RaiPlay 33
reach/dissemination 78
 see also breadth of voices
'ready-made news' 63–4, 160
Reckwitz, A. 18, 19
recognition as legitimate political actors 58
Reddit 39, 43, 45
Reed, T.V. 7
regulation, top-down 45
relationality, inherent in data 11–12

INDEX

relationship-building practice 90, 103, 124–9, 160–2, 165, 173–4
reputation management 2, 78–99, 179
resource constraints 41
retweets 41, 78, 133
rhythms of data sequences 31
Rome 151, 165
RSS 43
ruling elites 37
Ryan, C. 147

S

salience 38
sampling 188
Savolainen, R. 18, 32, 184
Schatzki, T. 19, 21, 22, 23, 127
Schrock, A.R. 94
Schudson, M. 97
Scott, S. 19
secret documents 117
security concerns 115–118, 122, 149, 156–9, 162, 165
  see also surveillance and privacy
Segerberg, A. 5, 98, 103, 104
self-censorship 90, 91–2
self-perception of activists 10
semi-structured interviews 183, 187
sensitive information 100, 117, 157–8, 163, 176
serendipitous information gathering 32
shares 68
  see also retweets
Shove, E. 18, 19
Signal 116, 117, 157, 159
Siles, I. 20
simultaneity 44
situated nature of practices 180
Skype 117
slow data 44–5, 53, 131, 174
slowing down and interrupting the data stream 112–15, 167
smartphones
  journalistic profession 155
  materiality and algorithmic visibility 94, 95, 99
  political organizing 101, 104, 107, 109–12
  self-imposed limits on use of 114
  and social movements 4
  surveillance and privacy 116
  sustaining connection 138–41
  writing on 138–41
SMS *see* text messages
social, practices as 20
social media
  advertising 84
  age of users 69
  algorithms 6, 42–3, 78–99
  as broadcast versus interactive media 68–9
  community-building activities 131–2
  data analytics 40
  freelancers 154
  gaining visibility 57, 66–70, 76–7, 179
  general climates of opinion 30–1
  individualization of visibility 90–4
  information gathering 29, 30–1, 177
  interactive affordances of 68–9
  legacy media accessed through 35
  as news sources 31, 38–43
  paid services/content 83–4, 87
  personal social media profiles 67, 79, 80, 90–4, 98, 134
  presencing 75
  public interactions, sustaining connection through 136–8
  reconstruction of grassroots political debates via social media and algorithms 38–43
  simultaneity 44
  surveillance and privacy 116
  sustaining connection 133, 134, 136–8
  temporalities of data 43–5
  timeliness of 29–30
  training in 78
  variety of voices 37–8
  see also Facebook; Instagram; Twitter
social media managers 143
social movements 4, 7, 17
social networks 39, 49
social news aggregators 43
sociology of media 16
solidarity actions 8
Spain
  acceleration of time 180
  alternative media 70, 72, 73
  data abundance 46
  data analytics 40, 53
  emails 135
  Facebook 123–4, 180
  friend vs non-friend news media 153
  gaining visibility 68–9
  instant messaging platforms 139–40, 170
  journalistic profession 147, 154, 162, 182
  legacy media 34, 36, 61, 62, 76
  Madrid bubble 151, 165
  making personal connections 123
  media and political systems 147, 148, 150–2, 153, 182
  organizational work 101
  personal networks 49
  slowing down and interrupting the data stream 113
  smartphones 104, 105–6, 107
  social media 43, 44, 67, 68–9, 78, 82, 88, 91–2
  surveillance and privacy 116, 118, 121–2, 156–9, 162–3, 165, 180

sustaining connection 131, 139–40
Twitter 2, 68–9, 76, 78
spatial dimensions of movement
   organization 13–14
sponsored content 79, 83–4, 87
stages of latency 7–8
stance, conveying a 67–8
statistics 89
Stephansen, H.C. 17
stereotyped characters 65
strategic communication 40
strategic interactions 125
street protests 58
subactivism 10
superficiality 46–7
supporters, nurturing connections with
   129–33, 142
supranational organizations, data developed
   by 14
surveillance and privacy 115–18, 121, 149,
   156, 162, 176
sustaining connection 123–44
   as front-stage practice 22
   interconnection of practices 169–71
   with journalists 145–66
   as key practice 21, 125–6
   as mundane practice 23–4
   symbolic aspects of practice 20, 39, 115, 132,
      150, 152, 183
sympathetic media 150

T

tablets 94
TeamSpeak 119
Telegram 105, 111, 113, 136
teleoaffective structures 71, 128
television 33–4, 37, 45, 49, 55–6,
   59–60, 76
temporal dimensions of movement
   organization 13–14
temporalities of data
   accelerated times of organizational
      work 100–22
   future research 180
   independent websites 71, 72
   information gathering 31, 43–5,
      51, 53
   interconnection of practices 169
   oral versus written communication 140
   smartphones 107
   static websites 71, 72
text messages 94, 108, 113, 124, 140, 143
Thompson, J.B. 75
TikTok 39
time as a precious resource 63
trade union organization 40, 82, 91, 100–1,
   107, 109, 118
trade-offs 57, 64–5, 99
traditional media *see* legacy media

training in media management 78,
   116–17
transparency 37, 105, 121, 177, 183
Treré, E. 5, 6, 70, 81, 106, 118, 172
trolling 91
trust relationships
   interconnection of practices 169
   journalistic profession 149, 153, 158,
      162, 165
   sustaining connection 123, 128, 130,
      139, 141
trusted information 48, 49–50, 76, 80, 86,
   87–90, 148
Twitter
   24/7 45
   algorithms 6
   breadth of voices 39
   data analytics 41
   filtered information 51
   gaining visibility 66, 68–70
   information gathering 39
   interactive affordances of 69
   journalistic profession 146
   presencing 75
   Spain 2, 68–9, 76, 78
   sustaining connection 133, 143
   temporalities of data 44, 45
   transparency 37

U

understanding of algorithms 53, 178
unfriending 114
US Supreme Court 97

V

Vaccari, C. 87
Valeriani, A. 87
validation of information 50
   see also credibility
Van der Velten, L. 10, 11
video communications 67, 82, 93, 95, 137
video conferencing 117
viral content 45, 162
visibility *see* gaining visibility
voice notes 64
VoIP software 119

W

wearable technologies 94
websites
   alternative media 59, 70, 71–2
   independent websites 70–2, 77
   movements' own 70–2, 134
   news websites 34, 35
WhatsApp
   becoming a data source for legacy media 64
   daily political work 105
   effect on use of phone calls 140
   immediacy 108, 110

information gathering 40
interconnection of practices 170
making personal connections 124
multiple uses of 175
political organizing 100, 111–12
surveillance and privacy 117, 157
sustaining connection 136, 139
World Bank 14
written communication 138–41

X

X *see* Twitter

Y

YouTube 33, 34, 39

Z

Zamponi, L. 8